Digital Fever

Advance Praise for the English Edition of Digital Fever

"Fake news, bots and foreign interference are just part of the new media landscape that is reshaping—almost daily—our culture and even the sense we have of ourselves. Newspapers have always been prone to scandal and "man bites dog" kind of stories, but today the digital flow is unlimited, instanteneous and disruptive. As Bernhard Poerksen shows, this means a radically changed and charged world as billions of people check their cell phone each day. Authority falls away because each person is now consumer, producer and distributor of stories—chosen for excitement rather than veracity. Poerksen tells us that there is a way forward but only if schools utterly transform learning and prepare students to dissect and understand this brave new world of endless digital flow."

—Jerry Brown, *Governor of California (1975–1983, 2011–2019)*

"No longer do journalists independently control the gateway to the public world, says Bernhard Poerksen in his new book, *Digital Fever*. 'The fourth power of traditional journalism has been joined by the fifth power of the networked many', which can be organised to reject and discredit the work that journalists do. Meanwhile, The Media, in his vision, 'short-circuit the private and the public awareness of things'. Poerksen's heady description of the communications world we are moving toward is unlike any I have read. It made me rebuild my understanding of what is going on. Try it against yours."

—Jay Rosen, *writer and Professor of Journalism, New York University*

"Bernhard Poerksen brilliantly guides the reader through a shifting media land-scape, without either simply accepting the new or nostalgically idealising the gatekeepers of old. Never afraid to evaluate, but never content to just evaluate, this book makes an implicit case for curiosity and precision as cardinal virtues of our age of informational climate change. Timely and deeply necessary."

—Adrian Daub, *Professor of German Studies and Comparative Literature, Stanford University*

Praise for the German Edition

"If we had more experts of Poerksen's stature, the debate would most certainly have progressed further, become more realistic."

—Tim Schleider, *Stuttgarter Zeitung*

"*Digital Fever* is not a piece of dry scientific prose but a long essay at the top level of analysis, differentiation and well-honed language. Many perceptive examples illuminate the points discussed. And Poerksen, as always, creates new terms that succinctly express his insights. It is a hallmark of media science in the present media world."

—Gernot Stegert, *Schwäbisches Tagblatt*

"Excellent media research that tells us, by way of many stories, about the 'cultural break of digitalisation'. It fuels neither alarm nor inflated feelings of euphoria and—a real benefit—articulates suggestions as to how journalism could save individuals, society, and democracy."

—Paul-Josef Raue, *kressNews*

"Compulsory reading for anyone who wishes to go through life and time with open eyes."

—Otto Friedrich, *Die Furche*

"Media scientist Poerksen has written the book of the moment."

—Michael Kluger, *Frankfurter Neue Presse*

"With this essay, the author presents far more than an up-to-date report on the existence and the effects of anywhere-and-anytime communication. It encompasses preparatory studies for a general theory of the digital age. And it is a passionate plea for an educational offensive aiming at the media-mature citizen."

—Gunther Hartwig, *Südwestpresse*

"It is 'the thesis of the "filter bubble"' that he explodes most convincingly, the thesis introduced by the political activist Eli Pariser, which in 2017 was discussed in practically every newspaper and at every party. It claims that the Web is fragmented into echo chambers in which one can only hear the reverberation of one's own assertions. Poerksen proposes his own thesis of a "filter clash", the assumption that the immediate media neighbourhood of diverging opinions will permanently generate collisions and conflicts. Person A gets excited about something and immediately person B gets excited about the excitement of A. A cycle of hatefulness whose regeneration can be experienced every day on Facebook and Twitter."

—Linus Schöpfer, *Tages-Anzeiger*

Bernhard Poerksen

Digital Fever

Taming the Big Business of Disinformation

Bernhard Poerksen
Medienwissenschaft
Universität Tübingen
Tübingen, Baden-Württemberg
Germany

Translated by
Alison Rosemary Koeck
Köln, Germany

Wolfram Karl Koeck
Köln, Germany

ISBN 978-3-030-89521-1   ISBN 978-3-030-89522-8   (eBook)
https://doi.org/10.1007/978-3-030-89522-8

Translation from the German language edition: *Die Große Gereiztheit. Wege aus der kollektiven Erregung* by Bernhard Poerksen, © Carl Hanser Verlag München 2017. Published by Carl Hanser Verlag GmbH & Co. All Rights Reserved.

Cover credit: eStudioCalamar

This Palgrave Macmillan imprint is published by the registered company Springer Nature Switzerland AG
The registered company address is: Gewerbestrasse 11, 6330 Cham, Switzerland

For Julia

Contents

The New Priesthood: A Preliminary Remark by Computer Visionary Lee Felsenstein

I am an old revolutionary—having helped a generation overturn a priesthood who exercised control of information technology. We were informed and encouraged in this by our own visionary text, authored by Ted Nelson. Through applying an ethos of sharing we made possible an infosphere based upon individuals' ability to publish electronically without constraint.

Now history seems to have come full circle as we confront the invidious effects of large social media companies utilising our efforts so as to amass fortunes while poisoning society's infosphere. This cries out for a new generation to storm the bastions of this new priesthood and render them obsolete.

Fortunately, we now have the text around which to rally thinking that leads to the needed action. Dr. Poerksen has laid out not only a critique of our degraded information commons, but a list of principles around which constructive action can be based. By redefining journalism as a function essential to the functioning of the commons of information he points the way to a very different future.

Our revolution did not rely upon structures of government to bring about the radical democratisation of information technology, and neither should this new revolution in building the processes and principles necessary for effective self-regulation of the information commons. This book should be studied and discussed by everyone who hopes to have a hand in moving our information society from our dispiriting morass to a better world.

Lee Felsenstein, designer of the Osborne 1, the first mass-produced portable computer, member and moderator of the Homebrew Computer Club, the formative force behind the personal computer revolution in Silicon Valley.

The End of Gatekeeper Complacency: a Note on this Edition

In another far-off time, investigators of the history of changing human mindsets may have to face the task of making sense of our present-day Tweets and Facebook postings as the traces of a bygone age. They may have to reconstruct our debates about refugees, climate change and pandemic shocks as they find them in blogs and podcasts, in internet magazines and standard newspapers, and pursue them even into the parallel media universes of hyped-up Telegram groups. In their endeavour to grasp zeitgeist mentalities they may hit upon our never-ending discussions about whether "anything" might still be said, or whether societies were drifting into an ever narrower corridor of opinions and finally emerging as some sort of moral dictatorship. And, through all this, they may recognise that the pervasive mood of great irritation in our time was an expression and a consequence of a deep-rooted rearrangement of our mass media and our power structures, managed and controlled by strange paradoxes.

For what we are living through at the moment is a sort of limbo, an interregnum of communication, informed by the simultaneity of discrepancies. On the one hand, each and every one now has a voice. Via functioning internet access, they can address a world public and seek to attract attention and commitment for ideas and issues. On the other hand, the emergence of digital giants (Twitter, Facebook, YouTube, etc.) has brought about a commercialisation of the communicative space never encountered before in media history. Mega-mass media operate their own stimulation systems to overheat the communicative climate, following the principle of human interest(ingness), not principles of relevancy, according to the motto: what emotionalises, functions. And what emotionalises catches the attention of the users whose data tracks can be evaluated and sold to the advertising industry. Furthermore, and this is also part of the confused appearance of our age, the time of gatekeeper complacency is over. Journalists can no longer independently control at the gateway to the public world what is to be considered interesting and relevant. Their authority and sovereignty of interpretation is broken because the pressure of the expectations of greater and smaller groups of consumers now takes effect more massively and directly than ever before, and what is more, these expectations are becoming glaringly visible for the first time. However, the traditional media order continues to exist, although it is subjected to ever more severe criticism and fiercer attacks in many countries of the world. Once again, what will future historians possibly say about this present limbo of human communication? Perhaps they will (which would be nice) acknowledge that it was the kick-off and the prelude to a novel kind of media maturity penetrating entire societies. For I am convinced that we are now still living in an intermediate phase, media empowered but not media mature. Established rules of communication are weakening. Contexts are collapsing. The fourth power of traditional journalism has been joined by the fifth power of the networked Many. Documents of enlightenment as well as of hate, serious facts and thoughts as well as banal narratives, are circulating in so-called social networks simultaneously, just clicks from each other.

The question of the moment is, therefore: How can we implement techniques of cooling down? And how can we accompany the gradual transformation of the old communication order not merely with hysterical lamentations but also with sceptical friendliness, critical detachment, and the inevitably required generous portion of confidence? The answer presented in this book is twofold. It is important, first, to describe and assess the ongoing changes as thoroughly and precisely as possible. And it is, second, the great task entailed by the current developments to work out a vision of media maturity that would fence off the negative effects of the dramatic changes involved. The pages that follow present pertinent ideas and proposals that can and will, as I sincerely hope, contribute to achieving media maturity not only in the future but in our troubled life and times.

Tübingen   Bernhard Poerksen
January 2022

1

Clash of Codes: Or the Age of Indiscreet Media

Not much appears to have really been happening, nevertheless an infinite multitude of events has actually taken place. As the Canadian media theorist Marshall McLuhan stated in a prophetic aphorism in the year 1964: "Today men's nerves surround us; they have gone outside as electrical environment."[1] This is certainly the case today. Any event touching the nervous system of other people anywhere in this world, anything moving, upsetting or terrifying them may also reach and upset us.

This is the time of a cybernetics of outrage, a time in which multiply entangled and mutually intensifying impulses converge to generate a state of permanent excitation and acute irritability. Anyone posting, commenting, sharing news and stories or uploading mobile videos is instrumental in finally obliterating the remaining limits of the excitation zones of the networked world. Not a single day passes without some disturbance, not a single hour without push notifications, not a single moment without some shocker. One cannot escape these digital fever attacks even if one wanted to. They dominate the public agenda of the established media and determine what is deemed worthy of comment. And for quite some time now a specialised emotion management industry has been registering exactly what works and goes viral so as

B. Poerksen, *Digital Fever*,
https://doi.org/10.1007/978-3-030-89522-8_7

to reinforce irritants systematically by means of cleverly adapted real-time ratings. So that, at the end of the day, millions of people are discussing a particular image, expressing their anger about a tweet, watching a special video, or laughing about the same joke around the globe.

The proposition of the present book is, however, that it is impossible to understand the working and the effects of a nervous and highly reactive media power system by merely reiterating the sequences of topical events, i.e., by exclusively considering actually debated content. This is not to imply that the events themselves are unimportant or just fictitious entities, chimeras born of the thunderstorm of impulses from the networked world. Obviously, one encounters any number of oddities and curiosities on this planet to either laugh or rant about. Obviously, the horror of terrorist attacks and shooting rampages is *really* shocking, independently of statistical probabilities. Those media theorists who can only see simulation and spectacle everywhere, who consequently seek to re-interpret events as media fictions, and who therefore want to banish such events to the realm of the irreal with formulations that may be as amusing as they are silly, are merely cynics intent on avoiding any association with what is happening.[2] Such media analysis is mental escapism, the legitimation of ignorance and indifference. It is self-evident: human beings are *really* bleeding, are *really* suffering from natural catastrophes, poverty and torture. They really die on the run, under massive bombardment, or from contaminated drinking water—independently of an act of media representation that possibly only consists of a blurred mobile video which, when reaching the privileged inhabitants of the world, is transformed into the subject of philosophical debates in the realms of meaning cultivated by academic clubs. Images of total poverty as well as of obscene wealth refer to a reality that simply cannot be reduced to blatant claims of simulation, and that must not be negated. However, in the background of the historical flow of events the interconnected digital media are at work as a kind of generally transformative irradiation; and precisely these media influences are the topic of the present book. As will be shown, they change the character of what we call the public sphere. They short-circuit the private and the public awareness of things. They generate their own special dynamics and dramaturgies of disclosures. They drive entire societies into phases of nervous frenzy and general confusion. They ensure that conflicts escalate at high speed and they sustain them because all of a sudden everybody can stoke the fire without any difficulty and can continue to fuel the general excitement once triggered.

An example? It is 12 January 2016, somewhere in the neighbourhood of Berlin-Marzahn. On this day, 13-year-old Lisa, who had been missing and unreachable for 30 hours, deals her mother a pack of lies.[3] Lisa disappeared the day before on her way to school. She did not spend the night at home, and so her family reported her missing. Her story is that three men with southern features had kidnapped her, had dragged her into a car, taken her to an apartment, beaten and raped her. It transpires later that the girl had had difficulties at school and that her parents had been summoned to an interview, the potential outcome of which had apparently alarmed the girl. It becomes clear soon after that there was no rape but just a sleepover in the flat of a friend who had not hurt her in any way. And the injuries that Lisa has supposedly incurred during the horror night turn out to be self-inflicted.

But by now the falsehood has already left the sphere of the conversation between two persons. It has suffused the digital world and begun to leave its traces in analogue life. On 14 January 2016 the internet is already seething. Lisa is of Russian descent, and within the Russian community in Germany, on Facebook and Twitter, rumours circulate that the 13-year-old girl was abused by migrants but that politicians and media were refusing to tell the truth and attempting to hush up the case. Only a day later infuriated Russians appear at the entrance to a refugee home in Berlin-Marzahn. Window panes are broken, a security guard is hurt. The irritation within the Russian-German communities, who generally still consume the media of their former home country, increases further when the First Channel, the most popular television station in Russia, takes up the case on 16 January 2016. The presenter introducing the broadcast states that there was now a "new order" in Germany. People were no longer safe; the refugees were flooding the country unchecked and would therefore no longer refrain from abusing even children. Violence and chaos would dominate the cities. The Berlin correspondent of the station, Iwan Blagoj, reports that foreigners had raped Lisa for 30 hours and then thrown her out "onto the street", and that the police had interrogated the girl for hours but did not undertake any action. All this spreads like wildfire. Portions of the television broadcast, translated rapidly, emerge on the most diverse websites and receive millions of clicks. On the same day, the right-wing party NPD organises a demonstration in front of the Eastgate shopping centre in Berlin-Marzahn. Another NPD assembly demands the death penalty for child molesters. A purported cousin of the girl laments in tears what has been done to her.

But is this witness for the prosecution to be taken seriously, can she claim to be authentic? Various sources suggest that all the different publicly presented relatives of the girl could actually have been actors—a claim that, though unverifiable, must nevertheless be considered as an indication of the general confusion resulting in the question of whether we are not all taking part in a grand stage performance. In any case, the Russian media quite mercilessly transform the story of the supposed cover-up of a crime into a dominating topic. Occasionally there is talk of five rapists and a sort of "sex-imprisonment". There are Russian-German demonstrations in various cities. 700 demonstrators appear at the German Chancellor's office building in Berlin. "Lisa! Lisa!" calls can be heard, signs with slogans are held high: "Today my child—tomorrow yours", "Our children are in danger!", "Protect our wives and children". On some of the T-shirts one can read: "Lisa, we are with you". In the digital parallel universe, conspiracy theorists and right-wing agitators have long taken possession of the topic. The attack is directed at the allegedly deceitful and collectively aligned front formed by police, politics and established media. A blurred amateur video circulating on the internet since 2009 showing young foreigners boasting about the gang bang of a virgin is considered a sort of documentary evidence for social conditions lacking all restraint. The case becomes more complicated with the revelation that the girl had actually had sex with a Turk and a German man of Turkish origin, but at an earlier date and, as confirmed by the investigators, with consent, which of course does not in any way alter the fact that a serious crime was committed, i.e., the abuse of an underage girl. However, an actual case as claimed never existed. Nevertheless, the story turns into an alleged certainty on countless web pages, and it is judged as potentially true even though still not verifiable in essential details. "This is war", appears for instance in a commentary forum of a right-wing online magazine, "In a war, propaganda ammunition is fired! ... Lisa is exemplary! Even though an act of rape may not have been completed, the girl was definitely kidnapped and tortured and could, of course, have been raped like innumerable others before. Yes, she could even have been killed as in all those many cases in which Germans had to suffer that fate from ethnic foreigners." On 26 January, the Russian Foreign Secretary, Sergey Lavrov, joins the general fracas and accuses the German authorities of being too hesitant about a thorough investigation of the crime for reasons of political correctness—an insinuation that was vehemently rejected by the German Foreign Secretary, Frank-Walter Steinmeier, and banished to the realm of fable by other members of the German government. The great irritation has thus now reached the halls of international diplomacy. A few days later, the public prosecutor conclusively declares that the girl simply invented the crime.

And so one could now let the matter rest. However, this story illustrates a bigger story concerning media depth effects. It makes visible the immediacy and speed with which parallel public domains clash under the conditions of modern media practice. It demonstrates how easy it can be for people to form alliances for the purpose of protest and to proclaim certainties from within their own self-confirmatory milieus, which then turn into subjective realities. It makes clear that the boundaries between the periphery and the centre of the public sphere are becoming permeable, that rumours suddenly enter the media mainstream and there coagulate into topics that eventually even necessitate a political reaction from the foreign secretaries of two states and various members of government. The events connected with the 13-year-old Lisa *would not have happened in this way* without the indiscreet media of the digital age. What does this mean? It is the digitalisation of data and documents together with easily accessible and barrier-free usable networking technology, which makes the mass media indiscreet in a twofold sense.[4] Against the backdrop of this set of conditions, the publication of what is still more or less private becomes much easier. Indiscretion in this case, therefore, means specifically: to reveal the confidential and the concealed.

More generally, the global spread of media technologies together with digitalisation and networking has already interlinked formerly discrete, strictly separate spheres of mental and practical life. Indiscretion therefore also means the merging of what is still more or less discernible. Such merging in the process of digitalisation, networking and the global use of digital media involves: the here and there, the past and the present, information and emotion, speech and writing, reality and simulation, copy and original. This is a decisive change in the global organisation of information, the switch from a more strongly *audience- and context-specific segmentation* to *integrative confrontation*. The more or less strict separation of informational spheres for young and old, children and adults, is abandoned; everything can now be seen by anyone. They can all permanently send and receive messages, at any hour, day and night, at work or in their spare time, from anywhere in this world. What we therefore find worrying are, on the one hand, the events that upset us, the wars, the dirty election campaigns, the symptoms of the decline of Europe, the return of authoritarianism, the escalating conflicts. And it is, on the other hand, the sudden visibility of horror that accelerates the diffusion of an atmosphere of great irritability. Networking makes us sense an underground tremor, a constant emotional confusion, from which we feel unable to escape.

Such an atmosphere of growing uncertainty, emotional turmoil and sudden outbreaks of fury was described by Thomas Mann in the now famous penultimate chapter of his novel *The Magic Mountain*, entitled "Die große Gereiztheit [Hysterical Passion]". The chapter paints the social and emotional panorama of a bygone age, the atmosphere in a sanatorium on the eve of the outbreak of the First World War, charged with neurotic outbursts and bouts of excitation. It runs like this:

> What was this, then, that was in the air? A rising temper. Acute irritability. A nameless rancour. A universal tendency to envenomed exchange of words, to outbursts of rage — yes, even to fisticuffs. Embittered disputes, bouts of uncontrolled shrieking, by pairs and by groups, were of daily occurrence; and the significant thing was that the bystanders, instead of being disgusted with the participants, or seeking to come between them, actually sympathized with one side or the other to the extent of being themselves involved in the quarrel. They would pale and tremble, their eyes would glitter provocatively, their mouths set with passion.[5]

As Thomas Mann describes, the residents of the sanatorium in the Swiss Alps, shivering in fever states, tormented by their illnesses, tend to break into rages due to a change in the climate of the epoch, due also to a feeling of discomfort and the premonition of a looming disaster that has infected even those who have taken refuge in this supposedly closed-off oasis of the sanatorium and tucked themselves away under lots of woollen blankets in their deckchairs. High up in the mountains they are not really lost to the world, their isolation is pure fiction because "Being is lived by its environment, it lives only putatively by itself", as the philosopher Martin Heidegger summarises the basic message of the novel in a letter to his lover Hannah Arendt soon after beginning to read it.[6] Today the climate of the epoch has been changed by the indiscreet media of our time, and our Being, to use Heidegger's extravagant term, is "lived" and disturbed by the fact of digital networking, and the inhabitants of the digital world are being visited by pains transmitted with the speed of lightning, which grant them no respite, just like the wheezing and screaming luxury creatures on the magic mountain with all their real and imagined ailments. Informational and thus emotional isolation is illusory in the digital age; this is the very media-historical caesura that fundamentally transforms the communication climate of a society.

Obviously, such diagnoses of novelty must be stated with caution and prudence. The invocation of epochal upheavals—whether referring to the invention of writing, the printing press, the telegraph or the telephone, radio, television, the internet—has long been a proper genre of enthusiastic time diagnostics. It has always remained a questionable enterprise because it tends to neglect continuities and to overestimate small-scale changes. Obviously, every new medium invented in the history of mankind has provided new opportunities and conditions to transform the moods and sentiments of societies, to render excitation public and keep it alive; there is nothing unusual about that. Already with the advent of print, with broadsides, pamphlets, books and newspapers, human memory became divorced from actual persons. Past utterances—possibly fleeting and merely ephemeral—could now be laid down for permanence.[7] A photograph captures the moment thus saving it from disappearance. Sound recordings and radio permit the authentic reproduction of an utterance, render an impression of voice quality and emotion, thus enhancing the belief in authenticity. Film and television generate a feeling of familiarity with what is actually unfamiliar because celebrities and persons of power, beamed into people's living rooms at prime time, suddenly appear to be personal acquaintances whose clothes or hairstyle one may critically debate and even get worked up about. But despite such dynamics of media-induced social transformation, every medium has so far been tied to a material carrier and thus been limited in its range as well as doomed to decay and destruction. Before the cultural disruption brought about by digitalisation, an automatic, sometimes possibly undeserved, good karma of active forgetting was at work, which made certain events simply vanish or disappear from general awareness behind the thick walls of a library. Things are different today. The indiscreet media of our time swallow up all the various other media, absorb all their particular properties of documentation and in sum produce a new level of situation-independent visibility, of permanent, non-localised presence and undeniable evidence. What is transitory can thus be secured and spread, barrier free. Anything available in digital form can be made accessible to a gigantic public at the speed of lightning, and independently of its original contexts. In the extreme case, a kind of de-territorialised simultaneity of event perception is created: millions of people dispersed all over the globe deal with one and the same topic, process one and the same content—inevitably, however, from the perspective of their own situation, in the context of their own culture or ideology.[8] The collapse of contexts and the blurring of the boundaries of situations and information due to the comprehensive penetration of the world by media effects entails, for one, that protected zones of invisibility and retention spaces of impartiality are diminished. And there arises, furthermore, a permanent clash of codes, the immediate confrontation and ad-hoc comparison of exceptionally different modes of perception.

The effect of such a basic re-organisation of the world of information is that the inhabitants of this world often move in on each other too closely and to an unbearable extent. They are forced to look at each other and can no longer avoid each other. They see each other in all their strangeness, their extremism and brutality, no less in their attempts to appease, to create tranquillity, in their indifference or their compassion. The inmates of the inner world space of networked communication are forced into a kind of neighbourhood and confronted with a transparency of distinctions that is ultimately more than they can manage. And one can say now that the global village, this romantic-sounding *Ur*-metaphor introduced by the media theorist Marshall McLuhan, is a world that programmes the clash of codes through the worldwide use of indiscreet media. We are irritated because we are hit by the stream of thoughts as well as the stream of consciousness of other people in a directness not known before, because we are subjected to the unfiltered expressions of the total mindset of all mankind or the ideas of a delirious American president fired as tweets at the rest of the world. We are irritated because we cannot be sure whether what we consider certainties at one moment will still hold sway at another; or who is manipulating data and documents for what reasons and towards what ends. We are irritated because, due to the workings of the technological media, we find ourselves in a permanent state of uncertainty and are therefore excitedly searching for anchor points and truths in the informational thunderstorm, which are however shaken up and demolished as soon as we think to have got hold of them. And we are irritated because civilising discourse filters have broken down, authorities have been demoted in quick succession, and because deep down we feel that one day we might possibly also render ourselves vulnerable on the globally observable stage of the internet, just like that girl from Berlin-Marzahn who was proved to be a liar before the eyes of the world.

It is this feeling of irritation connecting different political and social groups that I am going to analyse in the present book. My analysis will consist in the diagnosis of five types of crisis.[9] I shall open my presentation with the diagnosis of a *crisis of truth* and show that certainties have increasingly become questionable in a time of falsified images and videos, hired trolls, secret service activities, forged profiles, social bots and perfectly orchestrated propaganda. The traditional world of more hierarchically structured knowledge and media was shaped by comparatively powerful gatekeepers and a certain stability of materials and documents, and thereby implicitly supported classical concepts of truth that have meanwhile come under pressure. The fear of post-factual times and the current fake news panic are consequently symptoms of a more general feeling of insecurity with regard to information, a fear that all connections with reality may go up in smoke. The second chapter sketches out the contours of a *crisis of discourse* and makes clear that the limits to what can be said and agreed upon are undergoing rapid changes. One reason is that established journalism is losing its influence and interpretative power in many countries; another is that radical, outlandish and hateful messages can be made public with little effort. In the present phase of transition from a media democracy to an outrage democracy, everyone can present their views publicly, the anger about the anger of others having long become communicative normality. Everyone may ally themselves with others to establish either a merely subjectively felt power, or a real politically influential power, the *fifth power* of a networked world.

What are the consequences? The evidence shows that the great irritation has for quite some time also infected the discourse about discourse. Observers of societal phenomena fear a sort of communicative anarchy caused by the loss of civilising filters and are becoming increasingly nervous when realising that, due to the disappearance or weakening of gatekeepers, unrestrained aggression and uninhibited malice abound. The third chapter deals with the *crisis of authority* in the digital age and shows through examples of politicians that the current media conditions will inevitably bring to light the ordinariness, contradictoriness and faultiness of purportedly exemplary personalities and previously undisputed authorities. Authority and self-mystification always depend a good deal on the control of information, on maintaining distance, on largely unhampered stage management and hidden PR, on the effective prettification of the past. Precisely this kind of information control cannot be maintained in the digital age in the same all-encompassing manner. The indiscreet media of our time, from the smartphone to the pillory blog, function as instruments of systematic disillusionment and instant debunking. They pulverise authority, aura and charisma and allow for the permanent production of unsettling disclosures. How will transparency and total illumination affect the future of model personalities, one might ask? Will the new stars be heroes of ordinariness and prototypes of camaraderie and friendship? Will authority be transformed into the ideal of authenticity? Or will *heroes of negativity* populate the public stage, impressing their followers by flouting or attacking moral standards?

The jury is still out. It is indisputable, however, that under the current conditions authority is only just hanging on with a fragile consensus, supported by perhaps merely short-lived and no longer institutionally guaranteed approval. The fourth chapter—the *crisis of complacency*—will elucidate what it means for the networked person that originally local conflicts escalate unexpectedly and disproportionately, that contexts collapse and real life-worlds clash. (Following Eli Pariser's theory of the *filter bubble,* I shall introduce the notion of *filter clash* and expound why the claim that we all exist in closed and unrelated filter bubbles cannot possibly apply under present networking conditions.) One can see how other people live, one is exposed to images of riches, poverty, bloody protests, and the real-time documentations of disgusting bestialities (live streaming of assassinations, torture and rape videos, etc.). It is the immediate accessibility of information and news of all kinds that tears down the idyll of complacency and deeply impinges on social moods. This too is a cause of the irritation that in its own peculiar dialectics of cultural development generates a yearning for tranquillity, silence and digital detox programmes. In the chapter about the *crisis of reputation,* my point of departure is the assumption that reputation has become a fundamentally endangered value in the digital age, independently of social power and celebrity status. Under the given media conditions, even totally unknown individuals—for whom height of fall is no significant mass-media criterion—are rendered objects of unwelcome attention excesses on pillory sites and in social networks. The public itself, in league with the traditional mass media, has become a mighty player in the irritation arena of our time. It can set agendas, denounce grievances, attack the powerful and the powerless for well-founded or less convincing reasons. This is the new lightness of scandalisation. However, the crisis of reputation, like the other crises of the digital age described here, is ambivalent, two-faced. It creates new victims but, on the other hand, lends victims a voice to publicly expose their tormenters. It systematically undermines authority; it may even bring down dangerous charismatics and despots in surprise coups. And this means: it can be shown that the multiform world of digital public spheres and their crises cannot be properly evaluated – either from a position of boundless euphoria or from an attitude of equally boundless pessimism. Beauty and horror, ambivalence and polymorphism, media constraints and individual liberties, must be revealed in an equally balanced manner—this is the significant task. No victimology or digital totalitarianism will be offered. Media environments are a flexible corset in which each and every one may move in a responsible or irresponsible manner.[10]

At the end of this book, we must enter into an ambitious dream about a politics of education. For I am convinced that the current situation holds an as yet uncomprehended and still undeciphered challenge to education. We live in a phase of mental puberty regarding the exploitation of new opportunities, shaken by the growing pains of media evolution, and we must face them with conceptual shrewdness. We must mentally disengage ourselves from the small-formatted didactics programmes of media competence, which react to the cultural disruption of digitalisation with nothing more than a few seminars and the most recent technical gadgets in schools and universities. They lack fundamentally innovative ideas concerning the ideal of media maturity at the highest level of current developments, spring from all too limited dreams. In the last chapter of the book, I shall present the utopia of an *editorial society* for debate, a society embracing reflected decisions about publication where the basic questions of journalism, i.e., the questions of the credibility and relevance of information, have become part and parcel of general education. The basic questions of the reliability of sources, the process of research, or the mechanisms of unprejudiced information selection, are no longer specific problems for journalists alone. Today they are relevant for all of us, for everyone carrying a smartphone in their pockets has become a producer and transmitter of messages. And precisely herein lies the significance of the ideal conception of journalism for a politics of education: it provides a system of values for public speaking, it connects the act of publication with the rigorous checking of facts and their relevance, it offers elaborate research routines and forms of fact and source checking—all of which can propel one out of the personal box of presumptions and prejudices.[11] Good journalism will—in the ideal case—systematically lead to "a second nature of openness" (in the words of the journalism researcher Horst Pöttker) because it is aware of the general human tendency towards self-confirmation, i.e., the first nature of human beings, their mental laziness. And it aims at mutual comprehension and exchange. The societal climate, the ways and manners in which we talk and quarrel with each other, how we arrive at compromises, separate significant information from pseudo-news, facts from propaganda, rubbish and genuine scandals from idiotic shockers— all this will only be achieved if we can successfully create a kind of editorial consciousness. To achieve this, we need to introduce a special subject into schools, whose contours and programmes I shall sketch out (media history, media practice, power analysis and applied error science). A fundamental requirement here is that the journalism currently existing is fundamentally revised, develops a new, less asymmetrical and more transparent self-image, and orients itself by the ideal of dialogue. The relationship with the public must be conceived of in a different and less hierarchical way and geared towards realising a kind of exchange on a level of equality that I call dialogical journalism. And finally, the platform monopolists in a future editorial society must be prepared to allow the cooperative critical examination of their power and influence as well as of their ethical principles. (I propose the creation of a number of procedural instruments, e.g., the model of a platform council, an organ of self-control similar to the press council.) These are big and still hardly understood tasks for the organisation of education in the future, which must be tackled in a book of this kind because without such projections the position of the author might all too simply be classified as one of customary internet pessimism, which it is not. Calling for education implies believing in the capabilities of fellow human beings, trusting their developmental potential, and refraining from invoking hopelessness. Such is the universal pathos of all educational thinking. Calling for education presupposes a thorough understanding of the crises of the digital age, despite their distressing power, and in sharp contrast to any misguided culture-pessimistic interpretation, as a set of open societal situations that require material decisions about their future forms and functions. Such demands are calls for analysis and enlightenment to be realised on a path that leads to media maturity and autonomy in thought and action, demands that can be fulfilled, but must first be accepted and supported. Nothing is without alternative.

2

The Crisis of Truth: Or the Suspicion of Manipulation

The Modern Turing Test

Given the prevailing information conditions, it is difficult, often even essentially impossible, to decide whether something is true and whether something is false. In a situation of wide-ranging uncertainty, suspicion is rampant, doubts reign, and murmurs abound that pretend to offer insights but actually only reveal confusion and bewilderment. The special cognitive situation of the digital age and the general atmosphere of deeply sensed manipulation may perhaps be made more accessible by briefly recalling the Turing test, that experiment from the prehistory and early periods of the computer era. The procedure was first described by the brilliant mathematician and cryptographer Alan Turing in 1950. The test is designed to establish whether machines may be called intelligent, may have intellectual understanding attributed to them. To achieve this, a human being communicates with an entity that is not specified in detail. It can neither be seen nor heard, it may be a person or a machine. If the human subject concludes from the responses given by the entity that it is human when it actually is not, then the entity's intelligence is attested, according to Alan Turing's argumentation. This

© The Author(s), under exclusive license to Springer Nature Switzerland AG 2022
B. Poerksen, *Digital Fever*,
https://doi.org/10.1007/978-3-030-89522-8_1

test has been controversially debated by philosophers and investigators of the human mind for decades. Some of them consider the whole approach to be erroneous, because the responses presented under such extremely reduced conditions of information and communication could not possibly reveal anything about the intelligence or consciousness of machines, as they simply demonstrate that the experimental subject has failed and produced wrong judgements. This would therefore imply that the procedure does not actually reveal anything about the intelligence of machines, but quite a lot about the ability of human subjects to assess reliably the source of communicative messages. Others, however, think that Turing's experiment is practicable and so continue to work hard on the improvement of programs that are indeed frequently capable of creating convincing illusions of human communication. One of the latest pieces of news came in 2014 from the University of Reading, stating that a chatbot, i.e., a computer program simulating a conversation, had actually passed the Turing test. The chatbot was called Eugene Goostman and simulated the communication forms and knowledge of a 13-year-old boy from Ukraine.

Such triumphalist news items must undoubtedly be of interest to specialists in AI research. The procedure is, however, of explosive diagnostic relevance for an epoch in which the paradigm of the communication situation that it represents has become common practice. Today's networked individual, under the prevailing media conditions, constantly communicates with "entities" whose intentions and interests, whose integrity or status—human or machine, neutral observer or propagandist—cannot be assessed beyond doubt. So, there is a new, globally celebrated, Turing test inscribed into digital communication forms, which is guided by the question as to what can really be considered to be genuine, truthful and authentic communication—and what not. The place for this experiment is not the science lab and not the university building, but the digital public sphere. Here the networked individuals face the problem of whether they can identify at all the innumerable false and defective items of information that are being spread around. And we have all known for a long time: to produce and distribute these has never been easier than today. Under the conditions of digital communication, each and every one can now create fake identities, stage-manage personal histories with suitable refinement, and then try this out on the public in order to ascertain whether the media-constructed realities are accepted as genuine. Each and every one can now play with identities and roles, can hide behind masks, and can design particular selves or personalities as variable projections whose authenticity sways others—until they realise the trick or are shown the production secrets behind a successful manipulation. "On the Internet," says a legendary *New Yorker* cartoon from the year 1993, which shows a dog in front of a computer, "nobody knows you're a dog." How easy it is to deceive even close relatives and good friends and to dazzle them with a pretty story, was impressively demonstrated by the Dutch arts student Zilla van den Born in 2014 in the form of an amusing personal experiment, a modern variant of the Turing test under the conditions of digital communication.[12] Zilla van den Born informed relatives and acquaintances that she was going away to travel through Thailand, Laos and Cambodia. In due course she posted charming holiday items on Facebook and sent photos of white palm beaches and images of snorkelling tours in turquoise water. One could watch her eating with chopsticks or visiting a temple accompanied by a monk in an orange-coloured robe—holiday snaps of a young woman who had, however, camped for 42 days in her flat in Amsterdam, which she had kept redecorating for the Skype sessions with her family. With the help of Photoshop, she created the illusion of a whole trip, and later submitted a bachelor's thesis at the arts academy in Utrecht on what is called *fakecationing*—the simulation of a spectacular holiday.

Nobody was able to trace the arts student through the weeks of her supposed absence. She finally unmasked herself and her computer-generated holiday persona and filmed the dismayed reactions of her relatives and friends to whom she explained on camera the tricks she had used to simulate the weeks-long dream trip through Asia. She offered incontrovertible evidence of what was correct and what not, and how the illusion of a reality that did not exist was fabricated. But this double vision that first presents the trappings of a world of appearances, and then reveals the hidden stage and the mechanics of its production, is not always available. The normal situation of understanding in media worlds is quite different: we may be basically quite aware of potential cheating but we do not really have any means of private-personal authenticity control. One may sense that something is not right but one simply cannot look behind the curtain, one cannot supply definitive evidence, certainly not from mere personal observation and research. The diffuse intuition of dubious goings-on and a characteristic uncertainty about genuineness are fed and enforced by several factors. First of all, the gamble with the publicity-enhancing stage management of realities has been democratised; it is now available for anyone. Obviously, media images have at all times been popular objects of forgery. And the means for the digital manipulation of images have existed for decades. Today, however, anyone can comfortably perform small experimental forgeries, be it with Photoshop or some other software, and feed them unhindered into public circulation. We no longer need—in contrast to earlier epochs—darkrooms or chemicals, scrapers for retouching photographic realities, all we need is just a few clicks within a conveniently pre-configured structure. The possibility of forgery is thus covered by personal experience; this is the *private* empirical procedure of manipulation. Furthermore, the assumption that we can niftily be cheated in the *public* sphere is now part of the collective knowledge, or at least part of the collective speculation, of all media consumers. There are many reports about hackers and armies of trolls, about paid commentators sent out into the digital world by the great powers in order to manipulate the currents of opinion and attention, to instigate campaigns and to stir up emotions at a high-powered rate. It is easy to ascertain that even eyewitness videos, i.e., ostensibly highly authentic documents, have become instruments of propaganda and are purposefully used by NGOs and activists—whether in the war in Syria, in the bloody clashes between Israelis and Palestinians, or in other conflict areas of the world. It is well known that PR people celebrate the internet as a system that is easily manipulated, that businesses and lobby organisations pay for postings and recommendations of their products and positions, that they persistently reorganise Wikipedia articles, fake miracles of clicks and likes. And we also know that the British intelligence, cyber and security agency GCHQ is thinking about how to use social networks and blogs for defamation campaigns, and how click numbers and online polls and surveys could be effectively manipulated. (The relevant strategy documents have been secured by the journalist Glenn Greenwald.) Beyond all this, there are excellent reasons for asking ourselves who is actually speaking whenever the masses apparently raise their voices online. Is it human beings? Machines? Is it real persons, hired propagandists, or fake accounts—of which there exist, as some journalists suspect, up to 100 million on the big platforms? It is evident that the *integrity* and the *identity of the communicators*—central anchor points for the assessment of their credibility and truthfulness—have become profoundly dubious in the digital public sphere. The problem for the media consumers in front of the curtain is that, on the one hand, they know too much and can therefore no longer show unsuspecting trust, but that, on the other hand, under the given conditions of communication, they have far too little rigorous knowledge to be able to decide with whom they are actually dealing. Too much diffuse knowledge, too little rigorous knowledge.

This dilemma may best be clarified by considering a suitable example, the successes of what is called robot journalism. The expression refers to automatically produced texts that have been in public circulation for a long time, but can no longer be adequately evaluated or properly attributed. This is really a rather undramatic example, but it is a symptom of the typical knowledge situation of the digital age. For here again the question arises: who is actually speaking, who is actually writing? Is the reader possibly offered a machine-produced text? Quite concretely: when on 17 March 2014 an earthquake shook Los Angeles and the software Quakebot was alarmed by the signals from the US Geological Survey, Quakebot sent a message within seconds, which was published by the *Los Angeles Times* only three minutes later.[13] This means: a machine was warning the people, a software composed the message. The warning message was correctly marked, but what we really have here is the Turing test in camouflage, carried out under high-speed conditions in the mini-format of a message. And it is an established fact that the time-honoured American news agency Associated Press (AP) meanwhile is spreading thousands of—machine-produced—messages dealing with the weather, sports events or business news. The prospect is that up to 80 per cent of news messages will shortly be composed by computer programs. It appears only logical in this context that the *New York Times* once jokingly offered its readers a selection of text excerpts connected with the quiz question, which harks back directly to Alan Turing's original question: "Did a Human or a Computer Write This?" The question to be asked next is, however, what readers are to make of such puzzle games. Naturally, they can find appropriate answers with the help of the newspaper makers, but they are also quite clearly made aware of the fact that machines are now being involved in writing texts that they may still consider as creations of human beings.

Just how extraordinarily the uncertainty regarding the identity of communicators has grown under the given conditions is reflected by, among other things, the current public debate about so-called opinion robots, or in specialist jargon, social bots. There is an ongoing international discussion of their influence on political opinion formation, massively overrated, in all probability. Still, the debate is very revealing in itself because it shows features and patterns of widespread beliefs about manipulation.[14] What are the facts? Social bots are seemingly intelligent programs that imitate human modes of behaviour. Programs of this kind have been cleverly adapted by their designers to fit into plausible and unsuspicious sleep–wake rhythms and statistically inconspicuous communication rituals so as to prevent them from being recognised and switched off by machines. Masked by comic strips or profile photographs of human individuals, they create a certain mood on Twitter or in social networks. They take part in political debates. They endlessly post ready-made commentaries. They agitate and spread propaganda and simulate opinion power. All this is well known and constantly reported. And yet all those in front of the curtain or out and about in social networks, getting worked up by tweets or surfing around without purpose, are incapable of comprehending immediately that an armada of social bots is possibly just duping them into believing that they are part of a consenting majority. The more fundamental point is that the modern Turing test starts and finishes, as a rule, with a tantalising feeling of profound uncertainty. Instead of unambiguous conclusions as to what is the case and who is scheming under cover for what reasons in a situation with diffuse knowledge, feverish speculation and a deep sense of manipulation take over, so that doubt and uncertainty become the central effects of highly variable media reports. One collects *clues* but is unable to assemble these in such a way as to yield a clear image of *evidence* that would finally lead to a precise and incontrovertible unmasking of the agents behind the curtain. It is the constant suggestion of appearances under the given media conditions, the simultaneity of universal uncertainty and the possibility of immediate confirmation or at least plausibility of raised suspicions, that fuels indiscriminate mistrust and exacerbates the crisis of truth.

Principles of Information Laundering

One thing is certain: despite all the uncertainty, somewhere out there, at this very moment, intensive efforts are being undertaken to degrade the traditional idea of a message, the incarnation of serious information, whatever it takes. The social networks abound with freely invented assertions that are presented as news and explicitly flagged as such. We find, for instance, that Angela Merkel is in fact Jewish, that she wants to damage Germany, and that she has taken a selfie with a refugee who eventually became a terrorist. It is claimed that Barack Obama, the former US president, is in fact not a genuine American. We can read that vaccinations cause autism and that gangs from Eastern Europe in white vans kidnap children or even the dogs and cats of innocent citizens.[15] The world of fake news is a sphere of reality in its own right, a very special cosmos of sense, pervaded by feverish eruptions of agitation, where drama has become the new normality and the spectacular revelation the ordinary experience. But how does this business of fabricating messages function? Its central principle is to effect purposive confusion, which would then ultimately undercut the possibility of clearly distinguishing between verifiable assumptions and mere baseless rumours.[16] Thus the disseminators of fake news copy the design, the logo, the names and all the other authenticity indicators of the classic news media. A well-known platform for the circulation of bogus messages has therefore chosen the web address abcnews.com.co; the obvious intention of such a choice of presentation and style is to be wrongly identified with the news provider ABC News (web address: abcnews.go.com). The imitation is meant to suggest authority; purported photographic evidence and often nameless witnesses are adduced to claim actual possession of genuine factual evidence for the most abstruse assumptions. Objectivity is thus turned into a rigid ritual, a mere theatrical gesture, no longer referring to an external reality. One may now continue to ask: what is the motive? The main point of all these attempts to prove credible is, of course, to make money, for extensively clicked fake news generates advertising revenue. Furthermore, bogus messages serve politically motivated disinformation, the kind of extremely effective propaganda that has gained momentum in the digital age. The agents and groups responsible for its circulation are fairly diverse. There is the ideologue type, there are the pranksters who see fake news as satirical jokes but nevertheless contribute to general confusion. And there is the fraction of the cool calculators who in this great poker game for attention in the digital sphere want to make as much money as possible by flogging counterfeit stuff produced at the lowest possible cost. And classic journalism? Naturally this expert witness for truth and verification of the modern period is in no way immune to the spreading of incorrect news—be it out of negligence or slovenly convenience, be it for the failure to cope with the hectic daily business, or be it due to the clouding of the clear view of what is actually verifiable by the greed for clicks and scoops, and for the final disclosure creating the ultimate stir.

What is finally sent out to circulate—for whatever reason, from whomever—makes an impact, that is certain. In the aftermath of the last US presidential election campaign in 2016 that escalated into a mudslinging match, the power of fake news finally became glaringly apparent.[17] On Facebook, the 20 most successful articles about the US election generated 7.3 million shares, likes and commentaries in the space between August and Election Day, 8 November 2016. The 20 most shared trumped-up stories, however, were more successful and produced the enormous number of 8.7 million reactions. An analysis undertaken in 2016 showed, furthermore, that up to 75 per cent of Americans who were confronted with fake news could not readily expose them as lies, but thought they were more or less accurate descriptions of reality.[18] The inclination towards such erroneous belief was stronger the more frequently those interviewed relied on Facebook as their central information source. The fact that Donald Trump—who produced a whole tremolo of fake information and half-truths, and who in a one-hour speech at an election rally managed to utter 71 factual errors[19]—was recommended for president by the Pope, was considered as possible by 64 per cent of the interviewees. 72 per cent thought it possible that Hillary Clinton was in some obscure way mixed up in the murder of an FBI agent. 79 per cent believed that the claim that an anti-Trump demonstrator had received US$3500 for his stage-managed protest show was quite realistic.

All this, one must repeat again and again, is nonsense, rubbish.[20] But correction is so infinitely troublesome and fails all too often despite the valiant efforts of respectable media and voluntary organisations to secure the comprehensive checking of facts. The difficulty is that typical fake news content is narrated in the form of infectious, immediately comprehensible stories, often with shocking effects. They are believed because they function as ostensibly plausible arousers that confirm pre-existing prejudices. They combine the "wow" effect of astonishment with the sedative of the confirmation of what is considered right anyway. What emotionalises, the basic rule of social networks states, functions. What surprises and excites, what stimulates enthusiasm and anger, compassion and hate, will be shared, will be taken to be news from friends, who will therefore generally not immediately be subjected to doubt. The correcting message, the rather boring note "Incorrect!" does not invite further spreading, and the detailed and inevitably complex reconstruction of a bogus story is therefore unavoidably less spectacular. All this is shared less often, and thus generally reaches far fewer people, possibly even only those who had already been sceptical anyway.[21]

It must also be conceded that corrections are extremely unattractive—who likes to admit publicly that they have committed an error, sending a basically embarrassing signal in the act of sharing something, which is always a mini-sequence within the flow of personal-private self-presentation? And who is prepared to revise private prejudices? So even if the correction is actually noted, persons who have been taken in by bogus information may exhibit so-called "backfire effects", as has been demonstrated by various experiments. The consequence: the correction is devalued, the erroneous conviction perhaps even stabilised if not mentally rigidified in the process of debate, as individuals consider with great energy and dedicated stubbornness the reasons for upholding their false beliefs.[22] Another important factor facilitating the preponderance of fakes and hampering their discovery is the diminishing awareness of the quality of a source within the wider public.[23] One of the reasons for this is that information of highly different qualities is indiscriminately flowing onto platforms like Facebook, and appears undifferentiated, i.e., without accompanying quality and credibility signals, on the display of smartphones. This confluence of things that are different comprises an implicit relativism and shows a wordless ideology that I would like to call the *doctrine of equal validity of information presentation*.[24] This doctrine of equal validity creates the wrong impression that we are apparently dealing with equally significant interpretations, which are in legitimate direct competition with each other. Furthermore, the still visible news and media brands (is it an article from *The New York Times* or from a shady gossip portal?) lose in orienting power, because consumers hurriedly swiping their smartphone screens disregard them, or because the source link to a primary medium has been weakened or cancelled by the platform determining the mode of presentation of the news item; the rapid assessment and the credibility check by means of the meta-message indicating the origin of the piece of news thus becomes more difficult or totally impossible.[25]

And finally, one can observe—especially in the case of fake news—a process of gradual source shadowing, which one could call *information laundering*—by analogy with the business of money laundering, the speciality of criminals. What is meant here is that in the all-too-easy processes of copying, mutual quoting and linking, even completely frivolous messages may gradually gain in value and seep from at best marginal media into the central and the wider ranges of a society because it has become increasingly unclear from what strange channels and dubious sources the original message actually derives. An example from the late phase of the American election campaign illustrates this phenomenon of gradual acceptance and revaluation of completely spurious information in the process of its dissemination. At the end of 2016, rumours appeared on the internet that presidential candidate Hillary Clinton was active in a paedophile ring located in the Pizzeria Comet Ping Pong in Washington.[26] The speculations were triggered by e-mails hacked and leaked from the entourage of Hillary Clinton and her campaign manager John Podesta, which had been published by WikiLeaks. In these e-mails, it was rumoured, code words of a dark secret language were used. "Pizza" stood in truth for *girl*, "cheese" for a *young girl*, "sauce" really meant *orgy*, "pasta" referred to a *small boy*. And so on. It is most revealing that the first message about Hillary Clinton's supposed entanglement in paedocriminal circles to be actually picked up, was published on Twitter by a certain David Goldberg, who linked himself to a Facebook post containing these rumours, the origin of which could not be ascertained. Goldberg presents himself as a Jewish attorney in New York: an individual by that name is actually unknown, but does appear in circles of American neo-Nazis under the same pseudonym. The so-called disclosure then surfaced on the sites of conspiracy theorists (*Godlike Production, Lunatic Fringe*), was discussed in forums, spread by bots on Twitter and continually augmented by further "evidence" (e.g., statements by conspicuously anonymous insiders). A few days after the first publication of these freely invented claims, the rumour page *True Pundit* published the story together with further bogus claims, which enabled the originator David Goldberg to trumpet in a bizarre act of circular self-confirmation of one invention by another, that now everything had been proved: "My source", he wrote, "was right!" Now the story of the paedophile ring—on its path of gradual revaluation in the act of transmission—was linked by Michael Flynn, the security adviser-designate of Donald Trump, on Twitter ("must read!") and further recommended by his son, also active on the Trump team at the time: "Until #Pizzagate is refuted", his tweet said, "it remains news." The alleged scandal message, already translated into countless languages, circulated on Facebook, was vigorously spread through all sorts of forums gaining constantly in momentum; at the height of the frenzy the distressed employees of the Pizzeria counted up to five tweets per minute appearing under the hashtag #pizzagate. The hype that had thus been created through the sheer dominance and wide distribution of the fake message in diverse networks, finally freed it from the stigma of total delusion and successfully completed the process of information laundering. The end of the drama finally came in the analogue world. On 4 December 2016 a young man with a gun stormed into the Pizzeria Comet Ping Pong in order to see for himself, as he stated after his arrest.

The obvious diagnosis seems to be that empirical verification is beginning to lose its claim to validity, not only with the followers of Donald Trump. It became known that even the defence minister of Pakistan, Khawaja Asif, took a freely invented article circulated on the internet at face value.[27] It said that Israel would destroy Pakistan with nuclear weapons if Pakistani ground troops invaded Syria—note: none of which is true. Deeply astonishing, however, was the ad-hoc tweet sent by Khawaja Asif in response. Israel, so said his thinly veiled threat, should never forget that Pakistan was also a nuclear power. Here we are confronted with the real danger of fictional fantasies, which requires a reformulation of the Thomas theorem, that central social-psychological postulate stating that: "whenever human beings define situations as real, then their consequences are real as well". With reference to the universe of madly whirling and globally circulating bogus messages, the Thomas theorem must now be: "whenever something invented is rashly believed to be true, it may have fatal consequences for the real world". And the reflex reaction of the moment, triggered by the invention, will then transform itself into a genuine drama—culminating in the threat of nuclear war.

Fear of the Post-Factual Age

In view of such chains of reaction and the slender chances of effective corrections, it is hardly surprising that the World Economic Forum has declared that disinformation in the digital public sphere must be counted among the central threats to the human community.[28] Nor is it a great surprise to consider the diagnosis of a *post-factual age* as the signature of our epoch, determining the critical interpretation of our life and times. The immediate experience of the crisis of truth and the aggravation of the publicly fought wars about truth have created this term of alarm and boosted its rapid and meanwhile epidemic spread. We face the horror vision of the total implosion of all reality references condensed into a single concept.[29] *Post-factual*—a loan-translation of *post-truth,* and since 2004 current in the books of American intellectuals like Ralph Keyes and Eric Alterman—was chosen as the German word of the year in 2016 by a jury of linguisticians and critics of language; an *Oxford English Dictionary* jury had already chosen it on an international stage. In *The New York Times* (William Davies) and in *The New Yorker* (Jill Lepore), unquestionably among the leading papers and magazines, scientific statements claimed that the tsunami of fake news, the dirty tricks of the Brexiteers and the rise of Donald Trump, proved that the age of facts had reached its end.[30] We are now entering the phase of permanent sentiment scrutiny, of free-floating data being liberally interpretable to suit individual emotions and prejudices. We are entering the era of gullibility, where brash liars and shameless idiots can get away with everything unscathed. There may be a touch of plausibility in such statements, but a closer look shows them to be merely symptomatic, an expression of fundamental uncertainty, of challenged security, leading to an overexcited, superficially stereotypical interpretation of our life and times, seducing us to bottomless exaggeration.

Is the blanket assertion defensible that we now live in post-factual times in contrast to an era of facts? Certainly not, and for at least three reasons. Such a post-truth diagnosis is, first of all, historically blind because it claims, purely on the grounds of conceptual logic, that truth had once been the dominating regulative idea in politics and social co-existence. This would imply that in earlier periods truth was clearly decipherable and is regrettably no longer clearly decipherable today. Such a premise, to put it judiciously, does not adequately reflect all the wars about truth and the many bloody trails of phantasms (such as "Jewish world conspiracy") on this planet. And the excitement of analysing our life and times leads us to overlook, as a matter of course, that ever since media existed, bogus news has existed, and that especially the gossip and people magazines produced on an insutrial scale have from their very beginnings lived splendidly off the sale of appealing and entertaining lies—and still do.[31] Second, the concept "post-factual" suggests that its users are in possession of the facts in contradistinction to others who are not. The label is used to stigmatise those strange Twitter tribes that unfortunately do not know that empirical knowledge is more than a diffuse feeling of certainty. The word may be suitable as a finger-pointing concept, which is not really apt to encourage an effort to comprehend how others have reached their own particular ideas of truth that are so vehemently rejected as totally false. Such finger-pointing gesturing is analytically sterile, because it works for wholesale denigration but does not stimulate the differentiated investigation into how hermetically sealed reality conceptions are fabricated under the given conditions of communication. The third mistake of the diagnostic analysts of our era is that the possibility of knowing the truth is implicitly asserted without acknowledging even in passing, however, that what is called *factual* has since the earliest sceptics been the pole of attraction for fundamental doubt. The invocation of an epochal disruption—signs of great unrest, linguistic manifestation of shock in view of free-floating lies—is therefore naïve, when judged professionally by epistemology and the philosophy of science, an expression of pre-philosophical feature or column writing for newspapers, serving only the purpose of expressing personal alarm. For it must be asserted quite decidedly: truth is an intersubjectively valid construct, multiply conditioned, inevitably time specific, but still in no way arbitrary. It is this insight into the fundamental limitation of the process of human world perception that unites innumerable epistemological schemes and conceptions of our time, whether they are based on philosophy or on neurobiology. But one does not need to enter the field of epistemology in order to experience that perception can never be understood as the one-to-one mapping of reality. A cursory look at practical media work is quite enough. Anyone who publishes, realises immediately that they are arranging things felt and experienced, things researched and, in the extreme case, invented, that they are composing statements for effect, picking out stories and scenes, metaphors and images they consider important, pulling together strings of action, personalising and focussing. And they block out—through the very act of selection—a gigantic residual world classified as irrelevant. Thus, the central axiom applies even to those who strive for intersubjective validity and are reluctant to give up the concept of truth as an orienting norm: one cannot *not* construct. However, there demonstrably are conceptions of truth and reality of highly variable quality and trustworthiness. Should one accept this axiom of the fundamental relativity of reality constructions, and consequently seek to dampen the explanation hysteria, simmer down a little the hidden truth furore that is inherent in the proclamation of a post-factual age and in the concept of fake news itself, then there still remains—despite all relativising—the central finding that there is increasing uncertainty about what is right and who speaks with what intentions and interests. The networked individual is in distress and in a state of bewilderment because certainties are nowadays dissolving in front of everyone's eyes, because the marketplace of ideas and truths—the supposedly ideal public space, a sphere of argumentation and balanced judgement—has so obviously become accessible to propaganda, manipulation and forgery, which may very well be suspected but cannot really be pinned down. Truth today is more controversial and beleaguered than ever, not least because any individual—the single blogger, or the hardworking and unpaid Wikipedia enthusiast, or even the secret agent of a foreign power—can charge into the fray for the right outlook, and because the struggle itself can be experienced in all its ramifications, branchings and forms by anyone with internet access, although the complete picture may yet be very difficult to assess.

One can gain a clearer picture of this fresh discernibility of versions and variants of what is considered to be real by examining the truth wars, at times bordering on absurdity, as documented in the growth of versions of articles in Wikipedia. There the metadata (discussions, evidence, links to other material, etc.) clearly reveal the conflicting dissimilarities in the reality conceptions of the contributors. There the most divergent convictions are recorded about which fierce battles are fought, even if only the details are in question. There is, for instance, the type of the pedantic, small-scale, fanatically fought truth war in the English Wikipedia over whether the correct spelling of the Berlin Voßstraße is Voßstrasse, Vossstrasse, Voss Strasse or Voss-Straße. Another case in the same category is the months-long and disastrously intensified quarrel about whether the Danube Tower in Vienna is a lookout tower or—get ready!—a lookout tower *and* a television tower. It is also controversial whether the gulf between Iran and the Arab states is named the "Arabian" or the "Persian" Gulf. A further complication has arisen in the meantime as some Wikipedia authors have delegated the task of correcting alleged errors and mistakes to self-programmed editing bots that comb articles for alterations and then alter them again according to the wishes of their masters.[32] What emerges from these examples of edit wars fought by humans or bots is the diversity of world views, the unfiltered imminence of different realities. The upshot is clear: the silent central message of the digital era is the attack on the idea of a truth monopoly. The idea of ultimate certainty or merely the idea of a fairly stable reality consensus disintegrates and crumbles in public, visible to all and everyone, and in indisputable clarity. This is the "symbolic fallout" (an expression coined by the cultural critic Ivan Illich) and the implicit, directly comprehensible core statement of a pluralism that is manifesting itself in the media at breakneck speed. Consequently, both the experience of *informational uncertainty* and the impression of the fundamental questionability of knowledge and truth have obviously become inescapable. This experience is not just negative, however, because it can trigger most diverse effects. It can productively shake up the world picture of a dogmatic person, it can free people from the dictatorship of a mono-perspective, and it can be understood as an enrichment as well as an encouragement to make a fresh start in the direction of an autonomous creation of knowledge. But the confrontation with contingency may also upset and shock people, and this will perhaps be the more plausible reaction when the cosy sofa of firm truths is thus demolished for all the world to see. However, we must in any case proceed very cautiously in the exploration of the reasons adduced for justifying the fundamental questionability of knowledge and carefully reveal all the numerous facets of occasions and conditions. We need to operate with a broader picture and a more encompassing perspective in order to comprehend the crisis of truth in the digital age and to decipher the deep effects of confusion and uncertainty. The singular drama of forgeries and the hysterical-apocalyptic interpretation of these forgeries as the advent of a post-factual phase in human history are not yet substantial enough, because they are still too much tied to the surface of events and to curiosities and their weird effects. The history of media changes must be related in a form that tangibly demonstrates how the boundaries between fact and fiction are becoming blurred as a result of a tectonic shift of a complete architecture of information, and as a consequence of the *deregulation of the truth market*.[33] The history in question deals with nothing less than the fundamental re-ordering of the frameworks of relationships with the world and with human realities under the conditions of digitalisation.

The Catastrophe, the Terror and the Laws of the Digital Media

To arrive at a better understanding of this fundamental re-ordering of the frameworks of relationships with the world and with human realities, a number of worthwhile questions must be answered: How does information spread? And what do people make of it, how do they deal with it? Paradoxically enough, the laws of information *dissemination* and the fundamentally valid patterns of information *processing* in the digital age are most conspicuously exposed by reports about catastrophes and attacks, i.e., the confrontation with extreme events of different kinds. Such occurrences lay bare the normality in the extraordinary case, the rule in the exceptional example. A prime example is the story of the pilot Charles Sullenberger, because it provides telling indications of the predominant dynamics of dissemination today. On 15 January 2009, shortly after leaving New York's LaGuardia airport, Sullenberger's US Airways plane A 320 collides with a swarm of geese, some of which are caught by the plane's turbines, threatening to destroy the engines. Sullenberger then manages to accomplish one of the most spectacular emergency landings in the history of air travel. Realising that his plane no longer has enough thrust to reach an airport, he pilots it directly into the Hudson River, knowing full well that this manoeuvre could cost many human lives. The plane, however, does not break apart, the tanks do not explode. New York tour boats and ferries head for the sinking plane as if on secret orders and take all the passengers on board. Apart from the spectacular emergency landing and the immediate rescue operation, there is another sensational happening that, although obscured by the impact of the Hudson crash, has meanwhile become strangely normal— the operational process by which the information from the place of the accident was disseminated.[34] In concrete detail: At 15.31 the aeroplane hits the water surface of the Hudson River. Two minutes later the first tweet from Jim Hanrahan, who happened to watch everything, goes online, full of excitement and therefore with expectable spelling mistakes: "I just watched a plane crash into the hudson rive (sic) in manhattan." Five minutes after the landing, businessman Janis Krums takes the first photo from one of the ferries and sends it via Twitter with the words:

"There's a plane in the Hudson. I'm on the ferry going to pick up the people. Crazy." The classic media need 15 minutes to follow with their first reports. In the meantime, the first tweet and the first photo from the scene of the accident race around the world and are read and seen by thousands of people.

This example demonstrates three central laws of information dissemination, which shape our world view and our images of human realities. The first is that information under digital conditions is incredibly fast (*the law of lightning-speed dissemination*). The second law is that it can reach a world public unhindered (*the law of unhampered publication*). The third law is that it is capable, particularly in the case of highly emotionalising topics, of combinations and reactions of the highest order, is copied rapidly, transported from website to website, published in ever new contexts, and connected with other kinds of information (*the law of simple decontextualisation and association*). These forms of information dissemination are intrinsically neither good nor bad, but they are not neutral either, to use an illuminating formulation by the historian of technology, Melvin Kranzberg.[35] They can intensify and exacerbate, they favour and fuel a dynamics of immediate escalation and generate the shock of the direct present, the total presence of the event.[36] This media-produced here-and-now shock may have extremely positive consequences, when horrifying injustice is unexpectedly revealed. It can be tremendously educational, when faraway events are transmitted by smartphones and social networks in live mode and a world community of eyewitnesses is thus created that gets access to the unfiltered observation of what is happening in the streets of Cairo, Kiev or in the squares of Istanbul. However, these laws of *information dissemination* must unavoidably clash with the ideal of *information processing* and the struggle for the calm search for truth, the balanced prejudice-free checking of assumptions that can neither be confirmed nor refuted in an ad-hoc mode. "Information is fast", as the internet philosopher Peter Glaser characterises the dilemma of digital modernity, "truth needs time."[37]

We may be informed quickly nowadays that something awful has happened, but we cannot establish at comparable speed whether what we are told and shown is actually correct. This is particularly true in the case of reports about assassination attempts and terror attacks. Here we see the following patterns displayed with brutal regularity: instant reports, instant reactions, bogus messages on the trot, general disorientation, suspicions across the board, all on social networks but also in the established media and the classic editorial offices that are obviously trying very hard to compete in the contest for the speed trophy. And so it happened, for example, shortly after the terror attacks in Boston on 15 April 2013.[38]

On this day in April, explosive devices hidden in rucksacks detonated in a crowd of spectators lining the home stretch of a marathon track. Three people were killed, hundreds injured. What ensued was the spectacle of a feverish hunt for the perpetrators with practically everybody joining the fray. Platforms and websites like Twitter, Reddit, Facebook and 4chan for a prolonged moment became instruments of a modern witch-hunt. And even CNN and the news agency Associated Press (AP) disseminated false messages, infected by the race to find the assassin. The *New York Post* published the photograph of an innocent suspect on its front page. The outcome of this information disaster: rumours spread millionfold, fatal misinterpretations of grainy FBI mugshots and purported police radio messages, eruptions of hate towards the family of a wrongly accused student, who was suffering from depression and whom they had reported missing—he was actually found dead later—who found themselves suddenly in the public pillory, while still desperately searching and hoping to find their son. The constant barrage of faulty and undigested news messages had finally been rendered meaningless, wrote the journalist Farhad Manjoo in the online magazine *Slate,* in a critical analysis of this sort of reporting. His diagnosis: "We get stories much faster than we can make sense of them, informed by cellphone pictures and eyewitnesses found on social networks and dubious official sources like police scanner streams. Real life moves much slower than these technologies."[39]

What surfaces here, furthermore, is—apart from the speed damage analysed already—that the networked society has not yet developed a communicative register that would enable it to deal with the horror of the uncertainty that inevitably surrounds extreme events like assassination attempts and terror attacks. Of course, there are hectic, twitching live tickers, which are expected to bring enlightenment in real time. Of course, we are time and again offered special media broadcasts in which humility-displaying journalists proclaim in an endless loop that any of their statements and assertions must be taken with a big question mark. Of course, new formats of news message processing have been invented ("what we know—and what we don't know"), whose application is expected to help clarify the boundaries between certainty and mere speculation in a much more precise and transparent way. But the unexpectedness of an assassination or an attack in association with the thrill of buzz of the networked world and the craving for immediate clarification necessarily generate, as can be shown, a *fourfold information vacuum*, the reaction to which then consists of false descriptions, damage and injury to innocent and non-participant people, and misbehaviours of various other kinds.[40]

This fourfold information vacuum can also be easily illustrated by means of an example drawn from the more recent history of catastrophes. It demonstrates in an illuminating way the interplay of disturbing dramatisation and the desire of the public to know everything immediately and exactly. On 24 March 2015, pilot Andreas Lubitz navigates a Germanwings Airbus on a regular flight from Barcelona to Düsseldorf with deliberate intent against a mountain face in the French Alps. He himself and all 149 passengers are killed: the suicide of the pilot who was suffering from depression also sealed their fate. The coincidence of a catastrophe with elementary uncertainty and simultaneous broadcasting compulsion leads, first of all, to *a news vacuum* in the days following the event which, due to the lack of relevant news information, is increasingly filled with nonsense and pseudo-news ("Website of Germanwings not accessible!" "Comedian Stefan Raab cancels his programme!"). In such situations of elementary uncertainty, secondly, a *factual vacuum* arises, which is quite simply covered with bogus statements. There is very little precise information—and so assumptions and guesses are rashly and prematurely presented as certainties. It is for instance suggested that Lufthansa is somehow also guilty of the crash of its aeroplane. Due to its business policies and its joining a budget airline market characterised by fierce price competition, in order to cut costs it may not have done enough for the security of its planes—a claim that, despite the total lack of precise details of the circumstances of the crash, was presented as a more or less established fact. The hectic search for causes, the attempt to present explanations, motives and background information, creates, thirdly, *a vacuum of interpretation*. In the case of Andreas Lubitz, there was a choice selection of journalists, experts in aeronautical engineering, psychologists, and even a pizza maker who knew the pilot, who all helped with speculations and contributed the most varied interpretations concerning the causes of the catastrophe and the personality and mental state of the pilot. Finally, the general craving for pictures and the need for instant illustration of the horror inevitably generates, fourthly, *a vacuum of visualisation*. One wants pictures and images but there are none.[41] So what is served up in the case of an aeroplane crash? For example, a weeping neighbour, the home of the pilot and his parents, shocked and grieving pupils who have lost their classmates on the fatal flight and are huddled together in despair. These are shots presented in a strangely context-free manner, pictures apparently intent on combating not-yet-existent knowledge with a sort of protective invisibility cloak, merely simulating explanation, because the available images are only diffuse-depressing ciphers for the horror and unsuitable for creating insight and explanation. The superordinate pattern exhibited by such ad-hoc reports could tentatively be called the taboo-declaration of helplessness. There is no well-founded knowledge, but this fact must on no account be conceded. It cannot be admitted, either, that nobody is as yet able to say with any certainty what the actual meaning of what happened is, which items of news and which facts are really relevant, which interpretations and images are really meaningful. So, the question arises, why this state of uncertainty that is so easily generated in the digital sphere is cognitively so hard to bear. The answer is pure anthropological pessimism: human beings are in extreme need of sense and security, they are wrapped in their desire for approval, encapsulated in the cocoon of their judgements and prejudices, most energetic in their attempts to defend their own beliefs and merely vaguely sensed certainties (the American comedian Stephen Colbert very tellingly calls this understanding of truth "truthiness").

The unbearability of uncertainty in an intensively networked society capable of lightning-speed reaction may be demonstrated by another example. On New Year's Eve 2015/2016 massive acts of sexual harassment of women occur in the area between Cologne's main railway station and Cologne Cathedral (as well as in other areas of the city and in various other German cities), committed predominantly by men from North Africa and the Arab world. Once again, for days much about these occurrences remains in the dark. Established media, with the exception of a few local newspapers, report only hesitantly. The first police reports are dressed up. However, as soon as details about the extent of the attacks finally seep through and create a stir both nationally and internationally, a phenomenon becomes observable that I want to name *commentating instantism*.[42] We interpret instantaneously and much too fast. The inevitably still confused situation is glossed over by sharp ad-hoc commentaries formulated with maximum truth furore—as if in the act of commentating and instant interpreting a feeling of security could be won back, as if the still diffuse and unexplained event were a decisive opportunity to re-stabilise already existing patterns of interpretation quite unaffected by precise knowledge. As if one could, in fact, suppress the wait for solid facts by an emotional instant interpretation at the moment of general agitation. In the case of the attacks on New Year's Eve such commentating instantism is, interestingly enough, practised by all political orientations and factions. For right-wingers who speak of mass rape or see indications of a media conspiracy and the power of cartels of silence behind the reports, the circumstances seem to be as clear as for left-wingers who quickly warn of racism, fantasise about the sexual emergency of the attackers or demand a debate about the harassment of women as a general societal problem. Soon visual sham evidence is introduced, something equally typical of the overwrought instant construction of the certainty of already pre-conceived opinions. As an alleged item of proof, a photograph is circulated, which shows a fair-skinned girl apparently trying to ward off the embraces of a dark-skinned person while holding her nose. The photo, however, contrary to the attached claim, was not taken on New Year's Eve in Cologne but has been circulating on the internet for years with the caption "funny picture, smelly N*gger".[43]

What does all this imply now, in more general terms, for the mechanisms of information dissemination, information processing and the question of truth? We may fundamentally assert that human beings need truths and certainties and yearn for clear assessment. But it has also become very clear, furthermore, that the laws of information dissemination have the potential to destabilise this desire for certainty in a most direct and effective way simply because uncertainty and diffuse-threatening scenarios may be generated at high speed. Finally, the diffuse-threatening perplexity of a situation is often fended off by means of ad-hoc commentaries and instant interpretations, which are often enough exaggerated, i.e., exacerbate the crisis of truth.

The Unleashing of Confirmatory Thinking

However, the picture painted up to now of the knowledge situation of the digital age remains incomplete. Significant facets are still missing. We cannot only *generate* uncertainty at lightning speed, e.g., by instantly spreading horror messages, nor can we, as previously described, just *gloss over it* with greater or lesser superiority. Information engendering insecurity and uncertainty, possibly involving disconcerting "meaning threats" (an expression coined by the psychologist Travis Proulx), but conceivably also offering challenging and horizon-broadening opportunities for learning, may be technically rendered perfectly *invisible* today, quite in keeping with the fundamental craving for the confirmation of built-in beliefs and what is considered right or important. Potentially upsetting noise signals, which irritate or productively change personal worldviews, may for instance be rendered invisible by the personalisation of web search results by a web search engine like Google. The principle is simple but the underlying mechanism of algorithmic computation is extremely complex and not really transparent. It is quite unclear in what ways the algorithms of Google, Facebook or any other internet giant function, which present appropriately adapted search results and news messages to different persons. Secret recipes of reality construction are at work. All that is known is that personal web search history (what queries were dealt with at an earlier point in time), the profile of the inquirer's interests (what might they find interesting), the inquirer's location (from where in the world they logged in), and many further constantly optimised parameters are condensed into a personality profile, into a subtly spun web of probably pretty realistic hypotheses permitting statements about what might be of interest to the inquirer at a particular moment and what advertising offers might possibly be successful.

This kind of invisible curating of realities can only be experienced in its effects and not as a processual event. It may be demonstrated by an experiment that was carried out in 2009 (a small eternity ago from the perspective of today's internet progress), but that nevertheless clearly illustrates the explosive nature of personalised filtering. It is a rather amusing investigation with the somewhat awkward title "Personal Web Search in the Age of Semantic Capitalism – Diagnosing the Mechanisms of Personalisation", and it tackles the question of how the Google algorithm works and how it subtly and scarcely decipherably impinges on the reality image of the user.[44] To explore this in exact detail the researchers created the search profiles of three philosophers, Immanuel Kant, Friedrich Nietzsche and Michel Foucault. They selected one book by each thinker, generated search questions from key concepts of the works together with other wildly concocted subject headings and trained the Google algorithm accordingly through several sessions. In repeated run-throughs of their Google experiment, they thus simulated three different personality and interest profiles in several variably conducted search operations. The result was illuminating: Google personalises radically in a short space of time, focussing especially on the first ten search results shown to, and subsequently probably clicked by, the user. On average, around 64 per cent of the search results were specific, implying that the virtual search personalities named Kant, Nietzsche and Foucault gradually drifted into realities configured in clearly distinguished ways. What Kant was shown in first place was sifted out for Nietzsche or Foucault as potentially unimportant and irrelevant.

As suggested already, this may have changed drastically in the meantime (filtering algorithms are continually optimised). Top user adequacy of the information selected is obviously indispensable to contain the threat of anarchy in the data universe in as sensible a manner as possible. In addition, barely anyone will wish to contemplate the world solely and exclusively through the window and the mask of a search engine, i.e., relying solely on the information thus supplied, which could of course differ substantially from the information offered to neighbours who are occupied with other things. However, the fundamental danger of a radically personalised internet has not yet been ruled out by this approach. The fear is that people google themselves into highly personal reality bubbles. We do not have to agree with all the details of Pariser's scenario, condensed as it is into the horror of a society unwilling to learn and incapable of being stimulated; for this would presume that algorithms confirm only what is known, and that they are incapable of developing tempting calls directed towards the unknown and the unanticipated, which must be attractive simply for economic reasons— new needs, new products, new markets.[45] It would imply, furthermore, that we exist in just one informational environment at present, which seems highly unlikely considering the given conditions of media hyper-diversity and the effortless availability of the most varied news supplies. In short: the real danger is not the algorithmically determined filter bubble but the unleashing of confirmatory thinking in the gatekeeper-free zones of the internet. The problem is not a merely technical one, but a technical *and* social one. What is important is not exclusively or primarily the algorithmic determination of a world image, but its self-inflicted cognitive closure by virtue of new media technologies.[46] Everyone wishing to do so can now fashion their own fields of meaning, can win inner stability and greater self-assuredness in exchange with others, and can easily overlook, or continually verify, the corresponding mistakes of confirmation (*confirmation bias*). Once again, however, we must be wary of premature criticism. For the possibility of joining the internet at high speed and detecting multiple personally desirable milieus of self-confirmation is in many ways extremely useful. This is fundamen-tally good news, as it opens up opportunities for creating communities of choice. For now, all those who cultivate very special hobbies, who suffer from discrimination or a rare disease, or who simply seek enter-tainment, can perform exchanges and associations. The bad news is that in this age of digital modernity the hunters and gatherers also seeking confirmation for their peculiar brand of fanaticism are thus enabled to track down people of similar mind and orientation, i.e., ideologically related tribes. And they can quite decidedly enter spaces of resonance in which their private truths soaked in fantasies of violence and murder may be made to appear plausible, if not capable of winning majority support. This was made more than evident by the terrible 1516-page-long manifesto entitled "2083. A European Declaration of Independence" by Anders Behring Breivik, published on the internet shortly before he committed his murderous atrocities. Nine years, we are told, he had been working on it. For nine years he had copied and pasted together warnings of the "emergence of an all-controlling multiculturalism" and a worldwide conspiracy of Marxists, humanists and organisations for human rights, he had visited right-wing and anti-Islamic blogs, studied evidence and quotations from authorities, which he mounted in an endless sequence intended to lend his paranoia a stable foundation, a base for his hatred. He finally stylised himself as a crusader leading a "West European resistance movement". The last entry in the text is: "It is now Friday, 22 July, 12.51h". A few hours later he detonated a homemade car bomb in front of the Prime Minister's office in Oslo, killing several people. Disguised as a policeman, he then indiscriminately shot dead children and youngsters at a holiday camp on the island of Utøya, where he had summoned them, exhibiting the authority of a uniformed man, under the pretence of informing them about the bomb attack in Oslo. All in all, 77 people died. This is certainly an extreme example of the media-enabled self-radicalisation of a person with horrendous consequences. What emerged here, to use an astute expression by the internet theorist Michael Seemann, is a sort of *informational strongbox of opinions*, composed of personal commentaries, endless ramified references, hostile blog entries and hate commentaries by others. It is a homemade strongbox filled with opinions and hatred, which demonstrates the dangers immanent to a strictly self-oriented and individualistically-ideologically constructed reality.[47]

This bizarre, unique case reveals to what extent the commitment *to sources*, to *methods*, to *facts* and to *experts*, i.e., the set of a traditional,

classic, more or less hierarchically structured, but in any case, prefabricated and socially pre-given organisation of truth, can be shaken up
in a universe of freely whirling and arbitrarily combinable data so as to
justify a personal delusion. Is the internet therefore "guilty" of creating
the delusion? Certainly not, for such an assertion would negate the
responsibility of the individual, which is obvious in this example. Is the
internet consequently "innocent"? This question is considerably more
difficult to answer but is ultimately wrongly put because it insinuates a
strict causality that cannot actually be corroborated. The essential point
is a different one. It concerns the rather diffuse and unclear intellectual and social effects immanent to the media-generated communication
environment: the subtle moulding power of media environments. The
decisive question is therefore: does the internet—in comparison with
other media—favour and encourage ideological self-encapsulation? The
answer can only be affirmative because documents, once they have been
transformed into a stream of bits and bytes, become fluid and changeable. It becomes incredibly easy to combine and recombine them, to
spread them, to cut them loose from established forms and formats that
appear more or less complete and cumbersome (e.g., a book or a newspaper), and to use them consequently as building or tinkering materials
for ideologies of all kinds. Whatever is available as digitalised information may be changed endlessly, and it may therefore lose the character
of a resilient instance occupying a fixed spot in a pre-given organisation
of truth with its own special kind of shaping power. Physical-material
constraints are lifted in the digital space of realities, instantaneous transformation without context permanence may happen abruptly. What
seems firmly given becomes changeable without limits; it can easily be
sent, received and shared, and endlessly copied. "With digitalisation ever
more things that used to be tied to particular non-exchangeable materials
enter a new aggregate state", says internet philosopher Peter Glaser, "Cultural things in the widest sense – consisting of drawing boards, sound
studios, television sets, you name it – become data. And this digital
substance has a fundamentally new lightness. Digital things may be
much more easily and dexterously moved than before, may be sent and
received worldwide, changed, copied, shared with others and remixed."[48]

Printed and immortalised on paper, information is comparatively static and solid, it is difficult to access as a rule, may cost money, and does not possess a data body that can easily be split and transformed singlehandedly. In more concrete terms and by means of an example: publicity in the medium of the classic printed newspaper inevitably has the form of a bundle. Anyone reading the paper who has no interest in the business pages, must physically discard those pages. Any one who is bored by the arts pages can easily get rid of them but may still, even in an act of rejection on the way to the rubbish bin, catch a glimpse out of the corner of their eye of the existence of a particular canon of topics. This kind of feeble irritation in the organisation of information I should like to call the *soft paternalism of the bundled form*, because the diversity of the extraneous perspectives and the totality of the contents are thus presented as actualities that cannot be completely ignored. It must be emphasised here that it is the broadcasters, who tie the information and topics bundles on *their own* channels and who consequently proclaim the axiom of the agenda of relevance. The whole situation is pervaded by a sort of quiet insistence on dealing with strange perceptions, on taking them seriously, and on acknowledging them as existent in the first place.

The internet, however, re-orients itself from the logic of the broadcaster to the logic of the recipient. It re-arranges the world of movable data and documents, which are no longer fixed in a static order, in such a way as to fit exactly the direction of proprietary perspectives.[49] We can now construct our own realities without interfering with the agenda of the general public, unencumbered by ties to a world of perception organised from outside. This can—on the one hand—be conceived of as a kind of liberation engendering a new kind of mobility, it may bring about emancipation from static hierarchical conceptions of knowledge, because the previously existing constraints of the organisation of information have been lifted.[50] The principle of a public sphere of querying and receiving, created by information search governed by individual presumptions and prejudices (*biased assimilation*), on the other hand, tends to play into the hands of the craving for confirmation and certainty. Anyone who wishes to do so, whether alone or together with like-minded associates, can now seek out reasons justifying personal dogmas, which appear absolutely compelling to them at that moment. Anyone who wishes to do so, can profit from the wild variety of voices and, in an act of wilful choice, pay attention only to the confirming voices so as to barricade themselves into a self-created echo chamber or even an echo bunker.[51] This is now the strange paradox of the digital truth organisation and its ambivalent shape. It permits cognitive closure and a highly effective self-dogmatisation *because of* its openness and simple formability. This truth organisation seems, on the one hand, flexible as never before. It does not form a fixed or even oppressive system of certainties, no hierarchically executable ideology with special contents, but shows itself to be a gigantic prop house of fiercely competing realities. Hierarchies are levelled, the distinction between periphery and centre erodes, orthodox knowledge loses its modelling power. But this is only one side, the bright side. For this indulgent truth organisation that basically supports diversity, on the other hand, offers fanatics every possibility of presenting their disconcerting delusions as comprehensively well-founded worldviews and lending them the appearance of plausibility. Fanatics, together with like-minded associates, can wrench new dogmas and ideologies from whatever can be found in the prop house and then flood the public sphere with a plethora of insane ideas in the clear light of day for all to see.

3

The Crisis of Discourse:
Or the Diminishing of the Gatekeepers

From Media Democracy to Outrage Democracy

How is public discourse changing in the digital age? Who is gaining, who is losing influence? And who is allowed to speak at all? Here is the story of Martha Payne, a little girl from Scotland, who provides answers to such questions in a cheerful and friendly way—and thereby illustrates central mechanisms. The story begins in the year 2012 at the family dinner table. Martha, nine years old at the time, tells her father that she wants to become a journalist and would like to do some daily writing. Her father sets up a blog for her. In order to find something suitable to write about, i.e., to define subject matter and content for her daily production, she decides to report on the canteen lunches at her primary school. She borrows her father's camera, photographs the food in the school kitchen, notes what is offered—and develops, as a sort of freshly baked restaurant critic, a kind of evaluation system: the number of bites in every meal, her assessment as to whether the food is healthy, finally the number of hairs that she finds and that are not hers. Soon her first blog entry goes online together with the first photo.

B. Poerksen, *Digital Fever*, https://doi.org/10.1007/978-3-030-89522-8_2

This photo shows a single sad-looking potato croquette, a little bit of sweetcorn, a piece of pizza looking somewhat yellowed. Martha Payne notes: "I'm a growing kid and I need to concentrate all afternoon and I can't do it on 1 croquette".[52] Her father links the blog entry further via Twitter. Then everything begins to move very fast. Martha has at once thousands of readers. The first newspaper reports appear, the star chef Jamie Oliver joins in via Twitter. Schoolchildren from Japan, America, China, Korea, Finland and many other countries send images of their own midday food, and she publishes them. Everything finally comes to a head as Martha is one day summoned to the office of the head-mistress of the school. She is forbidden to take photographs of the school fare, as the school dreads further negative press reporting about awfully overcooked meals, the brutal evidence of glassy tinned pineapple and organised heartlessness. Martha then writes a blog entry entitled "Good-bye", saying that she is very sad about the ban and that she will have to stop. A Twitter storm of solidarity breaks loose. *The New York Times* and many international media pick up the story. Within 24 hours Martha's blog has more than a million visitors. So-called "rage donations" are made. Many people collect money for Martha and her project. And the school authorities are forced to learn the hard way about the law of novel asymmetry between incident and effect, between cause and effect: minimal communicative impulses may produce maximal effects. Natu-rally, the photo ban is also cancelled instantly due to the tsunami of rage. And Martha resumes her blogging. She succeeds in making the school meals improve. She collects more than £100,000 and uses the money to establish a school kitchen in the African state of Malawi. The moral of the story: a nine-year-old girl in cooperation with others can place a topic on the global agenda.

What is the upshot of this story? Each and every one of us has nowa-days become a transmitter and can, free from barriers, make public what is driving us. The media sciences call this phenomenon *disintermedia-tion*, which means that the gatekeepers of the old type, the guardians of the gates to the public world, hitherto embodied by journalists, may be bypassed under the present conditions of communication, and are losing their importance.[53] Everyone with internet access can now publicise their own topics in the hope of reaching an interested public audience. At the same time, however, the world is teeming with media and network effects as well as with new non-transparently acting gatekeepers that operate as largely invisible governing powers performing prefiltering, selection, weighting and potentially epidemic dissemination—a phenomenon that can be called the no less awkward *hyperintermediation*.[54] It is search engines and social networks that render it possible, in the first place, to detect all the ideas and insights, all the data and documents that may then be disseminated. They are used daily by billions of people. And they organise what becomes effective in public with the help of algorithms, thus functioning as world-view machines in their own right, as global monopolies of reality construction that have for quite some time now proved more powerful than the classic news manufacturers and the traditional mass media. Algorithmic prefiltering is, contrary to other opinions, not necessarily neutral. For example, when on 9 August 2014 the black youngster Michael Brown is shot dead in the course of a police raid in the American town of Ferguson, demonstrations, protests and street fights flare up. Images of these events circle the world. The American sociologist and blogger Zeynep Tufekci notes that the topic does not surface immediately in her Facebook news stream—in contrast to amusing news items about the next round of the Ice Bucket Challenge—but that it does appear on Twitter, although not upgraded to a so-called trending topic, despite its obvious relevance. This is due to the algorithmic filtering that determines what will rank uppermost in significance and therefore appear to be relevant. Classic gatekeepers thus lose their status, and largely invisible powers of information filtering and information distribution gain in importance. And the individual users—unconstrained by the pre-monitoring of journalists, but habituated by the non-transparent gatekeepers of the digital age—are entangled, with all their intuitions and urges, in a globally networked and highly sensitive communication universe that maximises their operations in a manner that is ultimately uncontrollable.

What does this entail for the climate of debates and the rules of discourse? There is the view, still voiced from afar and with a certain distance, that in the digital universe an open space has evolved that is characterised by barely controllable network effects and in which the *simultaneity of the different*, the diversity of sentiments and voices, can be accessed and experienced directly. There is a large number of astute analytical commentaries, and illuminating and entertaining contributions. There are inspiring debates on Twitter and Facebook, in blogs and commentary columns; we encounter relevant information and banal narration, reports about genuine grievances, abstruse claims, the senseless spectacle and the touching story. And we can meet with hatred, polarisation and the murmurings of conspiracy theorists who have armoured their thinking against every external influence. All these parallel public spheres are simultaneously present. The possibility of disintermediation with simultaneous hyperintermedation may have the effect, furthermore, that gradually new forms and formations of public discourse will evolve, which may tentatively be called *outrage democracy*.[55] The meaning of this will become clear by comparatively evaluating this development in contrast with the pre-digital mass-media democracy. In the media democracy of the old type, the big publishing powers maintained complete supremacy over interpretation and stage management. They could lay down—even before the cultural disruption wrought by digitalisation and the spread of Web 2.0 technologies—what had to be considered important, who might be heard in what manner, what forms and patterns of presentation were deemed acceptable. There were clearly defined, institutionally tangible centres of publicist influence in the form of newspapers, radio and television stations. The classic key media were the pacemakers of agenda setting, and the journalists were the gatekeepers. They organised the multiplicity of information material, they sorted the contents, they decided their relevance and importance, and their suitability for publication. They practised "a regime of control selecting what contents, generated by the production processes in the print and radio media, were permitted to reach the public sphere".[56] Already in the act of selection and certainly in the choice of the forms of presentation, they were channelling the public audiences' processes of judgement and thus delineated the boundaries of what could be said and represented in public, i.e., the essential guiding lines for public discourse. The public audiences remained comparatively passive, acted primarily as consumers and appeared in the actual processes of communication as, at best, the taillights. Anyone disagreeing with an article or a broadcast could lodge a complaint with the appropriate medium. These were practically the only opportunities of interaction and intervention. This world of media democracy is best characterised by the following quote from sociologist Niklas Luhmann: "What we know about our society, and in fact about the world in which we live, we know through the mass media".[57]

But the power of the mass media has certainly not been eliminated by digitalisation. Moreover, the media democracy of the old type still lives on as *one* form of organisation of publicity, although it has become much more strongly interaction related and public driven. We must keep all this well in focus so as to avoid premature proclamations about the looming end of the classic media. And yet the number of information sources dealing with the world in which we live has expanded explosively. The media as carriers of information have changed. In addition, a whole bundle of media and economic framework conditions—quite apart from the elementary processes of disintermediation and hyperintermediation—is effectively reducing the influence of the classic gatekeepers and the classic quality media. On the one hand, the PR industry has massively enlarged its resources, and the advertising revenue market has collapsed, because lucrative advertisements have been moved onto the internet and budgets have step by step been re-directed towards digital giants (in particular Google and Facebook). The print media and daily newspapers are meanwhile fighting a desperate battle for survival.[58] Their publication numbers are dropping; their capital returns are dwindling. Their core problem is that the fundamental question as to how to re-finance journalistic quality remains unanswered. A robust business model with a long-term perspective to compensate for falling income is still outstanding. There are of course the experiments with sidelines (travel, educational projects), the exploration of diverse advertising and marketing formats as well as mixed forms of news reporting (native advertising, content marketing). This might, however, damage the credibility of the whole business, because it will become systematically unclear in the process whether whatever is offered is a comparatively independent analysis or a paid message. So, paywalls are established on the internet, and diverse paid-content variants are tried out, but so far without really overwhelming success. On the other hand, we face further influential framework conditions, in that platforms like Facebook have meanwhile become so powerful that journalists are in danger of gradually losing the sovereignty over their distribution channels. Meanwhile, news messages are increasingly received via social networks, particularly by younger media consumers, no longer necessarily even from the original website or in printed form. This weakens brand loyalty and makes identification with the original journalistic medium and the actual source more difficult. It must not be overlooked, furthermore, that at a time when some of the media are fighting for their survival, when editorial offices are being merged and in ever more desperate coping strategies being economised to death, trust in journalistic information performance is undoubtedly decreasing. The numbers of ideologically radicalised voices are increasing that revile journalists as representatives of a *press of lies*, of *propaganda* and *system media,* and accuse them, backed up by hostile slogans like *MSM* (*Mainstream Media*), of being fundamentally bent upon manipulation. Various national and international surveys show that, especially in these present times of a noticeable re-ordering of the conditions of communication and power, journalists and established media producers are losing societal acceptance and basic trust, the very foundation of their work, for only if the public trusts them can their disclosures actually have an impact. The preliminary upshot here is therefore: the interplay of an economic crisis with the rise of platform monopolists and the fact that trust in journalists and their reputation is slowly diminishing, particularly in certain milieus, are palpably changing the climate of discourse.

The author Sascha Lobo holds the opinion that the traditional media democracy—despite the massive transgressions of the gutter press—overall represented a sphere of moderation, a world of precisely and considerately calculated emotional reactions. Emotionality was offered in a relatively static system of presentation forms and thereby domesticated, because a clear distinction was drawn between information (news) and commentary (opinion, certainly not without emotional colouring). In the media reality of our days, the primacy of emotion has become predominant over the primacy of information, driven primarily by the social networks. "What we know about the world", Sascha Lobo parodies the sentence by the sociologist Niklas Luhmann, "we know through a small screen that presents to us socially, editorially, and algorithmically processed information tending to favour sensationalised, exaggerated, radical matter, all self-reinforcing through the echo chambers of the public sphere of the Net."[59] Everything can now become visible immediately, whatever is stated may be commented on and criticised—without mass-media prefiltering. The sovereignty of interpretation of the Few has thus become the bitterly fought battle of opinions of the Many. And the gatekeeping of influential media (the journalistic act of weighting, of publishing or suppressing information) changes into the permanent and often ad-hoc sort of publication that I would like to call *gate blowing*— in analogy to the filtering processes of the mass media. Sometimes a single link is enough—a Twitter message sent in seconds, a Facebook posting, a video about some mishap, or a hastily produced report—to blow open still precariously protected spaces of information and to feed documents of embarrassment and demolition into the global, barrier-free circuits of agitation. So, it is no longer a single key medium that rules, but instead we have a *network of effects*, a network associating editorial and social media, integrating opposites into a mutually stimulating communal game. Publicist power thus loses a firm address and an institutionalised form. It turns systemic and epidemic, and is unexpectedly everywhere. Who is allowed to speak? Practically everybody—as was shown by Martha Payne's story. The spaces of discourse have become generally accessible through the transition from a media democracy into an outrage democracy.

Deterioration of the Communication Climate

And yet the experiences of Martha Payne now appear to us like a romantic tale from a distant past. This is due to palpable changes in the climate of communication. The great irritation has in the meantime reached the discourse and the discourse about discourse. The fear reigning today is that anxiety, mistrust and anger might ruin the great societal discourse and pull the public world into a maelstrom of senseless attacks and malicious gossip. The gradual deterioration of the communication climate can be illustrated by picturing three phases of atmospheric change, three stages in a society's reflection on the consequences of digital communication. The first picture stems from the early phase of the internet age. It is a utopia of communication hailing back to Howard Rheingold, one of the original computer hippies and co-founder of the first online community in the world, which arose in the 1980s in Sausalito. There in the California sun, somewhere between a few houseboats and sheds in the harbour, protagonists of the counterculture met with the gradually rising computer culture. There, hippies and hackers found each other.[60] And Rheingold was enthusiastic about the new possibilities of exchange and community formation: as we cannot see each other, ran his assumption, because we are invisible to each other with our bodies, our ailments and our skin colour, descent and skin colour, status and sex become less important; and all this will favour the genuine, true and discrimination-free encounter in an egalitarian space enabled by digital communication.[61] The second picture symbolising the gradual change of the social atmosphere is still at least moderately euphoric. It is from *Time Magazine* of the year 2006. In that year the magazine's editors decided to honour the networked person as the person of the year. They did not print, as in other years, the photographic image of a famous and influential person on the cover but a computer screen reflecting the observer's face. Look here, was the message, there you are in your own right, capable of publishing and protesting, setting your own agenda and changing the public agenda. It was said that this was an open-ended experiment enabled by Web 2.0 technologies and the chances of universal participation. This experiment should not be romanticised prematurely, of course, but we were about to cross the threshold to digital democracy and an epoch of universal participation. The third picture is from the year 2016, also from *Time Magazine*, again a cover story. What is now shown on the cover is a malicious-looking troll with a computer—a figure symbolising hatred and senseless raging aggression. This time the headline expressing the state of carelessness and the boorification of discourse announces: "Why we're losing the internet to the culture of hate."

The question therefore arises: what really happened with the exchange of the emblems and the transition from euphoria to disillusionment? How could the utopia of the beginning turn into the dystopia of discourse that informs the descriptions of the public internet sphere of today? The general answer has already been suggested. It is this: the classic filtering and sorting authorities of media democracy have broken down or have at least been recognisably weakened, and the boundaries of what can be said have been shifted. There are those who make themselves heard in a loud and aggressive way, uttering impudent irrationalisms. There are those who wince and are terrified by what is being said. And there are those who waver, who are insecure and who finally allow themselves to be driven along or swept away. One indication of the shifting of discourse boundaries is the extent to which conspiracy theories are spread and supported today—even in middle-class circles. We must obviously concede that real conspiracies exist, real conspiracies in history and in our present time. But this is not what we are concerned with; it is the attraction of great suspicion, the discursive power of diffuse whisperings and claims of manipulation that are proclaimed as disclosures lacking any serious evidence. Plainly, however, the tatty appearance of the kind of imprecise thinking that proceeds combinatorially, immunises itself against refutation and links everything with everything else, is beginning to fade.[62] Various studies and analyses show that indiscriminate claims of conspiracy, in times past argumentation patterns of self-isolation that would certainly and quickly have relegated their upholders to the lunatic fringe of discourse, are becoming increasingly popular.[63] Is it the intelligence services of foreign powers that attack us in social networks, distraught people will ask? Do cartels rule the mass media, people irritated by the media may suspect? Do obscure groups pursue specific plans to implement a sort of *population exchange* in Germany through uncontrolled immigration, as some confused minds on the right-wing margins think? Was the government of Donald Trump torpedoed by the *deep state*, and under attack from a group of putschists within the administration intent on toppling Donald Trump, as some of his advisers and followers believe? Such questions discussed on a grand scale reveal that conspiracy fantasies are gaining in influence. In any case, set pieces of conspiracy thinking have already long been diffused through popular culture—from cult films like *Matrix* to series like *The X-Files* or *House of Cards*.

Against this backdrop, it may be stated in neutral terms that the distinction between orthodox and heterodox knowledge, and the difference between a discourse centre and a discourse periphery, have become labile, porous. However, one must state in a less neutral tone that vast amounts of maximally anomalous views are still being spread around in public. A concept coined by the political scientist P. Overton makes the diagnosis of a crisis of discourse as resulting from discourse shift and largely uncontrolled discourse expansion even more precise: that of the so-called "Overton window". This is a sort of corridor of opinions and utterances that marks the boundaries between what can be said without incurring sanctions and what is publicly tolerable.[64] Is an utterance described as reasonable, as reflected and as wise? Or is what is being said labelled as too radical, as unthinkable, as dehumanising? In the media democracy of the pre-digital era, the yardstick for deciding what was permitted was defined primarily by journalists and protagonists coming from the societal and political elite, whose utterance style always implicitly contained an additional meta-communicative message: "One can speak in public in this (and only in this) manner!" In this way was discreetly laid down which positions appeared to be just about acceptable and which positions must be rejected as completely unreasonable, ideological and as too radical. There existed therefore a sort of publicly celebrated style manual, a clandestine paternalistic instruction, dealing with the rules of the game of the grand public discourse itself, illustrated by the case in point. Anyone who violated the general consensus concerning what could be said was deemed intolerable, was attacked and criticised. There were comparatively powerful central authorities in the debate that selected topics, specified a focus by means of grand centralising gestures, but were also in a position to secure the observance of taboos. In the open discourse spaces of the outrage democracy, however, as the internet sociologist Zeynep Tufekci explains in an essay, the Overton window is smashed because the power of the classic gatekeepers is dwindling and because it is no longer possible to exclude offensively radically deviant views and points of view, which could not have been articulated previously.[65] This is not just downright negative. We need not advance sweeping complaints against the wider expansion of debates, for obviously not merely bizarre conspiracy theories but also valuable and hitherto unjustly marginalised and disregarded points of view now stand a chance of being dealt with. Nor does this mean that we must wish a reinstatement of sanctions to secure the limits of what is permitted by means of ad-hoc punishment and immediate exclusion of offenders from the community of the well-meaning. But it does imply that the mindset of networked individuals has been altered by the encounter with what was previously unsayable or still taboo. Nowadays nobody can escape direct confrontation with the elementary contingency of communicative standards, i.e., the experience of the "constant confrontation hailstorm" (Sascha Lobo) of utterances demonstrating how infinitely much more has actually become sayable. It is not surprising that the networked individual becomes nervous and acts in a stressed and agitated manner because established rituals guaranteeing calculability and traditional boundaries of communication have been undermined or even torn down. The horror vision of discourse anarchy resulting from the loss of civilising filters is bound to be upsetting and frightening.

It can come as no surprise, therefore, that those who present critical and controversial positions on the internet not infrequently show feelings of anxiety and pessimism. They fear incalculable communication effects and consequently try to consider in anticipation, already in the act of utterance, potentially excessive reactions and asymmetrical attacks. What will happen when they say what they think? Who will become outraged, who will attack? "This story is not a good idea" was the first sentence of the already mentioned cover story of *Time* magazine from the year 2016 about the hatred of trolls, written by the publicist Joel Stein. "Once it was a geek with lofty ideals about the free flow of information. Now, if you need help improving your upload speeds the web is eager to help with technical details, but if you tell it you're struggling with depression it will try to goad you into killing yourself."[66] Disregarding for the moment whether users in a moment of despair are really challenged to commit suicide, surveys have, in fact, shown for many years that insult and harassment are widely current in the internet. 73 per cent of adult internet users, as early as 2014, admit that they know someone who has received online threats. 40 per cent have experienced such threats themselves, 27 per cent of them were insulted and harangued, there were attempts to embarrass them publicly (22 per cent), to attack them physically (8 per cent), to stalk them (7 per cent) or harass them sexually (6 per cent).[67] It is more than evident that such experiences in the open communication space of the digital world will unavoidably tend to intimidate and frighten people.

Against this backdrop it is worth posing the basic question, independently of concrete provocative topics, as to what it is that can cause discussions and debates to go off the rails. What is poisoning them? What drives them into unhealthy overheating and polarisation? On the one hand, it is the feeling of anonymity that removes inhibitions, as the psychologist John Suler has shown.[68] He distinguishes two forms of disinhibition, a benign one and a toxic one. In a positive perspective, communication under the cover of anonymity allows people to explore their deep desires in a restrained and tentative way, as it were, e.g., sexual identity or the pining for a different way of life, or whatever else. In a negative perspective, anonymous communication lowers the inhibiting thresholds of a verbal attack because people believe—in many cases erroneously—that they could not be persecuted or could not be held responsible for what they say, and their display of aggression would be without risk. Furthermore, the addressed counterpart is usually not visible so that empathy-creating signals as well as immediate reactions expressing the distress actually inflicted cannot be perceived and evaluated. Furthermore, as people do not know very much about their counterparts, they can transform them more easily into projections and fantasy figures and interpret their own actions as merely virtual games without real consequences. Suler points out, finally, that unfortunately, recognised authority figures who would be capable of checking and implementing the norms of communication directly are rarely active online.

On the other hand, however, and that is also one of the given factors damaging the discourse climate, the public sphere of the Net is basically an instrument and a catalyst of aggressive polarisation—in free analogy to the motto of the media theorist Marshall McLuhan: "The medium radicalises the message".[69] For today, those who were once marginalised may now associate with people of like mind and overcome their fear of isolation, which might previously have inhibited and intimidated them. And anyone who wishes to do so will in today's outrage democracy speedily pounce on the chance of finding or creating a forum for presenting and promoting their own ideas. Even lonely citizens busily cultivating their ragings in solitude can now discover confirmatory evidence and seemingly sound reasons for their own agitation at lightning speed— without having to pass these through the sort of official credibility and reality filters employed by classic media democracy. The implication is, therefore, that the structuring power of the public sphere in the democracy of outrage is now ultimately the individual user. The individuals have become the directors of their world experience, they are now able to construct their private realities, and these realities will rapidly metamorphose from a personal reality into the generally valid reality. Individual thinking can in this way flexibilise and dynamise itself against the horizon of an incredible multitude of free-floating interpretations, but it can also of course armour and encapsulate itself in self-built echo chambers, where hate-soaked messages will be resounding from all sides. The law professor and publicist Cass Sunstein has given detailed descriptions of these echo chamber and polarisation effects in his studies. His central findings are that every individual can now, without causing friction with the views of the general public, generate an information and communication situation in which three different amplifier mechanisms come into play. First, one only has access to a strictly limited number of views and lines of argument. Second, the group's internal conformity pressure reinforces the potentially already extreme position by preferring not to reveal or file for discussion any still remaining doubts so as not to become exposed to the presumed majority in a negative way. And third, the compliance of others augments confidence in one's personal judgements, and one therefore formulates and acts with greater assuredness because, wound up by the assent of the like-minded, one is led to assume with absolute certainty that one is in the self-evident right.[70] The consequence of these different amplifying mechanisms is inevitably that positions and fronts rigidify.

A detailed analysis of the communication of rage and hatred on the internet shows that it is, time and again, particular groups of persons and representatives of particular professions that are attacked to an excessive degree. There clearly seems to be a limited repertoire of enemy images.[71] It includes preferably refugees, foreign-looking persons and members of minorities. Furthermore, journalists and politicians, who are suspected of serving the purposes of the establishment or the interests of foreign powers, but definitely not the interests of the population. It is also revealing that the frantic statements of the enraged networked citizens abound with indiscriminate *system mistrust* (in contradistinction to well-reasoned *special mistrust* based on particular cases of misconduct), a sombre and darkly flickering anti-feeling that is directed against "those up there", as is similarly apparent from international surveys concerning the loss of trust and reputation of politicians and journalists.[72] Politicians and journalists are made to appear—from the perspective of critics formulating without restraint and roaming the internet wishing them either to the devil or to the gallows—to be members of a plotting elite, i.e., they are no longer perceived as fundamentally antagonistic forces but as part of a diffuse phalanx, a sphere of power, which must be fought as one unity. Moreover, successful and actively feminist women, in particular, attract rage and hatred and are in extreme cases threatened with rape and murder. The purpose is obviously to remove them from the public sphere by all available means and marginalise them as participants in public discourse, not least with suppression fantasies, the beastliness-soaked game with deep-seated primal anxieties, the threat to harm them in their innermost selves. *Silencing* is the name of this technique from the toolbox of intimidation. The threats come from individuals or from whole groups of trolls that conspire to hunt down individuals as long and as massively as possible until they flee in shock to protected forums or give up completely. It would be a mistake to ennoble by quotation the hate postings received by active feminists or prominent women; they are—in an operation of counteroffensive through publication—partially documented on special proprietary platforms.[73] And it would be absurd to illuminate spheres of a media underworld called "Chokeabitch" or "Rapebait"[74] or to reproduce photographs showing men displaying battered and unconscious women like trophies after a big game hunt. This would unnecessarily potentiate the cruelty glorified in this media underworld. It is of supreme importance, however, that the existence of all this is made publicly known, and that it can even be easily verified in minutes by a Google search. No prophetical gifts are needed to see that the unfiltered presence of horror will inescapably change the mentality and awareness of networked individuals. Anyone who enjoys the experience of disgust and wants to relish the horror of internet debates that are no longer debates, will be rewarded with many opportunities. And they will be offered a plethora of evidence, possibly inducing them to despair of the minds and hearts of the outlandish and hardly avoidable inhabitants of the inner communication worlds of the internet, as they puke their hatred with drooling jaws.

The Many Faces of the Fifth Power

But is this now the complete and also appropriately fair picture of the discourse conditions in the democracy of outrage? Is the "personality" of the internet introduced by the publicist Joel Stein in his essay really adequately characterised by the indication of hatred and incitement? Naturally, these are rhetorical questions that show, however, a particular danger connected with an analytical diagnosis of discourse itself: the hatred may contaminate the analysis because the uninhibited aggression may, with its sheer momentum of intrusive virulence, compel the researcher to pass inappropriate sweeping judgements. And suddenly— following Gustav Le Bon's culture-pessimistic mass psychology and his consequently promoted mass contempt—the *mob* is everywhere, the *riffraff* publishes without inhibition, and the evil-minded *trolls* attack out of the darkness of anonymity. Other catchwords deal with *crowd stupidity* or with the ideology of *digital Maoism* that devalues the individual and celebrates the collective, with the *cult of the amateur*, the *hour of the dabblers* or the *confusion of the Many* who have transformed the digital public sphere into a breeding ground of verbal violence and unleashed irrationality. "The vulgar riffraff enters the arena of action again with renewed self-confidence", we can for instance read in an exemplary agitated interpretation of the present communication conditions. "The anonymity of the Internet therefore signifies a regression of civilisation in the direction of fascism and the middle ages, towards pogroms and witch burnings."[75] Another author writes in a book with the telling title *Meute mit Meinung [Horde with a View]*:

The relationship between publicists and public has been fundamentally changed by the networked society. The exchange of opinions is now no longer restricted to high-plateau media because now everyone can barge in, in real time, via Twitter, Facebook and the commentary columns of the Internet. And the general public is given the ubiquitous invitation: "Join the debate!" The consequences are predictable: Who allows the riffraff in, will suffer riffraff treatment. Who allows the mob to participate will be mobbed.[76]

Such sentences make clear that discourse analysis and discourse criticism may themselves be made instruments of a rhetoric of escalation and that, consequently, the anger about the anger of the other side, *outrage of the second order*, has meanwhile become a communicative normality. The problem of such aggressively degrading blanket statements is that we continuously produce injustices ourselves and that we trans-interpret the indubitably horrible extreme by means of a few catchwords into a phenomenal totality, as if the digital public sphere consisted solely of outrage junkies and idiots, who behave and mob excessively in disgusting ways, practise hate or lose themselves in bizarre conspiracy theories. This is misguided, of course, and all those in forums and blogs who operate differently, sensibly, arguing in a rational problem-oriented way, will experience such attacks as unfair and offensive. Therefore, in a time of an increasing pluralism of voices, we must raise the serious question of the generalisability of our own diagnoses, lest we simply fuel the general agitation even more. Whose story counts? The story of a nine-year-old girl or the story of the trolls that pursue their victim in a bestial manner? In the public worlds of the digital age the simultaneity of the different has become visible in a measure unknown before. Therefore, "the" personality of the internet simply cannot exist, as there are only very differently dominant and differently loud or soft-spoken but certainly not per se representative partial personalities. If we take this premise of fundamental difference in the digital world seriously, then the consequence can only be that the devaluating generalisation is always unjust and bound to create new offences, because extremely dissimilar characters and temperaments articulate themselves, as a rule, on one and the same platform. And this also means, of course, that a sweeping diagnosis, if it is presented in a suggestive and forceful manner, will only exacerbate the tone and increase the hysteria of the debates. The presumed analysis of outrage is then itself a trigger of outrage and will function as a catalyst of an endlessly continued game of agitation that contributes little to clarification but more to a further rigidification of the various fronts. Analytical mobility and material fairness can be better achieved by choosing a double perspective of description, which concretely identifies criticism and deciphers tendencies but is cautious with generalisation and blanket claims. On the one hand, the indications of degeneration must obviously be criticised, but it must be stressed, on the other hand, that a public that has won media power and those who have now acquired a voice on the internet, are all fundamentally quite different. A discourse analysis that is trying to implement such a view will therefore always start with the basic admission: we are dealing with a radically pluralistic sphere of power and influence, a *fifth power*, which is now establishing itself—as a publicative power in its own right—alongside the executive, the judicial, the legislative, and the fourth power of traditional journalism.[77] This fifth power of the networked Many is both beautiful and ugly, both sensible and cruel, it sometimes operates extremely brutally and sometimes shows moral involvement in a touching way. It initiates campaigns and creates counter-publicity. It does not orient itself by a single ideology, it has no unifying grand theme, but it has communally used platforms and instruments—social networks, wikis, websites, smartphones, high-performance computers, i.e., the whole spectrum of digital media. One cannot emphasise often enough that it is not very reasonable to present the networked Many simply as *mob* or *pack* and thus as a threat to discourse, even though they control and dominate the mobbing spectacles. But it is no less appropriate—and this is the other extreme—to rave abstractly about a digital grassroots movement that will finally put the world to rights with its notebooks, and that will alone be capable of formulating enriching and eternally meaningful discourse contributions. Between these two extremes of valuation, we can identify diverse balanced amalgams and mixtures, diverse patterns of action, and diverse forms of influences changing the public sphere.

It is now first of all necessary to record the obvious. The networked Many set agendas, they provide suggestions and material for further processing, they are energetically supported by the classic key media that pick up what the Many are debating. Simple internet publicity (a trend wave on Twitter, a shitstorm, overheating rumours in the social networks) has long been a public-directed news factor and an argument in the journalists' justification of topic choice. The motto reads, then: "Look what is going on!" In addition, the fifth power proves to be a topic supplier, also an opinion corrective and a media-critical authority. Mistakenly chosen film extracts are criticised, then stagings in the form of symbolic photos, exaggerations, exacerbations, banalisations. The underpinning of commentaries and articles is aided by the new possibilities of the precise documentation of mistakes and oversights. The media journalist Fritz Wolf notes

> Everyone can now download films, can watch them in the media store, can halt them. What used to rush by unnoticed in earlier times, can now be halted and even watched more closely in an enlarged format. This is often laborious petty work that can hardly ever be performed by the editorial offices themselves. ... Now nothing gets lost on the air as one was wont to say in editorial offices some time ago, if a mistake had passed unnoticed. When something is wrong in text or image then it no longer just simply disappears. The images, the texts, the gestures are all stored somewhere and can be retrieved and re-examined.[78]

The Russia reports, the so-called alleged or actual demonisation of President Putin, the presumed prejudices of the public service stations, and the kind of selection and weighting of news, are core activities of the ongoing media criticism on the internet. Special media-critical initiatives point out mistakes, numerous users comment in the commentary columns of the editorial offices what they favour or, more frequently, what annoys them.[79] It again becomes clear that there is a very heterogeneous picture if one cares to take a closer look; the bandwidth of utterances is enormous. One encounters analytical, careful and well-informed media critics who topicalise grave mistakes, who lament the missing distance between media and politics, but one also discovers the ideologically radicalised conspiracy theorists, the *press-of-lies* shouters as well as the interminably raging ideologues threatening with violence and suggesting that all journalists should be thrashed.[80] There are both prudent commentators and fanaticised accusers, who are equally active and tirelessly fire off complaints. Sometimes their anger is directed against the whole profession, the journalistic craft, sometimes at a particular person. Thus, enraged spectators at the beginning of the year 2014 attacked the talk-show host Markus Lanz, who had been declared a symbolic figure of mindless histrionic television after a disastrous interview with left-wing politician Sahra Wagenknecht. Hundreds of thousands joined an online petition and demanded his dismissal. Many commentators working for the classic media, however, reacted with horror and criticised the asymmetry between the comparatively marginal occasion of a failed interview and the drastic punishment demanded, i.e., the dismissal of the talk-show host. This divide between *public outrage* and *media outrage* is characteristic of the actual communication conditions, because each and every person today has their own channel, their own platform, on which emancipation from the majority opinion can be put into living practice. The consequence is that both the estrangement among the discourse participants and the criticism become manifest in a different degree of clarity. This kind of estrangement may also have existed in the past but it is undeniable now, because it is ever present and public. It is this *transparency of the difference* that basically shapes the discourse conditions far beyond the particular concrete provoking message, beyond concrete topics and particular contents. We now know whether we understand each other, whether we value each other, or whether we do neither. Criticism, once made public, has become a factor as well as a fact and cannot simply be edited out or negated. The obvious drifting apart of public outrage and media outrage thus becomes an everyday communication reality.

Another discourse-changing action and role pattern of the fifth power is in-depth investigation and targeted suspect hunt. In accordance with the principle of crowdsourcing—collective work in a crowd—together we speedily glean the fragments of an information puzzle and organise everything around a target of knowledge and disclosure of actual interest. Is it a question of identifying paedophile men after they have been lured in front of a camera by television producers where they might appear in a sloppily anonymised form? Can one identify them? Is there a new case of plagiarism that requires a crowd trimmed for strict detection work in order to accomplish appropriate unmasking? Must a terrorist be arrested after an assassination attempt? Can one find indications in photographs or videos on an individual's mobile phonethat have so far been overlooked? In such cases, too, the new powers and the new hobby detectives of the digital age are ready for immediate action, sometimes with good results, sometimes significantly more quickly than traditional journalists who are tied down by deadlines of printing and broad-casting or are hampered by lack of resources, sometimes with catastrophic consequences for innocent people or outsiders who are rashly accused, condemned and unjustly pilloried.

The Power of Connectives

So now the problem arises as to how the fifth power can be called to account in doubtful cases, or how the media public with all its acquired power might quasi-civilise itself—lacking an institutional address and accessibility regarding its ethos of responsibility. The communication scientist Tanjev Schultz is quite right, writing that the fifth power

> does not at all act solely as a controlling and a counter-power that pursues justified claims and provides attention for positions that have been unjustly marginalised. It often hides interfering insistence, populism, extremism, dilettantism, prejudices, conspiracy theories, disinformation, propaganda and mobbing. In short, the periphery of the periphery when elevated to the fifth power is both opportunity and risk for the deliberative democracy.[81]

Who will therefore have the means to control this new controlling power in the universe of discourse? Control is in actual fact barely possible because there are, as a rule, no clearly identifiable individuals and no calculable sequences of steps in the relevant procedural processes. One cannot simply pick on an individual as the central agent and make this individual accountable simply because the network effects cannot be personalised in this way. The power of the networked Many manifests itself in circularly interlaced chains of effect and in the energetic interplay of diverse forces, which may make a single incident explode into a big event. Examples of spontaneous mobilisation without clearly identifiable leaders and the discourse-shaping effect of suddenly penetrating impulses are the so-called #aufschrei debate and the #metoo movement, which have catapulted the topic of everyday sexism onto the level of a general agenda. How did it all start? The first answer is: there was a general rise in awareness of the topic of sexism because magazines like *Der Spiegel* and *Stern* had reported abusive approaches and offensive sexist language. The second answer is, however: everything began—in a climate of heightened sensibility, naturally—with a single tweet. During the night of 24 January 2013, internet activist Anne Wizorek reads a message from her online acquaintance Nicole von Horst which deeply shocks her: "The doctor who pawed my bottom when I was in hospital after a suicide attempt." This extremely reduced report of an abusive attack moved her to consider the idea of collecting similar experiences of sexist brutality under the hashtag #aufschrei. And suddenly numerous stupid remarks of the same kind are publicised, but also reports of violence, beatings, attacks. As ever more women come forward and relate their experiences, Anne Wizorek writes, overwhelmed: "I am crying just now, but please do not stop." 60,000 tweets are assembled in only the first two weeks—shocking mini-narratives told in the format of maximally 140 characters. Here we have, grouped around a hashtag, an organisation without organisation. There is a pulsating community created by sharing information, ever changing in intensity and size, that one could designate—to distinguish it from a strictly hierarchically shaped *collective*—a *connective*.[82] Collectives (for instance a party or some enterprise) act on the basis of clear agreements, common principles and strong ties, oriented by clearly recognisable decision and power centres. Orders and prescriptions are possible. Connective action, in contrast, is rather less determined from outside but far more strongly oriented by individual-personal self-expression, facilitated and shaped by digital media. There are no clearly defined internal–external boundaries. A connective cannot be given orders, common procedure cannot be enforced and membership cannot be determined in an authoritarian way. Nobody can say: "Okay that's it for now! Now change direction!" Connectives possess the shape of an *individual mass*; they combine the impact of a communal presence with personal self-expression remaining visible unfiltered and not pressed into a pre-set schema. They are *Me–Us communities* whose secret of attraction lies in the mixture of the membership promises, openness, and the offer of individualisation in the form of personal histories, images, films and contributions.

But one thing must be added immediately: the ad-hoc formation of such connectives does not at all mean that collectives—NGOs, professional campaigners, institutionally stable interest groups—are rendered superfluous, and that only the unstable crowd formation remains in control everywhere; crowds form spontaneously and at some stage collapse again into the nothingness of disorganisation. Classic collectives (naturally including powerful individuals and smart PR strategists) are able to inspire the formation of connectives in a more or less targeted manner—and so shape debates and discourses. They supply the Many who may suddenly attach themselves, armed with prefabricated materials, pre-formulated protest letters, shocking images, simple mass-effective messages, and animate them to tweet and click. In this way, for instance, the environmental organisation Greenpeace, a classic collective, used social networks offensively as campaign media for the first time in 2010 and thus managed to get the giant company Nestlé on the run with prepared online petitions and shock videos. The company was urged to abandon the purchase of palm oil from those producers who were involved in the illegal clearing of primeval forests in Indonesia. The strategy of comprehensive mobilisation was successful. Outraged consumers and clients tweeted an endless stream of protest messages, articulated their anger in social networks and linked the shock videos showing the death of orangutans in a destroyed primeval forest. Nestlé finally caved in. This means, once again in a more general perspective: the power of the network Many cannot be considered in isolation. Agitation may be triggered due to the societal atmosphere in connection with the impulse of just one individual, or it may be due to a campaign idea that suddenly generates resonance. As a rule, it is the classic mass media that create the connection between micro- and macro-publicity and supply the agenda setting with the necessary power.

It is quite undeniable in all these processes of influencing discourse, however, that the once faceless army of media consumers, condemned to passivity, has now adopted an active role, and that the use of the collective singular suggesting homogeneity—*the audience*—has been rendered meaningless through the transition from the media democracy to the outrage democracy. Here we have "the People Formerly Known as the Audience", as the journalist Jay Rosen formulates.[83] They are now shaping the great public discourse that a society conducts with itself with varying intentions and concerns, relaxed or angry, constructively or destructively.

4

The Crisis of Authority: Or the Pains of Visibility

Expansion of the Observation Zone

The comparison of two different scenarios of news reporting can be helpful for gaining a good impression of the effects of the power of new media and their potential to pulverise authority and reputation. The first scenario is from the far-removed media past, during the years 1933–1945 and shows, in contrast to the present, how the development of media brings about a subliminally effective perceptual revolution. Franklin D. Roosevelt is in office as president of the United States of America. In this phase of his presidency, he is wheelchair bound, probably due to a polio infection, and can walk only a few steps in extreme pain with the help of metal leg braces, propped up by assistants, always in danger of falling. What is peculiar from today's perspective and is in fact totally unimaginable is that his actual state of health remains more or less unknown to the majority of the population during his lifetime, because very little of his private life becomes publicly known.[84] There is some knowledge of a past illness and there are a few newspaper articles in which

© The Author(s), under exclusive license to Springer Nature Switzerland AG 2022
B. Poerksen, *Digital Fever*,
https://doi.org/10.1007/978-3-030-89522-8_3

a wheelchair is mentioned, but there are practically no photographs that could substantiate these scant pieces of information and influence the general perception. Roosevelt is able to control his public image—in case of doubt with the help of security officials, who force the photographers to hand over their cameras in order to destroy the films. The metallic leg braces sticking out of his waistband are concealed as well as possible. He is never photographed when being heaved out of his car by his helpers. At public appearances the curtain is only raised when the president is already securely seated at his desk. And whenever a few steps in front of the eyes of the public cannot be avoided at all, then Roosevelt saunters about as relaxed as possible, taking his time for casual conversation, leaning on a walking stick or the arm of a trusted assistant that he uses like a crutch as he slowly and with extreme discipline steers towards his goal. He is a good actor, as he acknowledges himself, whose stage management can only function, however, because he is in a position of authority to determine what may become visible and what must remain hidden.

The second scenario of news reporting is connected with a precise date: 11 September 2016. On this day a commemorative event takes place at Ground Zero in New York for the victims of the terror attack of 11 September 2001. Presidential candidate Hillary Clinton is also present.[85] It is the culminating phase of the election campaign, a hot and muggy day. The Democrat politician, who is suffering from pneumonia, as emerges later, leaves the event early. She has to wait a few minutes for her car, surrounded by members of her staff who are propping her up. When a car approaches, the hobby photographer Zdenek Gazda, actually a supporter of the candidate, in a reflex action pulls out his smartphone and films the scene. And he happens to create a video of just about 20 seconds that will prompt a global stir in an election campaign charac-terised by rumours and naked aggression. One can see how Clinton's legs give way and how her assistants grab her under the arms and with great presence of mind form a circle around her to guard her against prying looks. Zdenek Gazda posts the video without further reflection on Face-book. A few minutes later Fox News reporter Rick Leventhal, claiming an anonymous source, tweets that Hillary Clinton possibly suffers from some ailment, had to leave the commemorative event prematurely and probably fainted on her way to the car. The tweet suggests that there were apparently diverse observers of what happened now beginning to feed the media. What is still lacking, however, is the evidence of an impressive image or film. Shortly after, Monica Alba, reporter for NBC News, raises the question on Twitter as to where Clinton was at that moment because she had left the ceremonial event half an hour before. One of her spokespersons says that it had become simply too hot for her. Barely two hours after Zdenek Gazda had posted his video it is discovered and immediately finds its way into the mainstream media. Television stations show the pictures, also YouTube, and they are shared on social networks. Google search queries like "Hillary Clinton collapsing" or "Hillary Clinton 9/11" keep shooting up. What makes an attack of faintness and the ensuing news reports so relevant from the point of view of media analysis and the critical evaluation of our life and times?

The answer is, first, that this total illumination of the ordinary life of a politician shows that the protected spaces of intransparency, the spheres of vagueness and impartiality, are disappearing because everything is under permanent observation, is filmed or photographed, because each and every one can now broadcast and post and supply fresh material for the archives of our time.[86] In conjunction with the classic media, a glaring over-illuminated world arises in which hardly anything can remain hidden. The media power that still had a clearly identifiable centre in the analogue world is suddenly everywhere. It wanders from individual persons and single institution into situations. It is contained in the smartphone and in the digital camera, it reveals itself in a millionfold clicks of videos, it can be experienced in the unexpected effervescence of attention excesses. And it shows itself in the form of a highly nervously reacting network of effects, a world-encompassing nervous system, which needs only a slight irritation in order to produce hardly manageable waves of agitation, thunderstorms of impulses that may start on the social networks and on Twitter but live on in hectically pulsating live tickers, television stations and newspapers. Sometimes a simple 20-second video suffices as a first minimal impulse that flares up and in no time leads to an explosive drama. On the other hand, and this is also demonstrated by Hillary Clinton's dizzy spell, the example makes clear to what extent the development of the media determines the perception of events. In another media epoch, only stories would have been related by people present at the event, stories that might possibly have been rejected, relativised or even flatly denied by official spokespersons. Without the experience of the evidence of filmic documentation, there would have been a lot of quarrelling about the details of what actually happened and the significance of the event. Eyewitnesses would have come forward and would have presented different versions and interpretations. The possibilities of instant recording and the ad-hoc dissemination of films with the aid of mobile phones are of course comparatively new. When Hillary Clinton in 2008 tried for the first time to run for the office of US president, the iPhone did not have a video function. In 2012 one could make videos but only 45 per cent of all Americans possessed a smartphone and the publication of videos was not supported by Facebook or Twitter. By the time of the recording at Ground Zero, however, the publication of videos had become central to social media activities, and 77 per cent of Americans were already in possession of a network-capable mobile phone. Worldwide there are now (2021) about 3.8 billion smartphones users. And finally, what happened around Hillary Clinton is of explosive importance to media theory. Joshua Meyrowitz, a pupil in spirit of Marshall McLuhan and Erving Goffman, has developed the necessary tools for the analysis and interpretation of key events of this type. He distinguishes, on the basis of a reinterpretation of the interaction sociology of Erving Goffman, between the *downstage* and the *backstage* of behaviour, but does not envisage these stages, as Goffman does, as primary places of a strict static-spatial kind but as comparatively variable interaction systems and as potentially changeable worlds of perception, changeable for instance by media and communication instruments.[87] In this conception the backstage is not a strictly definable and forever delimitable space, where one can feel unobserved and relaxed, but a sphere that is inevitably under threat from the modern media. What happens here must not become public. The downstage, however—the sphere of what is generally visible—is ruled by the postulate of role- and norm-conforming behaviour in specific absoluteness. Here one must function, must orient oneself by what is publicly expected. Here one must never lower one's guard nor show weakness. Here one must conceal the tricks and methods of the stage management of desired impressions. The basic thesis of Meyrowitz is that microphones and cameras are increasingly endangering the clear distinction between backstage and downstage—thus damaging persons of authority through the effect of public embarrassment. He writes:

> Now, physically bounded spaces are less significant as information is able to flow through walls and rush across great distances. As a result, where one is has less and less to do with what one knows and experiences. Electronic media have altered the signifi-cance of time and space for social interaction. Certainly, physical presence and direct sensory contact remain primary forms of experi-ence. But the social spheres defined by walls of the mightiest fortress no longer define a truly segregated social setting if a camera, a mi-crophone, or even a telephone is present.[88]

Such considerations allow us to interpret the dissemination of the 20-second clip as the symptom of an unlimited media world. Hillary Clinton is waiting for her car and wants to get in, leave the observation zone of the public and enter the protected world of the inside of the car. But she is no longer strong enough to perform this transition without a mishap, which is not in accordance with the required permanent demon-stration of power ("never show weakness!"). Zdenek Gazda documents a disruption of the stage management in this attempted escape to the back-stage. His smartphone, both observation and dissemination technology, in conjunction with the other media of a largely networked world, oper-ates as a kind of *situation liquidifier* producing a *mixed zone* obliterating the apparently clear distinction between backstage and downstage. The boundaries and traditional distinctions within the world of communica-tions become fragile and porous: between the public and the private, the stage management and the effort to protect it, between the small number of bodily present people and the big number of spectators in the whole world.

Now the general upshot would be: Franklin D. Roosevelt, in the years of his presidency from 1933 to 1945, was able to conceal to a large extent what shape he was in. There is only one film of a few seconds and there are three photographs showing him in his wheelchair. (The film excerpt was only discovered in 2013 by a researcher in an archive, and it is inter-esting to note that the wheelchair cannot really be seen, but it is more

or less confirmed by the height of the seat and the sliding movement—
sailors standing around obscure the field of vision.) The case of Hillary
Clinton is completely different. Her attack of faintness is registered
directly and becomes a globally discussed image disaster. Two days after
the event *The New York Times* publishes an article dealing with the question of how healthy the candidate really is and quotes from the medical
report of her doctor. "Mrs. Clinton's pneumonia affects her right lung's
middle lobe, according to Dr. Bardack, a location that suggests that it was
caused by bacteria, commonly pneumococcus," the passage reads. "Mrs.
Clinton received two preventive vaccines against pneumococcal infection: Prevnar and Pneumovax. Neither is 100 percent protective against
pneumococcal pneumonia. ... Mrs. Clinton has been treated with two
antibiotics, first for a lingering cough and then for pneumonia. The first
antibiotic, which was not identified, was prescribed short term on Sept. 2
after she experienced a low-grade fever for 24 hours, along with conges-
tion and fatigue attributed to an upper respiratory tract infection related
to her seasonal allergies."[89] One can read this written statement as a kind
of health certificate. Oh well, one could say, one is informed and kept up
to date. At the same time, however, such an article is no doubt a proof of
a radically transparent world, an illustration of the idea of enlightenment
taken to its extreme, an idea that lays all of us open to attack, renders us
vulnerable, and inflicts the peculiar pains of visibility of the networked
society as we experience it today.

Collateral Damage of Transparency

A few years ago the writer Hans Magnus Enzensberger called for "pity
on the politicians" and in an angry and sparkling satire poured scorn
on those who live off politics as a largely isolated marginal group as far
removed from real life as the inmates of a psychiatric institution. "Like
the inmates of an institution the politicians are watched all the time," we
may read there. "To the peephole or the panopticon of the classic penal
institution corresponds in their case the eye of the camera, and the role
of the guards is taken by journalists and public prosecutors."[90] Enzensberger here refers to a thought model of the philosopher Jeremy Bentham

in order to illustrate the suffering of hounded people.[91] Bentham developed the concept of the panopticon in order to optimise and perfect prison regimes. The essential features of the panopticon are that the prisoners can never know with certainty whether they are being observed in their cells or not. The basic principle of this architecture of surveillance is that the guard is invisible to the prisoners and the cells are organised in a ring around a watchtower in the middle. It is the *potential* visibility that acts as the controlling and disciplinary force, simply because everyone must at any moment reckon with observation from outside. In his 1992 essay Enzensberger, like Michel Foucault earlier,[92] interprets the conditions of visibility strictly in accordance with the logic of this traditional panopticon model: there is one single central instance of power and the inmates of the institution and the prison are helpless and completely at its mercy. They are objects, not subjects, and participants in the surveillance situation under which they suffer. This means: Enzensberger pursues a line of argumentation with clear oppositions and easily identifiable asymmetries that no longer exist in the same way. In his analysis there are powerful media people with their cameras that lean over prisoners like prison warders. His ironical and condescending plea to pour maximum pity on the politicians derives from the idea that they are—at the moment of observation—simply victims and certainly not perpetrators.

There are good reasons to doubt that the circumstances in the field of politics have ever been so clear and unambiguous, they have certainly become more complicated and multi-coloured today. In our digital modernity a sort of panopticon has emerged that has been fabricated by ourselves and others and that has made the relationships between guards and guarded, between observers and observed, flexible and thus even permits a rapid exchange of roles. *Surveillance* and *sousveillance* take turns.[93] There is no longer the single central watchtower but a multitude of possibilities of exploring each other, of pursuing others right into their spheres of intimacy and privacy and of documenting their behaviour. All of a sudden, the guards are everywhere, standing at every street corner, smartphone in hand. Ever smaller, ever cheaper and ever more powerful media and communication instruments permit comprehensive illumination and 360° observation. Storage density, processor speed and the possibilities of searching and linking data are continually expanding. At the same time, those who are surveyed, for instance politicians, who were perhaps once driven carelessly or perhaps with cool calculation to instrumentalise these media for their own purposes, make public what they do and think. They tweet their thoughts and streams of consciousness, they document their ordinary life by means of postings, photos and films, and sometimes reveal even private things, embarrassing and intimate matters, in exchange for a form of publicity that they consider suitable to make them appear more humane, more normal and more approachable.

Finally, from a purely quantitative point of view, there is now ever more material, more data and documents that are being disclosed. One can easily make oneself aware of these changes by simply looking at a few representative figures of the photo industry. In the year 2000 the firm Kodak announced that about 80,000 million photos were made around the world. In the year 2010 the figure had risen to 300,000 million images, in 2015 to one billion, which is more than 2700 million images per day and 122.5 million images per hour.[94] For the year 2016 the Photo Industry Association announced a new record of 1138 billion photographs, taken frequently no longer with classic digital cameras but with smartphones. About 40,000 photographs are posted every minute on Instagram, to which must be added what is posted on Facebook, Flickr or Snapchat. Over a 24-hours period worldwide 1.6 billion images are simply sent with the messaging service WhatsApp. Gigantic mountains of material are created this way. And one does not have to be a prophet to imagine that among this mass of photographs can certainly be found embarrassing poses and scenes from the world of politics predestined for the discrimination and the discrediting of people. These are ideal preconditions for the optimal illustration of resentments. Every affect directed against "those up there" is supplied with a justifying reason, because whenever needed one can constantly bolster the great narration of the corruption and the general degeneration of politics in this way. One can certainly always find a suitable symbol or an image to serve as evidence.

Is it therefore appropriate to pour pity on politicians in the panopticon created by ourselves and others in our present time? Is pity required?

This is actually the wrong question because it blinds us to the elementary ambivalence of the transparency that meanwhile, in the age of ubiquitous digital media, has reached a novel level of evolution and escalation. For transparency is in itself neither good nor bad. It may serve extremely positive purposes—in the right dosage, in the appropriate context, focussing on a particular topic, and coupled with the question of societal relevance. Considered in reverse, however, impenetrability and intransparency can under certain circumstances offer an advantage or even a necessary condition for the success of difficult negotiations that are existentially dependent on confidentiality and the careful and discreet exploration of positions and possibilities of compromise. Some of the forms "of the undercover eliciting of potential consent" may often only become possible under conditions of trustworthy seclusion, as pointed out by the communication psychologist Eberhard Stahl, who has written about "*Lob der Intransparenz*" [Praise for the lack of transparency].[95] The consequence is that the wholesale jubilation of the transparency enthusiasts is just as false as the plea, coloured by culture pessimism, for the dark and the mysterious, for the heavy-blooded romanticism of concealment that seeks to stand up against the illumination of existence and sweepingly defames even the act of publication as pornographic. Transparency is an *instrumental* not an *absolute* value and must be discussed in a framework of means-and-ends relationships and with regard to our greater superordinate goal (e.g., the clarification of responsibility and accountability).[96] It can most certainly only be welcomed that cases of corruption and scandals are disclosed and that journalists together with bloggers point out how power is abused when individuals document and publish what cases of injustice they register. It would ultimately be extremely inimical to democracy to diminish or fundamentally negate this positive function of transparency and publicity—the precondition of an effective self-purification of societies. Once again: the act of disclosure and unmasking is or can be useful and necessary to correct negative developments and to open up opportunities so as to learn from them.

Heroes and Anti-Heroes in the Internet Age

So where does the problem actually lie, one might ask? The problem is that in some diffuse way we know, or at least imagine, too much so as to preserve a certain radically sobered capability of veneration. And that we know too much is the result of the fact that under the conditions of digitalisation an *absolutism of transparency* has come to rule that not only undermines the acceptance of authorities in concrete cases, but undermines such acceptance in a fundamental fashion. Whatever may be said and done can now become public with an ease hitherto unknown and can, once digitalised and put onto the internet, be searched without trouble, no longer really be censored and controlled. Authority, however, needs the protected and controllable space if it is to last. It needs the targeted selection of what is accessible, it needs visibility, and it needs a certain measure of distance because too much proximity and accessibility inevitably lead to disenchantment and profanation. Joshua Meyrowitz writes:

> An examination of hierarchal roles suggests that all people are, in a sense, "ordinary". An image of greatness, however, can be maintained by not allowing one's ordinariness to show ... High status depends on conscious or unconscious strategies for controlling situations. The high status person can maintain his or her status only by carefully controlling information and by hiding the need for, and the techniques of, control. Yet if one's strategies for appearing important are exposed, one loses one's image of importance. All techniques of creating awe, therefore, bring with them the danger of shame – shame caused by the potential revelation of the need for technique. The reliance of authority on privacy suggests that hierarchies are usually supported by media that foster a clear distinction between leaders' personal behaviours and public actions. Hierarchies will be undermined by new media that expose what were once the private spheres of authorities.[97]

And there are more succinct descriptions of the basically contradictory nature of the situation:

In pursuing our desire to be "close" to great people or to confirm their greatness through increased exposure, we often destroy their ability to function as great people. "Greatness" manifests itself in the onstage performance and, by definition, in its isolation from backstage behaviours. Yet when we say that we want to see what authorities are "really like," we generally mean we want to see what they are *least* like, that is, both how they behave least often in the role they perform for us, and also the least they can be in social terms. In intimate spheres, people are often very much alike: They eat, they eliminate, they get tired, they sleep, they make love, they groom, they indulge in whims and self-involvements.[98]

It is a fact that today politicians are regularly also seen in bizarre poses or at least in the garish light of commonness because the indiscreet media of our time operate as instruments of systematic disappointment and dis-idealisation. They pulverise charisma and permit the permanent production of disquieting disclosures. Model characters and heroes that seemed still unreachable suddenly turn into *dwarfs*, the publicist Torsten Körner formulates, because "the aura of difference" and otherness can no longer be preserved and because in the internet "every identity can be unmasked" and the "story, the historical greenhouse of the charismatic personality, dissolves into myriads of moments and points in time all of equal weight".[99] All of a sudden politicians are seen as the simple workmates next door, swearing savagely at the filling station, displaying their pot bellies on the beach, totally devoid of the aura of the enigmatic and loftily mysterious that gives life to the charismatic personality. And just imagine that we discovered on YouTube a blurred video taken by a mobile phone showing Willy Brandt, the former German Chancellor, in a hotel in Warsaw diligently rehearsing his genuflection in front of a mirror under the direction of a PR consultant? Would his performed gesture which became so widely known throughout the world still exhibit that infinitely grief-stricken dignity, would it still be effective at all?

To ascertain the connections between digitalisation and the crisis of authority in more precise detail, one must take a broader view for a moment, so as to realise that the peculiarities of media communication produce corresponding forms of visibility and therefore vulnerability. The written record is already public memory. It makes mistakes and slips and embarrassments of all kinds available across space and time. But only its transformation into the mobile, reaction- and combination-ready aggregate of the digital world makes it permanently consumable for an arbitrary and freely shifting public. And the carrier medium of paper delimits its own range and permits a comparatively high measure of information and communication control. Paper can be blackened and burned, it can deteriorate and yellow, disappear in archives or behind the high walls of libraries, and is therefore accessible only with compara-tively high effort. The photograph freezes the moment and tears it from transience, it has the quality of evidence and generates the impression of reality even though one knows how easily it can be forged. Using sound adds the acoustic dimension, making the emotions of speakers experi-enceable in novel immediacy. Film and television produce a paradoxically glittering kind of *distant closeness*: one feels close to politicians as human beings all of a sudden, one interprets their facial expressions, hears their voices, can see every drop of sweat on their foreheads, the trembling of their hands, every involuntary twitching of the corners of their mouths.

In the digital age, the era of combination and globally available multi-media presentation, the assailability and vulnerability of politicians has again increased, because now all these so easily usable and generally accessible media with their qualities of special documentation may be condensed into an experience of evidence of a special kind. The blackout in a television programme or the rowdy outburst in a talk round, the flood of tears in a press conference, the theft of a biro in front of the eyes of a camera (Vaclav Klaus), the spontaneous gesture with the middle finger (Peer Steinbrück, Sigmar Gabriel), the sagging trousers of a prime minister (Winfried Kretschmann), the disastrous stage manage-ment of an election campaign (Martin Schulz)—anyone who wishes to do so can now recover any amount of embarrassments, disruptions in style and self-presentation, alleged or genuine transgressions and norm violations of all kinds, which by now somehow radiate a peculiar and essentially media-produced permanent freshness. And just try the Google test in order to reduce politicians or other authorities of your choice to normal size at the speed of lightning or even make them crash to the ground from their pedestals. There are pillory sites with plagia-risms, special blogs of demolition, debunking films and whole series of disclosure stories available online, videos evidencing vulgarity, cruelty or fraud, testimonies of hypocrisy in all imaginable sorts of variants and variation. One can find ridiculing videos just as easily as sexting documents (Anthony Wiener), scandal films that show politicians snorting cocaine or smoking crack (Rob Ford). One can discover films and undercover sound recordings documenting blaspheming, sexist or racist utterances or—for example—the boundless arrogance shown towards a taxi driver who does not behave in a humble enough way (David Mellor). One can find online protocols of police interviews as evidence for using prostitutes (Eliot Spitzer), can recover detailed reports about affairs and sex parties (Silvio Berlusconi), SMS messages to a stripper (Ilkka Kanerva), the disclosure story about a politician's one-night stand (Christine O'Donell). Thus, whole lives are reduced to a shameful and embarrassing moment, to a context-free presentation of a shrunken biography, which may potentially shape the public image of a person forever. Everyone can construct such a shrunken biography by means of intensive research, can then, for instance, assemble the findings on a proprietary site or use them to supplement the relevant Wikipedia article on that person with these evilly glowing messages. Everyone can with a few clicks uncover quotations and contributions from which contradictions can be constructed, when needed, from which an accusation of personal inconsistency or hypocrisy can be cobbled together. The searchability, the relative persistence and the sheer quantity of data and documents provide the information-technological preconditions for the general demystification of authority figures. They are all of a sudden confronted with the fact that there is a discussion in the communications space of the digital public sphere dealing with some of their previous views, perhaps their leanings towards luxury, their drinking habits, or their SMS messages to strippers, because someone has simply felt like publishing what they came across on the internet. In short, one must always reckon with an unmasking under these conditions because the discrediting documents may be made visible at lightning speed, diverse statements of one and the same person can be compared and contrasted with each other with little effort. The *ad-hoc manifestation of obvious contradictoriness* is the preliminary basis for the constantly and increasingly loud accusation of hypocrisy and mendacity.[100]

According to analyses by different authors concerning forms of memory in the digital age, we are threatened by a kind of comprehensive recollection that encompasses every tiny stirring moment of an individual life and will never release it from the corset of its prehistory.[101] Under the present media conditions the past is now forever "our pasts are becoming etched like a tattoo into our digital skins", we can read in an essay by the publicist J. D. Lasica; the Net "has forgotten how to forget".[102] This assertion, however self-evident and seemingly plausible it may seem nowadays, is certainly not correct in this absoluteness, because the internet does of course forget, but not in a controllable manner that can be governed by every single individual. Even in the case of grand and global events, as is shown by a study of US computer scientists, 30 per cent of all sources are no longer traceable after about two and a half years.[103] And everyone can surely confirm the experience that links suddenly stop working ("page not found"), that applications and programs age and that storage media start deteriorating right up to the moment of sudden unusability. Bruce Sterling, science-fiction author and internet expert of the first hour, has quite correctly called the digital era "the Golden Age of dead media",[104] because every innovation inevitably produces vast cemeteries of suddenly unusable gadgets and implements. Technical advances, the very tightly calculated production cycles, opaque algorithmic prefiltering and the increasingly active interest on the part of the public, the manipulation of search results by PR tricks—all this shapes and programmes the process of remembering in the digital age, transforms it into an anarchistic game ruled superficially by feedback loops, hits and hypes, or simple accidents and emerging innovations. The internet as a whole, to use an illuminating formulation by the media scientist Roberto Simanowski, is not an *archive* that is controllable by an individual, but an *anarchive* consisting of an infinite number of ramifications—a highly dynamic memory machine, constantly subjected to a permanent plebiscite of search questions and the emerging emotional climate of the moment, a machine that is fed in a self-organising way with ever new masses of data and bundles of documents.[105] What has just mercifully been lost in broadcasting and what has been thought to have been forgotten may one day emerge again, be posted again, be brought up to date, and then compete again with other impressions for predominance over the concrete moment. There is the EU politician Violeta Bulc, who just at a pivotal moment of her career is reminded publicly of her training as a shaman and of her esoteric-sounding blog contributions that report running over glowing coals and the power of positive energies. There is the German–French politician and publicist Daniel Cohn-Bendit, who in a 1975 book and in a bizarre talk-show appearance on French television in 1982 prattles about the eroticism and the sexual appeal of small children and relates his own experiences in a children's shop—and who is therefore suspected online of being a pederast, because nobody believes his intense pleading that his statements were time-bound idiocies and that none of the alleged things had ever happened. There are the scandals about the German Prime Minister Stefan Mappus, who shortly after his election orders the hard disk of a computer to be destroyed, unaware that someone—as usual—had made a security backup and that incriminating e-mails would soon become publicly known. It is this *potential* and no longer controllable presence of the past plus the accident-prone power of the anarchive that influences the image of politicians in the here and now in a scarcely predictable manner.[106]

Abstracting now at this point from all these individual case stories and trying to gain a certain distance so as not to get lost in specific scandal and gutter stories, we can recognise a fourfold effect of the disclosures and the general over-illumination that have thus become so easy and effortless.

First, authority under the conditions of ad-hoc attacks will become the result of an inevitably fragile consensus of self-organised, at best temporary, and not primarily institutionally guaranteed acceptance.[107] It will without much expenditure be given a moment of the questionable and doubtful, beyond the official protocol and the more strongly hierarchically organised streams of information. Authorities can then be controlled much more effectively but can also be put under pressure when required and forced to criticise and discuss their ideas and modes of behaviour in public.

Second, there will probably be boundary and threshold values of scandalisation and disclosure, never quite precisely definable but nevertheless existent, whose transgression transfers the suspicion originally restricted to a concrete case and condenses it into a fundamental negative judgement of whole groups or "those up there". "The regularity of the repetition of the singular arouses the suspicion," writes the political scientist Herfried Münkler, "that something more general is at the bottom of it all."[108] In other words, one cannot really believe in the exception, but views it as the normal, because the pace of the sheer number of disclosures itself seems to be a solid piece of evidence for the general deterioration of the leading personnel.

Third, it is becoming obvious that there is no escape today from the continual and systematic challenging of politicians. Anyone who wants to be permanently unassailable would have to show the courage to escape to a lonely valley, totally inaccessible to media, and there encapsulate themselves in a closed communication system with a strictly controllable public—inconceivable in this digital era. The conception of total reclusiveness and control, the information-technological precondition of unquestioned and totally undisturbed reverence, is clearly characteristic of a different epoch of media and human history. Fourth, and in conclusion, the experience of a diffuse public sphere of course impacts on the attitudes to life of politicians, who must constantly reckon with being caught in some misconduct or some act of cheating and being consequently publicly exposed as hypocrites or simply pilloried as embarrassing and somehow dubious figures. What is at stake here is the right of informational self-determination. Everyone must have the right to define who is to be allowed to know what about themselves, as was clearly decided by Germany's Federal Constitutional Court in a fundamental judgement on the census on 15 December 1983, because otherwise a societal climate of pre-emptive conformity, of anxiety and fear would be created.[109] We need the certainty not to be under continual observation in order to be able to lead a life in autonomy and freedom. In a world in which the absolutism of transparency is in power, this right can no longer be guaranteed and enforced—at least not for politicians who have reached a certain measure of prominence. Thus, the ideal of *informational self-determination*, promising the possibility of protection and withdrawal, becomes under the prevailing media conditions the experience of *informational uncertainty*, entailing the constant threat that one could be observed in an unfavourable situation and thus be open to instant attack.[110] This is now the current media reality of politics. What is to be done, how can one react to such observation pressure? The escape into the catchphrase or a suitably insipid kind of rhetoric, the constant effort to avoid public outrage by means of smooth stage management and self-censorship in the direction of what just about qualifies as consensus seem to be consequential reactions against this background, a smart strategy to avoid provocation and negative attention. But the cringing of the fearful, who desperately try to satisfy barely achievable standards and ideals of perfection, need not be the only possible reaction. It is possible that *prototypes of comradeship* and *heroes of ordinariness* will emerge, who present themselves as approachable and whose suggested or actual authenticity essentially replaces their authority because they have realised that the aura of otherness and the stage management of difference are prone to invite attacks.[111] They are therefore trying hard to protect themselves by saying: "Look here, I am quite normal and totally open and I have no secrets!" It is quite possible to imagine, however, that ever more *heroes of negativity* will appear on the public world stage, impressing (some) with their uninhibited aggression, their refusal to adapt and accommodate and their snottily proclaimed meta-message that they do not really care about what the critics and the media may say. They make their mark because they are trying to control the absolutism of transparency by virtue of cold ignorance and the open ridiculing of moral standards—freely following the motto of the boorish-babbling anti-hero Donald Trump, who counters attacks and accusations with a sentence like: "I've been challenged by so many people and I don't, frankly, have time for total political correctness."[112]

It is also conceivable that a less demanding dis-idealised idea of authority will surface in due course, simply due to habituation effects on the part of the media public, and that the mass of slips will at some stage mutate into the unspectacular normal case and the accepted shrugged-off permanent event, because the deviation has become visible for everyone and has thus established itself as the new normality. This is the thesis presented in a careful and enquiring presentation by Joshua Meyrowitz, who writes:

In the long run, the continuing disappointment in many authorities may lead to a new, lower conception of most of our social institutions. Not long ago, the natural bias of the communication environment was to limit information about politicians and other authorities. Politicians had to act to get a message across. Indeed, the major role of public relations and advertising, in general, was once that of getting information to the public. The intent was to make certain aspects of people, institutions, ideas and products visible. Other aspects were kept invisible through simple neglect. Now, however, public relations is becoming more and more an attempt to restrict information or to counteract information that is already available ....[113]

If Joshua Meyrowitz is right, then the consequence is that the continuous media-technical innovation is transforming existing norms and leading us to the insight that embarrassments and norm violations have become everyday occurrences, inevitable and somewhat normal, so that one would learn to live with authority figures that have weaknesses, that are vain, sometimes exhausted, in a bad mood, undisciplined, and whose past life or entire personality is not particularly amiable. Ideals of perfection and archaic longings for heroes and luminaries would thus appear—from this perspective—to be a robust indication of the fact that the actual media reality has not really been understood and that, furthermore, the many-layered, morally vacillating nature of human beings remains misconstrued, too, because otherwise one would have to admit that an honest closer look makes it quite clear that nobody can really satisfy these ideals, and everybody is one way or another embarrassing or rather common. One can pose the question now whether in the future there will be more elastic role models, treated with leniency, fallible and obviously broken heroes and injured idols, who are admired despite their totally ordinary appearance and perhaps even because of their lapses?[114] Or will the larger public continue to uphold high ideals, demanding at the same time approachability, openness and transparency, i.e., will it formulate demands that are hardly reconcilable and manoeuvre every politician into a dilemma? Or will the boorish-ignorant anti-hero become the new messianic figure for a public that has become weary of the tremolo of continuous disclosures and that wants to protect its interests in reverence, and its capability of admiration, by simply suppressing criticism and objections, or by re-interpreting them into problems of the media that transport and transmit the discrediting messages?

None can know. It is certain, however, that until the diverse contradictory lines of development in the field of conflict oscillating between the loss of aura and anxious accommodation, of spiteful ignorance and general value change, can amalgamate into a somewhat stable tendency, the permanent publication of acts of misconduct will continue in an unbridled way, and we will as soon as tomorrow be hearing about a ridiculous and ambiguous gesture, an embarrassing tweet or Facebook posting, or a real scandal that once again fuels public outrage. Permanent disappointment and anger about the moral failure of the political elites will continue until further notice to be counted among the collateral damage of a garishly illuminated media world. We will have to wait and see whether under these conditions a radically clear-headed idealism and possibly even a new kind of tolerance will develop, or whether we will enter an era of transitory authorities and instant icons who will be frenetically applauded at first, only to be shortly afterwards sucked down into a maelstrom of disclosures and negative reports.

5

The Crisis of Complacency: Or the Collapse of Contexts

Filter Bubble and Filter Clash

The only thing that is known for hours on the evening of the 22 July 2016 is that something horrible has happened in Munich. A shooting at the Olympia shopping centre, that is certain. A young man streams live images from the scene of the incident with his smartphone via the internet platform Periscope. "There was a gunman, they say" is his comment from the scene of the incident. "There now, two policemen with machine guns … A woman arrives, has been crying … Sick shit." 100,000 people watch his images, multiplied shortly afterwards by television stations. There is a volley of desperate terror warnings and a series of diffuse messages of fear on Twitter and in the social networks. Rumours of a shooting in the city circulate. A man with the Twitter name @itsflyingbird writes that he has heard shots at the Stachus: "am just now at the Stachus, shots here too" he writes. Others claim to have heard an attacker shout "*Allahu Akbar*". Others again report that there were several armed men, but these are later identified as police officials in mufti. Hours pass in a sort of state of emergency, fuelled by breaking news reports on all

© The Author(s), under exclusive license to Springer Nature
Switzerland AG 2022
B. Poerksen, *Digital Fever*,
https://doi.org/10.1007/978-3-030-89522-8_4

media, by rumours and news messages on social networks, images and hectically pulsating information relayed through WhatsApp, Snapchat or Instagram. 113,000 tweets are published throughout this night of uncertainty about what may have happened in Munich, up to 336 per minute. Panic breaks out periodically. People injure themselves trying to escape from the Munich Hofbräuhaus when suddenly a man appears shouting "shooting, shooting". Photographs circulate that are alleged to have been taken in Munich but turn out to be photographs taken after an attack on a shopping centre in South Africa and at a terror exercise in Manchester. Even a photograph of the alleged assassin is disseminated, but it is a photograph that had already been used on the internet for gun rampages in the United States. All along the police try to calm the situation on all media channels, but with little success because nobody can yet work out exactly what actually happened. For a few hours the megacity of Munich seems to have been captured by terrorists.[115]

What really happened? It transpires that 18-year-old pupil David S. killed nine people and then himself when the police hunted him down. There was a precisely planned gun rampage at the Olympia shopping centre in the suburb of Moosach, not at all a coordinated citywide series of terrorist attacks, as was initially believed. What happened that night shows how easily under the present media conditions agitation can turn into panic, how quickly communities of fear emerge, and how instantly fear can spread and hold the general consciousness as a mental hostage. This is also shown by an essay filled with melancholy and sadness posted by the blogger Patricia Cummarata on 23 July 2016, the day after the incident.[116] The text, entitled "I don't need live tickers", ostensibly deals with violence and terror and the actualities of the moment, but its undercurrent has to do with the end of complacency in a networked world, in which "our planet's collective neural wiring would create a single 24–7 blobby, fuzzy, quasi-sentient metacommunity", as the writer Douglas Coupland once formulated.[117] Patricia Cummarata, who grew up in Munich, is in a cinema in Berlin when the first bits of news reach her mobile phone and she follows the news reporting in a state of shock. The day after, she writes about the tranquillity of her childhood, about gathering mushrooms in the Bayerischer Wald and life in the blissful world of ignorance. Only reports about the nuclear catastrophe at Chernobyl and the second Gulf War had nebulously penetrated her world at the time, had reached her at all. "Apart from all that, my childhood was completely carefree. I never noticed anything." Nowadays she has a smartphone and is tied to the internet via Twitter and Facebook. And now she has no clue any more as to what she should be afraid of first—the terror slowly reaching Europe, a president called Donald Trump, the consequences of the putsch in Turkey, the circumstances in other countries from which human beings are fleeing. "Can journalism, please, be more than the hasty voicing of a suspicion and the publication of the first photograph," she writes. "Live tickers, images, nothing of this sort really helps."

Her ad-hoc reaction to the gun rampage is of broader significance. Patricia Cummarata experiences networking as a situation of permanent alarm. *Networking means distress*, is the message of her melancholic reflections. A general experience of our times and our media becomes tangible here. I shall call it *filter clash*, in analogy to the concept of *filter bubble* introduced by internet activist Eli Pariser.[118] It means that the most diverse variants of world perception clash with each other in radical immediacy, caused and enforced by intensively networked communication. People inevitably live in pre-filtered worlds of information and communication, in which they have prepared cosy private worlds of their own. These worlds are conditioned by their biological constitution (we do not see, hear or feel "everything"), by cultural circumstances and epoch-specific traditions, by societal and ideological milieus, by personal life experiences and personal interests. Some of these filters are part of human nature, others are variable as they can be altered and newly configured according to personal opinions or external influences. It is precisely these variable filters of a person, moulded by media and information technology, that can easily be disrupted in an intensively networked society and flooded with news messages of the most diverse kind—with the effect that realities and perceptions collide with previously unknown brutality. If we really wish to grasp the distressing simultaneity of modern ways of being as well as the alarming permanent experience of shrill contrasts under digital conditions, we must set aside the one-dimensional deterministic concept presented by Eli Pariser in his intensively debated book *Filter Bubble*. Personalised filtering with the help of algorithms, as he intends to show, means that we are lured into a tunnel of self-confirmation, as it were, which makes us see only what interests us. We only experience what confirms our personal presumptions. We are animated, to use a word by Miriam Meckel, to build and use a "short-sighted world view" because the personal close-meshed matrix of perception is permanently confirmed.[119] The world, according to this dystopian assumption, consequently appears to be essentially a small selection of pieces of news and opinions that we have created by our own search history. The blogger Patricia Cummarata demonstrates, however, that we cannot shrink the world under the given conditions of communication according to the patterns of personal predilections or even systematically exclude it. The elementary effect of networking is precisely that the idyll of inaccessibility is destroyed and that the terror of the moment reigns absolutely in full force. We can be reached even in our own informational universe, conditioned by algorithmic prefiltering, whether we like it or not.

Simultaneity of the Disparate

Once again and now in detail. The conceptual image of the filter bubble that has meanwhile come to rule small-talk about societal analysis and tends to dominate the countless debates about the quality of public discourse is wrong and misleading—and for at least three good reasons.[120] The idea of extreme isolation contradicts, first of all, our daily experience of information. Anyone who surfs, is active on blogs and forums, keeps receiving newsletters and posts messages, is certainly aware that the essence of the internet is linkage. And every link is—potentially—a ticket to enter another reality. It needs just a click. And you are right there.[121] The idea of the filter bubble contradicts, second, the insights of network theory known since the 1970s, which show that the better people know each other, the more predictable are the messages shared. Weak ties and loose relations (in the sense of network sociology) are particularly useful for the very reason that they confront us with varied, unfamiliar and totally unexpected information.[122] And the internet is definitely the relational universe of weak ties. Offline human beings may have only a few friends; online, however, possibly very many. Naturally algorithmic filtering cannot be switched off, but the probability of being confronted with different kinds of information increases dramatically in such weak tie networks. Numerous weak ties (considering only the many Facebook friends young users are typically connected with) programme the kind of information pluralism that can be reduced autonomously (by way of a self-organised echo chamber). Third, the filter bubble theory is refuted by all the empirical studies published so far, which show that our universe of information is much more wide-ranging than is generally assumed. These studies demonstrate furthermore that what we call *filter bubble* is always also a symptom of our informational behaviour, an indicator of our personal intentions and fascinations.[123] Human beings search, read and spread what concurs with their convictions, or anyway, with what they want to believe in.[124] The fact is, as already explained in the chapter on the crisis of truth, that the internet panders heavily to the universal human desire for self-confirmation and thus allows for the stabilisation of obscure and more or less marginal positions. The possibility of unpacking and "thinning out" information favours the construction of illusory realities by recipients, whereas the well-wrapped packets of printed matter tend to programme surprise and irritation more strongly. Just a few clicks google people into their personal self-confirmation milieus, where they can then, without much effort and without much friction with the agenda of the rest of society, find their own experts, their own media and platforms as well as ideologically related tribes of like mind—from the political extremist to the anti-vaccinationist. Information and communication environments of this kind engender majority power illusions. Here the regulative power of social taboos vanishes. The natural human fear of isolation diminishes, and human individuals who are prone to being wound up by applause and consent in such a deeply sensed communicative mainstream cosmos begin to voice their feelings and opinions in an ever more demanding and aggressive manner, additionally fired on by the likes and the comments of all those who think and feel in similar ways. The distorting mirror of light-handed infinite multiplication suddenly transforms ways of speaking that had traditionally been ostracised and stigmatised into common and acceptable modes of expression in the catacombs and echo chambers of the internet. The limits of the sayable are shifted in the direction of the normalisation of extremes simply because the self-confirmatory milieu resounds with voices of support and compassion and thus nurses the erroneous belief that what is being posted and published is quite okay. All these different findings may be condensed into an interim summary yielding the following insight. What we experience now is the simultaneity of general human self-siloing *and* permanent confrontation with ever-changing variant views, together with greater and smaller ideologies under networking conditions. The adequate comprehension of this emergent dynamics and of the deep-rooted causes of universal irritation requires us to grasp this *simultaneity of the disparate*, the pulsating simultaneity of closure and opening, siloing and confrontation. For there is without doubt a vast number of milieus for special groups and exclusive madness. And yet the various communities are not completely isolated but coexist in direct friction, often only a click away. How can one possibly reconcile the co-existence of opening and closure? The internet theorist Michael Seemann offers an answer.[125] He distinguishes between positive and negative filter sovereignty. Positive filter sovereignty means that one can freely rig up one's own personal world view by googling together all the pseudo-evidence supporting whatever one thinks and wants to believe unconditionally. Negative filter sovereignty, by contrast, means that one can seal oneself off against any undesired irritation and retire into the private cosmos of one's preferred world perception. And this is downright impossible. It is like living under constant siege in a valley while still being able to see the bright or dark valleys of others.[126] For the self-constructed filter bubble is violently opened again and again and the cosmos of complacency is torn apart the more strongly the formation of the personal mindset shifts from the analogue into the digital sphere (14-to-29-year-olds are now using the internet for up to six hours daily). In brief: the networked world favours the mindset of a fragile fundamentalism. It renders the *filter clash* inevitable, i.e., the clash of parallel public spheres and self-confirmatory milieus. After every criminal attack or assassination, we painfully experience how rumours and anti-rumours create a seething poisonous primal soup of disinformation and how the most diverse groups and parties at cyberspeed re-interpret happenings in the pursuit of their own goals, in turn corrected and attacked by the opposite side, annoyed and bewildered by such reactions to the reaction that challenges their own certainties. Social networks demonstrate this equally well when a single thread exhibits the most wide-ranging positions. And extreme events create the same experiences when they explode into a great drama on the world stage of the internet.

On the one hand, the news messages flow in via the classic media, which are meanwhile also present in the public sphere, as a matter of course—just think of the television screens in railway stations and airports or in pubs, of newscasts in trams or local trains. On the other hand, everyone can be reached by e-mail, through Facebook, Twitter, WhatsApp. They arrive in the form of push notifications or breaking news headlines, but they sink in anyway. The excessive use of mobile phones (heavy users reach a figure of six to ten times per minute, and younger people, on average, look at their smartphones more than 160 times per day) together with the fear of missing out on something important, generates a state of nervous attention and tense wakefulness. *FOMO* (*the fear of missing out*) has become a general phenomenon of culture. It is of course an optimal precondition of being ready to receive news messages and being receptive to informational contact at all. Numerous persons, as is shown by relevant studies, are online more or less all the time and even take their smartphone to bed. And they experience, even when nothing is happening, so-called phantom calls, phantom vibrations or phantom hummings of their smartphones, which means they have the impression that they are being contacted and sent news messages even though this is not the case at all. Information is something that one is prone to miss all the time, is what they believe.

But it is not only the massively intensified use of media, the constant expectation of news messages and the gradual penetration of everyday life and public spheres by media, that programme the filter clash. It cannot be evaded simply because of the fact that the constantly increasing networking and the digitalisation of materials and documents creates elementary changes in the ways and manners of accessing and disseminating information. Suddenly—assuming there is functioning internet access—we are confronted with the most diverse life-worlds, we experience the contingency and the complexity of realities after only a few clicks. Naturally we experience strange realities also when reading books or newspaper articles, we are irritated and inspired, touched and surprised. Even the press, as was noted by Marshall McLuhan, "presents a daily image both of the complexity and similarity of human affairs",[127] and thus creates a sense of the new and the other, and in the act of communication reaches beyond ourselves in a surprising and potentially even alarming way. Programmed surprise and the effect of distress have become key features of media communication. But in a pre-digital, primarily print-determined world, one kind of information structuring is significantly more important, which will be called here the principle *of audience-specific segmentation.* Not everyone can see everything in such a world nor access information in the same easy way. The peculiar paradox is that the contents are made available in printed form on paper, but that their comprehensive dissemination—due to the carrier medium of paper and its particular slowness and materiality, the demands of literality, and the orientation by special target groups—is at the same time hampered by certain obstacles.[128] There are books for children and adults, magazines for women and men. It stands to reason that the diverse worlds of information are therefore not completely detached from each other and that there is of course mixing and exchange, mutual inspiration and undoubtedly even massive irritation.[129] But digitalisation and networking also opens up possibilities for re-organising the flow of information in different ways. It is no longer the public-specific segmentation that divides a society into different worlds of information and perception, but the *principle of integrating confrontation.* Everything is potentially shown to everyone. Everything becomes visible for everyone else, in the extreme case independently of age, sex, origin and social status. Everyone is confronted with the most diverse kinds of information concerning life-worlds, ideologies, sexualities. And it is now possible to shift and wrench apart with hitherto unknown ease and speed still remaining enclaves of information and perception, bubbles of worlds and realities that may be determined algorithmically or in a primary social, cultural, or world-view- and ideology-dependent way—with the consequence of the general alarm and distress of a systemically conditioned crisis of complacency that is brought about not simply by events themselves, but also by the fact that one cannot sidestep other, strange, shocking life-realities and cannot evade them.

What we see today on a global scale has been condensed into a remarkable description in a report on the life and the literature of Walter Kempowski by the journalist Iris Radisch:

> Walter Kempowski, who had been sentenced to 25 years hard labour by a Soviet military tribunal in 1948, was sitting hungry and dirty in a freight train carriage, which was to take him to Bautzen. At a stop, he sees through a gap in the planking a married couple walking by, the wife in a floral dress, the husband in knickerbockers, both carefree in the sunshine. The view shocked him into the recognition of the simultaneity of what was incompatible. How much happiness and unhappiness, how many harmless and tragic, life-threatening and idyllic moments are stacked on top of each other in every second of world existence! This is as immeasurable, as inapprehensible as the numbers that lie between one and two.[130]

This very experience of the shocking simultaneity of the incompatible has by now, in the age of collapsing contexts, merged into our everyday experience, and it is changing the social temperature of networked societies, provoking disharmonies by the instant confrontation with other life-worlds and possible lifestyles. It causes, in view of the growing awareness of social distinctions, of the privileges of the Few and of forms of discrimination, the more forceful articulation of demands for justice and equal treatment. Those who have been excluded and deprived can now explore their situation with greater clarity and acuteness and will perhaps no longer be prepared and willing to adapt to existing circumstances nor to accept living with their lowly status: they know now what others have and how they have to live themselves.[131] Furthermore, as just shown by the scene from the life of Walter Kempowski, happiness and unhappiness, the harmless and the tragic, life-threatening and idyllic moments, are equally present, all characteristic of a boundless and barrier-free accessible public sphere. Random surfing exposes us all to images of obscene riches, of poverty, blood-stained protests, the real-time documentation of human beastliness, total banality and harmlessness. A few examples can serve as *chiffres* of the simultaneity of what is incompatible, sources and triggers of dissonance caused by information and media technology. There are—on the one hand—the *Rich Kids of Instagram* or also the *Rich Kids of Tehran*, who boast with all the insignia of their riches.[132] They exhibit themselves surrounded by champagne bottles, in their bathtubs, parade their designer clothes, present their watches, their expensive cars, their credit cards, their gilded iPhones. They document their party life with images of helicopters and private aeroplanes transporting them to their holiday destinations—in free association with the self-created motto: "our everyday life is better than your best day." The counter-programme is just a few clicks away, the *Poor Kids of Tehran*, images symbolising abject misery: we are shown cheap watches, derelict cars, dirty bodies and children apparently living in dire poverty, who are cowering on the floor together. The transparency of difference that makes tensions unavoidable applies not only to social status, however, but also to the political worldviews and ideologies that immediately clash with each other under the conditions of networked communication. Opinions and claims that in the pre-digital age would only have been voiced at the pub counter or in the catacombs of extremist sectarians, which nobody would ever have encountered in public, are now suddenly recorded and moved into close proximity as documents, even right inside the addressable space of our very own sphere of communication. They now reach us on the media channel that has up till now been primarily used more for rather private communications with friends and acquaintances. On Facebook and possibly on our own timeline on Twitter we may thus not only become confronted with cheerful holiday snaps, puzzles, cat videos, funny GIFs and news messages from friends and acquaintances, but may also hit upon racist-sounding commentaries, "Auschwitz selfies", triumphalist images and provocative photographs of the Berlin Holocaust Memorial, bizarre pornography, or the snap of a woman who photographs herself in front of the Brooklyn Bridge in New York while in the background someone is about to commit suicide. We can effortlessly discover the postings and tweets of people who are thrilled by the drowning of a Syrian child, who revile dissenting people as "ticks", "lice" and "rubbish", who want to gas refugees and advocate the re-activation of concentration camps. "Social media, by blending spontaneity and documentation, enable us to look into the heads of people", the internet publicist Sascha Lobo states summarily. He advances the view that the direct contemplation of spontaneous communication will ultimately destroy the idea of shared basic values on which a society depends, even if only in the sense of a friendly illusion. "Heinrich von Kleist in 1805 wrote his famous article *On the gradual production of thoughts whilst speaking*. And now we can watch people at this gradual manufacturing of their thoughts and feelings when commentating on what happens in the world."[133]

But it is not only the total mental condition of a society that suddenly becomes visible and destroys the illusion of moderate circumstances, potentially even quite directly within our own communication habitat. We can experience the shock of the simultaneity of what is incompatible perhaps most directly when we watch the images of violence, the documents of humiliation and torture, which have become so easily accessible now. Pictures of beheadings carried out by the Islamic State can easily be found. There is a film showing the burning to death of a Jordanian pilot which the American station Fox News deliberately published on its website in order to maximise the terror of resonance of strategically working violent criminals. We can discover a mobile phone video documenting how an American policeman engaged in traffic controls shoots an innocent man dead in front of a four-year-old girl and the man's partner. On the forum 4chan we can see the photographs of the bloodied hands of a 19-year-old man who has just killed two people. There is suicide in front of a running camera, the rape of girls and women, the confessions of a murderer who has just capriciously shot an older man dead and filmed his deed, a father who hangs his 11-month-old daughter and records the deed on two videos for publication, the torture of a disabled person by youngsters lasting several hours—all such matter can be watched live on Facebook and on the internet. In short, anyone who is on the lookout for anthropological shock experiences and searching for the triggering stimuli of secondary traumatisation will find a multitude of materials.[134] In such situations indifference is no real option. In free association with Paul Watzlawick's axioms, the communicative axiom of our intensively networked world now states that one cannot *not* react to all these reports about strange or damaged lives that are flushed into our minds in such an unhampered fashion. There is, however, no unconditional automatism of reaction. What we see and experience will frustrate some and anger others, it will create feelings of powerlessness or encouragement, of hate or fear, it will mobilise and animate us to protest, it can catapult us all out of our self-centredness on our own perspectives. Under any circumstances it will throw the great number of those participating in the general communicative noise into a collective experience of difference and dissonance and ruin the feeling of self-indulgent complacency. These differences and dissonances may certainly be dampened in the short run, they may be anaesthetised for a while, but we will certainly never be able to evade the shock of the simultaneity of what is incompatible.

Digital Butterfly Effects

The butterfly effect is a metaphor concerning the asymmetry of cause and effect, of source and result. The single beating of the wing of a butterfly, *chiffre* for the weakness of a first impulse, may trigger a thunderstorm or even a tornado—this is the basic idea. Under the given conditions of communication and media, a phenomenon can be observed that might be called the *digital butterfly effect*. Minimal impulses, when linked to provocative topics, may produce maximal effects and generate an explosive mixture of agitation and violence, seemingly disproportionate to the triggering moments and the hierarchy of forces. Ordinarily, a cause produces roughly calculable effects more or less linearly, and strong, massive effects are therefore necessarily based on strong causes that consequently appear suspended. Sometimes the provocations of a single individual are sufficient to cause a global tremor, as will be shown. How one can proceed with the production of digital butterfly effects and turn journalists and commentators into accomplices was demonstrated by Terry Jones, up until 2015 a pastor of a mini-community with only a few dozen members in Gainesville, Florida.[135] Terry Jones represents the figure of the rabble-rouser and firebrand who can, however, only be effective if others supply his actions with the absolutely necessary *oxygen of publicity*.[136] It is on 12 July 2010 that the pastor, who is quite capable of pulling out his gun while consumed with anger during one of his confused speeches and who is also known for a book entitled *Islam is of the Devil*, sends a tweet to his modest number of followers. He declares

11 September 2010, the anniversary of the Twin Towers attack in New York, to be the international day of Koran burning. The text of the original tweet is "9/11/2010 Int Burn a Koran Day", and it triggers an unprecedented cascade of conflicts, which is fuelled by the classic mass media and a horrified public.[137] He also publishes this announcement in his own Facebook group, claiming to have acquired 700 members. A few dozen websites and blogs report his plans. CNN takes note and now a mechanism starts up that the American PR and campaign professional Ryan Holiday calls "pulling something up through all levels".[138] This means that some news item is first published on a few unimportant websites and then begins to climb up the hierarchy of attention until it makes contact with the classic key media, finally reaching the top through the nervous interplay of all the relevant players. Soon after the first announcement the firebrand from Florida is interviewed on CNN in front of a worldwide audience. It is his breakthrough. During the following weeks he gives more than 150 interviews, several camera teams visit his community, journalists the world over report, not least because there is at the same time a fierce ongoing debate about the setting up of an Islam Centre near Ground Zero in New York. And Jones thunders on all channels that this Centre must be stopped and that the Koran burning was his signal. At the beginning of September 2010, the first protests flare up in Jakarta and Kabul. With ostensible signs of nervousness, military, religious and political leaders try to induce Terry Jones to give up his project. On 6 September, David Petraeus, US Supreme Commander in Afghanistan, warns of outbursts of violence, should the book burning take place, followed on 7 September by NATO Secretary General Anders Fogh Rasmussen. On 8 September, criticism of the pastor's plans is voiced by the German Federal Chancellor Angela Merkel, the US Secretary of State Hillary Clinton, the Afghan president Hamid Karzai and the Vatican. On 9 September, Pakistani demonstrators burn the American flag and broadcast the threat in English that the burning will be the beginning of the end of America. The very same day, former British prime minister Tony Blair and American president Barack Obama call on the leader of a petty community of sectarians to refrain from setting fire to the holy book of the Muslims. The US Secretary for Defence Robert Gates calls him personally on the telephone. Finally, Jones cancels the

performance. However, the Westboro Baptist Church, a group of religious fanatics from Kansas, shortly afterwards spreads the message that they will take over the pastor's mission.[139] Rumours claiming the Koran had been burned cause violent protests in the Indian part of Kashmir on 13 September. Images of Barack Obama go up in flames, a Christian school is set on fire, 16 people die.

Things go quiet around the pastor after that, at least for a few months. At the beginning of January 2011, however, Terry Jones posts another video in which he announces an International Judge the Koran Day for the month of March. It is to be a kind of tribunal, and in the case of a conviction the Koran will be "burned, shredded, drowned or shot". This time, however, there is no media hype. One reason is that after the excessive reporting of the first round a debate took place among journalists and a phase of reflection and self-criticism set in.[140] Furthermore, the Imam Muhammad Musri, who lives in Florida, had contacted journalists and asked them to simply ignore Jones in future. And this strategy of purposive ignoring nearly succeeds. On 20 March 2011, the day of the so-called tribunal, only a single journalist is present. It is Andrew Ford, a 21-year-old student and freelancer for the international news agency Agence France-Presse (AFP), who observes how in a bizarre proceeding the sentence is passed and a copy of the Koran is set on fire. His article about the incident is online only a day later, it is linked by Google News and Yahoo News and picked up by various media and websites. And the news item starts circling the world. Pakistani and Indian media publish reports. The presidents of Pakistan (Asif Ali Zardari) and Afghanistan (Hamid Karzai) criticise the Koran burning and fan the flames of outrage. Finally violence erupts.[141] At least 12 people are killed in demonstrations in the north of Afghanistan, among them seven employees of the United Nations. And again, as if following a ready script, journalists reflect and debate the responsibility of the media and their own role. "It took just one college student to defeat a media blackout and move a story halfway around the globe within 24 hours", the journalist Steve Myers states in his summarising analysis.[142] For the publicist Carolin Fetscher, the lesson to be learned from the media appearances of Terry Jones is that it is imperative in certain situations not to report. She writes, "Although serious mass media specialising in news reporting have an obligation to record, there are events the respon-sible treatment of which requires abstinence, distance or the refusal of details."[143] *Forbes* editor Jeff Bercovici regards the whole sequence of events as an indication of the de-professionalisation of journalism in the digital age. The lay publicists celebrated by cyber-utopianists would now dominate the public agenda.[144] Bercovici formulates the key thesis of his text on Twitter in the following way: "When journalism 2.0 kills: the report by a student is the cause of 24 dead in Afghanistan." Such an assertion is nonsensical simply for the reason that Andrew Ford was not active as a blogger in his own right, but had been hired by the time-honoured classic news agency AFP. Furthermore, it was not he who killed the people in Afghanistan but ideological-religious fanatics, who were incited by their religious and political leaders, and an agitator oper-ating via media of news reporting. His contribution is worth mentioning, though, because it shows a typical pattern of scapegoat identification. Bercovici personalises network effects, constructs cause–effect relations according to a simple stimulus–response schema. It is his moralising mono-causalism, however, that makes crystal clear that digital butterfly effects can only be understood in the context of systemic frameworks of effects. It needs the first tweet, the provocations of the pastor, a mingling of accidents with a general emotional climate, the observation excesses of the media, the stepwise upgrading of the provocation by all partici-pants involved, and finally the readiness of fanatics to turn to violence, justified by the insults expressed. *Conflict avoidance* and *conflict miti-gation*, it turns out, becomes ever more difficult under the conditions of worldwide networked communication, whereas *conflict escalation* is facilitated, if only for the simple reason that the number of those who feel entitled to participate in firing up things cannot be strictly delim-ited. (As soon as Terry Jones had announced desisting from the burning of the Koran in 2010, another hate group rose up to take action, as was already mentioned.) In addition, a self-organised news lockdown, however desirable it may sometimes be, cannot really be kept up for long, nor is purposive ignoring a really practicable solution. Finally, nobody has the authority over, nor the necessary recognition by, all participants to contain the conflict or even terminate it and to force the protagonists to accept and observe a robust moratorium.

Another case will show how attempts to settle conflicts under the conditions of networked communication and collapsing contexts can escalate into confrontation on a stage that is globally observable. It happened on the evening of 9 April 2008, on the Duke University campus in America. Two groups of demonstrators clash. What at first appears to be an insignificant quarrel finally creates a stir in the USA and in China.[145] What happened? On that evening in April, months before the Olympic Summer Games in Beijing are to take place, a group of pro-Tibet activists want to stage a vigil to raise awareness about the destruction of Tibetan culture and the violations of human rights by the Chinese. The group is confronted by Chinese demonstrators who demonstrate against the pro-Tibet vigil and do so in an ever more excited manner. On her way to the library, 20-year-old student Wang Qianyuan happens to pass and, noticing familiar faces in both groups and also because she speaks both English and Chinese, tries to mediate between the two groups in conflict. She repeatedly runs back and forth between the two fronts, being photographed and filmed all the time. The pro-China demonstrators, however, suspect her attempts at settling the conflict to be a kind of partisan manoeuvre simply for the reason that she also speaks English and not just Chinese. They shout at her, want to know her name and her place of birth. One of them wants to know what school she went to. Wang Qianyuan readily answers these questions at first, with no second thoughts. In the further course of events one of the pro-Tibet demonstrators, a friend of hers, who has taken off his shirt, asks her to write the slogan 'Free Tibet' on his back with a felt pen, which she does, but not without exacting from him the promise to join the pro-China demonstrators and to talk with them. The same evening, the police have to be called to escort Wang Qianyuan to her lodgings because she has received serious threats. In the early hours of the morning, she writes an open letter and posts it on the online forum of Chinese students at Duke University, trying to explain the situation. She pleads for tolerance in encounters with the Tibetans and, quoting Taoist and Confucian wisdom, reminds everyone that oppression only leads to rebellion and unrest. But this attempt at explanation and reconciliation fails as well. On the same day, the witch-hunt starts on the internet. "Snuff it, shameless thing", the commentaries run on a popular Chinese forum.—"Makes us lose face in this way? Execute her here and now."—"Has perhaps fucked too many foreign devils. Where does such rubbish come from?"—"Alarm customs and make them capture her, and if she has family, find it and beat its shameless children to death so that they can never again damage the Chinese people." A video of the demonstration also showing her is now circulating on the internet and is considered to be evidence of her betrayal. Those who have published the film declare her to be, without the shadow of a doubt, on the side of the pro-Tibet activists. More photos are posted, most of which show her in conversation with the American students but not with the Chinese demonstrators.—"Betrayer of our race! Traitress!", someone writes. "Sooner or later your whole family will pay for this." And this threat will actually come true for the family. Unknown people discover the address of her parents, smear excrement on the entrance door to their house and spray the following sentences on the walls: "Kill the whole family. Kill traitors to our country!" Soon her telephone number, e-mail address and other personal details are circulating on the internet. Her former school strips her of her school leaving certificates, her parents are forced to go underground, and she herself is said to be put on a black list and would no longer be allowed to return to her home country without incurring punishment. China Central Television, the country's biggest television station, introduces a rubric with the title "the ugliest Chinese student abroad", together with a picture of her.

This excessive reaction and the brutality of the attacks, on the other hand, generate outrage in the USA and fuel anger about the anger of the other side. Her American fellow students defend her in articles and comments. They praise her for advocating dialogue and freedom of opinion and they criticise the threats as signs of the intolerance of a violent regime brutally persecuting dissenting views. *The Washington Post* prints several articles about the case. *The New York Times* devotes an analysis to her fate and places it on its front page. At this point in time, the central agents involved in the confrontation have been transformed into symbolic figures. Wang Qianyuan, from the Chinese point of view, is a traitress who lacks national consciousness, who adapts and kowtows in order to belong. From the point of view of American media, she is a representative of tolerance and freedom of opinion, who must be protected against an intolerant regime. It is this *symbolic charge* that lends the confrontation additional meaning and buoys up polarisation and camp formation on all sides. It is particularly significant that the mini-scene of her writing the words "Free Tibet" on the friend's back is interpreted as the ultimate proof of her partisan position. For on the internet a photograph is circulated showing her writing this slogan, to which the expression "traitress to your country" has been added. This means that the favour she did her fellow student is all of a sudden seen as an anti-Chinese act, a plea for the independence of the Tibetans—as if she had campaigned for the separation of that country from China. "I was not advocating Tibetan independence", Wang Qianyuan explains in an article published a good month after the events on the campus. "I am not an expert on this subject and have not researched it deeply nor ever even traveled to Tibet so I would never form such an extreme view based on no personal knowledge.. ... Regardless, I never imagined that the act of writing the words "Free Tibet" would come back to haunt me so powerfully."[146]

The mechanism revealed to be at work here will be named *context violation*. Context encompasses the totality of expected and expectable communication conditions. Context violation means, therefore, that talking and acting in other circumstances is abruptly attributed a different meaning that is no longer under personal control. The fact that the words "Free Tibet" are twisted into a confession of guilt and into a proof of lack of loyalty would certainly have been totally unimaginable for Wang Qianyuan at the moment of the incident.[147] The context she thought to be operating in was the context of an ephemeral, spontaneous and in fact differently intended kind of action, and this context was violated by the photograph and its ensuing interpretation.

Space	Protected spaces of information are broken up, data made available worldwide for simultaneously receiving communities, *de-territorialised*
Time	Temporal boundaries erode, the past turns into an enduring present, data and documents are *de-temporalised*

(continued)

(continued)

Public	The public can no longer be delimited, it turns into a potential world public
Publicity	Intimate and private matters become public, secrets are revealed. Personal publicity—e.g., in the form of a blog contribution—can no longer be controlled
Culture	Cultural contexts may be shifted at the speed of lightning. What is considered normal in one culture may—after its transfer into a different sphere of interpretation—appear objectionable, disgusting and insulting
Mode	Seemingly volatile orality is fixed and preserved to last; ad-hoc utterances and situation-bound actions remain present but gain a different meaning within new frameworks

The diagram shows different forms of context violation[148]

We may now well ask what all this has to do with digitalisation? It would naturally not be very plausible to claim that digital media per se are guilty of the escalation of the conflict around the student Wang Qianyuan. The driving force of nationalism and the thinking in friend–enemy patterns is obviously quite recognisable in this case. However, it must still be remembered that data and documents, from the moment they are available in digitalised form, possess a new kind of weightlessness and mobility. They can be removed from their original anchoring context, they become shareable, combinable, transferable, and are suddenly freed of the ponderousness and sluggishness of their original materiality. The digital age is also the age of the undying violation of contexts, of the continuing entanglements, misunderstandings and embarrassments, not least for the reason that one can so easily wrench data and documents quickly from their original material framework and make them available worldwide and for all time. All of a sudden, a single photograph may create a stir, or equally a particular sentence, or that single minute from a film that apparently shows it all. The internet philosopher Peter Glaser writes: "The transition into the digital aggregate first produces a kind of primeval soup of fragments and atomised cultural goods, which is however highly susceptible to reaction. It resembles the free radicals in chemistry that seek to unite with each other in an aggressive way."[149] Snippets of text, particular photos and snapshots, once transformed into a stream of bits and bytes, can be sent round the world at high speed. They may then engender excitement there. Gestures that can easily be misunderstood, but also satirical nonsense, provocations and insults, verbal attacks directed at religious leaders and secular authorities, which might only cause a slight wagging of heads in one part of the world, can in the extreme case be interpreted as insults and humiliations in another part, which call for punishment and even revenge. What does it mean, however, when the resounding space for utterances expands ever more incessantly and when the contexts of reception collapse? The answer is: as the inhabitants of the networked world, we must live with the feeling of the loss of control, perhaps also with a diffuse fear of escalation resulting from the *clash of codes*, i.e., the clash of different systems of reality interpretation. And we must pose the question as to how to uphold our personal values and norms without unreasonably violating those which have in the meantime come so insanely close.

On the Rise of an Industry Managing Emotion and Agitation

This is a story about the laws of the modern industry of agitation, of the economy of emotional infection.[150] It begins in the early evening of 26 February 2015. Cates Holderness, working for the media platform BuzzFeed, receives a tip-off about an ongoing debate on the internet. On the blog platform Tumblr a debate has broken out about the colour of a wedding dress. Some say the colour combination on the snapshot of the dress is blue-black, others are certain that it is gold-white. Holderness feels confused herself. She sees a blue-black dress and re-posts the photograph together with the quiz question as to what colour the dress now really is. As a hype begins to grow on the dashboards of the editorial office, the BuzzFeed team reacts at lightning speed. During the same night the article is translated into five languages, and everybody is thrilled to watch how the dress story jumps from network to network and from platform to platform, spreads through the USA, Great Britain,

India, Germany, Spain and other countries. One team seeks to identify who posted the original photograph in Scotland and also conducts some interviews. Other team members gather comments from scientists who are trying to explain the phenomenon of differences in colour perception. Others again who specialise in the celebrity business write about the acrimonious quarrel soon raging between stars and starlets on Twitter. The communication department relays successive statements that push the hype even further. The result in figures: in practically no time, BuzzFeed produces 40 articles that are seen 52 million times. About 40 million accesses are registered for the original puzzle posting around the world, as shown by the analysis of the enterprise. The story of the dress, produced at the speed of lightning and at low cost, is a perceptual spectacle of the internet age, a battle for attention on a global scale.

We may consider this as amusing or simply trivial, but that is not the point. What emerges here is a special cybernetics of excitement, a heating-up of the public world driven by feedback loops and signal flashes. It is a mechanics of emotional infection, self-organised at first, then amplified at lightning speed by professionals. On the one hand it shows that click factories have the capability of starting and running campaigns. On the other hand, this quiz spectacle shows a business model of digital publicists that is radically geared towards the individual success of information particles that first alarm in some way and then suddenly appear everywhere. These digital publicists have become powerful instances of agenda setting because they control the technologies of trend and topic analysis as well as the tricks of emotionalisation. And they thus contribute to the formation of what appears important and dominates the public world. They can introduce serious content but they can also feed nonsense stories with enormous power and amplify spectacles in such a way as to change the communicative climate. Millions of people then suddenly discuss a single strange photograph, watch a single touching video, and become outraged about a single directly comprehensible and immediately rousing cruelty arresting their attention at least for the moment. It is a particular attitude to life that is propagated here: what is happening on the planet appears to be a hit list of strange, bizarre and exciting things and events. The world is, according to this message, the sum total of isolated curiosities and skilfully orchestrated éclats.

Just a few examples of what we can observe on the digital boulevard of these platform publicists. We can see sweet little dogs with their skin hanging from their bodies in bloody flaps because someone has maltreated them. A giant shark has apparently been sighted somewhere, and a woman presenting herself as an ardent feminist claims to use her vaginal bacteria as a substitute for commercial yeast when baking bread. At times the actual news scene crops up and we can see a few terrorists rush into a picture or we are offered listed articles, so-called *listicles*, which may be the "25 snappiest Egyptian demonstrators" or—it is history now—a well-ordered survey of "the craziest genocides of the 1990s". The conflict in Syria is explained by a series of grisly swearwords for the benefit of all those who still have no idea what is going on, the history of the Egyptian revolution is presented as a collection of Jurassic-Park GIFs. A young man in tears is playing the piano for his mother who is suffering from cancer, and a cat stroking a baby into sleep. Even the Dalai Lama appears. One cannot say that the marginal group of the enlightened masters is marginalised in the battle for attention on the viral platforms of the internet. His "wise words about farting" can be found in a video clip from a lecture on the platform Upworthy where the Dalai Lama speaks about how to avoid annoying noises in the presence of others on an aeroplane while still managing to relieve oneself. This clip, too, has the sole purpose of being spread and shared freely according to the motto of a world-view reduced to curious details: amazing what's out there! Sascha Lobo concludes:

> In the virtual space of the Net the governing rules differ from those in the traditional media landscape. Up to the present time, editors have selected what appeared significant to them. In the Internet now, all sorts of things are flushed up because they are found interesting by sufficiently many people. The editor-driven diktat of relevance is now supplemented by the diktat of interestingness. Thus, a new filter threatens the power of editors. The collective of the Net selects by means of this age-old instrument of recommendation what it considers to be interesting enough to be disseminated. All the social networks from Twitter via Facebook to the totality

of weblogs are based on this recommendation: 'Look what interesting…I have here!'[151]

However, in describing the supposed democratisation of agenda setting, Lobo overlooks the fact that these recommendations can themselves be observed most exactly, can be scanned most specifically, can be condensed into real-time diagnosis of tendencies and mentalities, all of which can then be amplified in various systematic ways—until the diktat of interestingness displaces the classic concept of relevance, not simply supplementing it, however, but marginalising it, because trash and serious news (even in unbundled and singularised form) compete in the digital universe in direct immediacy. Tabloidisation is an attractive programme, particularly in times of fragile business models. And more clicks, likes and commentaries produce, as can be observed, ever more articles on the same and similar topics in a self-propelling cycle. The entire internet is, from the point of view of a self-generating, globally operating industry of agitation and emotion, a gigantic "data bank of intentions and fascinations", as was once formulated by the publicist John Battelle. Battelle's central consideration is that everything that is searched, commented and shared, can be interpreted as information about needs, wishes and interests, which one can take up and exploit in order to serve them as directly as possible. He writes:

> This information represents, in aggregate form, a place holder for the intentions of humankind – a massive database of desires, needs, wants, and likes that can be discovered, supoenaed, archived, tracked, and exploited to all sorts of ends. Such a beast has never before existed in the history of culture, but is almost guaranteed to grow exponentially from this day forward. This artefact can tell us extraordinary things about who we are and what we want as a culture. And it has the potential to be abused in equally extraordinary fashion.[152]

One certainly need not use expressions of monstrosity in such a general way, but it is definitely true today that we are now able to measure in a hitherto unparalleled way what is fascinating, what headlines are clicked, what articles are read up to what paragraph, and how often particular teasers and texts are shared and commented and in what ways the whole perceptual and life-cycle of a particular story unfolds. The live surveillance of reception movements allows us to establish and to test which stimulating words ("sex", "mystery", "drama") and which qualifying adjectives ("inconceivable", "crazy", "bizarre") are working particularly well, which images, GIFs and videos absorb attention and create likes on Facebook. Enterprises like Chartbeat, Spike, Crowdtangle, Linkpulse, 10,000 Flies and Google Analytics grasp more precisely than any classic analysis of publication figures and quotas the reaction and interaction forms of users, condense them into pulsating, nervously vibrating statistics and offer their services to media enterprises across the world. They indicate stories exploding virally in a particular part of the world, which might well be worth taking up elsewhere. They produce rankings of articles ("most read, shared, commented…") and show with the matchless authority of click numbers and shares with what intensity even at best half-true pieces of news, rumours or satirical nonsense are disseminated ("At last: Chuck Norris starts ground offensive against IS – three countries already IS-free"). And by means of their scales of favourites they clearly demonstrate that most people are more interested in an uncanny giant squid in a Japanese harbour basin, a curious animal friendship ("Siberian zoo tiger spares goat offered for food") or the selfie-video of an American woman in a Star Wars mask (more than 140 million views within a single week!) than in the conflicts in the Near East or the war in Afghanistan. In short: it is real-time quota and precisely analysed reception movements that shake up the publicist world. They have suggestive power in a world that is fascinated by thinking in rankings, by measurability and quantifiability, and they animate us to replace the principle of soft paternalism ("we show the reader what we consider important!") step by step by the principle of smooth popularity oriented by the current mass taste ("we only provide what pleases!").[153] It is obvious that this does not only concern particular media platforms like, for instance, BuzzFeed, certainly one of the giants in the business with millions of users and a central player in the industry managing emotion and agitation in the digital age.[154] There are differently oriented media producers like Viralnova or Upworthy, which co-determine the business of attention in the digital public sphere. Some focus upon special topics, for example, The Dodo, which scores with stirring animal stories—like the sensational one noted the world over about a mastiff in France which was buried alive by its owner but discovered just in time before dying of thirst. Others, like Playbuzz, concentrate on quiz and guessing games invented and finished by users in unpaid micro-work, because they function so well on Facebook. Again others, like the German-language platform Heftig, compose very few articles per day with gleanings from the internet, but sometimes outrange traditional boulevard media with hundreds of employees. They all play a sort of attention poker game in front of a world public, usually with boulevard and nonsense content and very rarely with serious information or even investigative stories, driven by the aim to land the next viral hit and trigger the next epidemic of excitement, in order to turn the measured range into advertising revenue. They all operate with the materials freely floating in the digital universe, which are easy to recombine, invite frequent easy reaction, which—in the jargon of platform publicists—*perform really well*, i.e., generate clicks, trigger commentaries and will be spread further on the initiative of a media-empowered public. The death of a police horse struck down by a car in Houston, which is while dying hugged by a policeman, can thus become a news item that suddenly circulates the globe. The video of a group of dolphins supposedly stranded on an unidentified beach in 2012 and pulled back into the water by helpers, can years later still be presented as an item of emotionalising supernews on the platform Heftig and numerous other websites. And we may read: "He only wanted to do a little filming on the beach, actually, but then he could not believe his eyes". There is the purported miracle healing of a prematurely born baby through a single embrace in the incubator somewhere in the US state of Massachusetts, which since 1995 has been diffusing the analogue and digital public spheres—a photograph showing that embrace is still posted in repeated spurts.[155] The story around this particular picture, a classic urban legend, runs as follows. Twins Kyrie and Brielle Jackson were born 12 weeks prematurely. One of the twins at some stage begins to show signs of approaching death, starts having breathing difficulties and changing colour. Standard apparatus-based medicine proves ineffective. Finally, a nurse against all rules obtains permission to place both twins into one incubator. There the life-saving embrace takes place, a kind of miracle healing by touch, which is of course recorded on a photograph by a photographer who accidentally happens to be present. The twin in a better state of health places an arm around his dying sister. And everything is all right. In 1995, *Life Magazine and Reader's Digest* are the first to report this event, then diverse other media follow. Finally, the story starts to circulate on the internet, and from 2011 onwards it is still repeatedly published on numerous websites, as Google research shows. The television station CNN picks it up, it appears in blogs and forums like Reddit. This endlessly repeated story has, however, a few flaws. The nurse who allegedly fought against the tangled web of the medical bureaucracy to be allowed to put both babies into a single incubator, did not have to do very much to realise this idea. She simply asked the parents whether it was okay, as was reported by a journalist who took the trouble of researching the story in more precise detail.[156]

And the one twin supposedly near death was never ever at the point of dying. So, strictly speaking, the miracle healing that has now been celebrated for over 20 years simply did not happen. But who cares? The story still scores points in the scramble for attention and the bullshit bingo, it is still clicked with passion.

Of course, one can now point out that even classic journalism is in no way free from the pressures of quota and the alignment with mindless entertainment, freely invented shockers and publication numbers. This is certainly the case. One only has to read the so-called yellow and gutter press that is available at any railway station stall. But this is not the point. Of decisive significance is the publicist collateral damage caused by a form of organisation of publicity that is governed by the principle of total popularity and the measure of success of informational particles. It becomes clear, on the one hand, that a politically informed public sphere cannot emerge in this way at all, for the political public sphere requires relevance in the form of an idea, of an axiom. It lives off the effort for the bigger picture and the totality of topics, and it must recoil for idealistic reasons alone from the radical un-bundling of contents in the information streams of the great platforms. It feeds on the pathos of self-assuredly claimed importance and a kind of evidence that may only be sensed intuitively, does not rest on empirical confirmation, and refuses to be impressed by popularity values. But in the very fight for the inevitably limited amount of attention this public sphere is forced into a relationship of direct competition with the players of a modern industry of excitement and agitation, who—from the perspective of the history of ideas—do not possess the slightest inkling of publicist responsibility. The sole vying for popularity values, on the other hand, for purely economic reasons enforces the jazzing up of stories by all possible means to mono-topics and to advertise constantly with dramas, tragedies, big emotions and eye-catching cliffhangers. "Watch the first 54 seconds", a millionfold-accessed video about street children that fabricated musical instruments out of garbage, announces on Upworthy. "This is all I ask of you. I swear you will become an addict." Of course this is the basic pattern: the superlatives of announcement become normality. What is claimed is the total surprise, what is supplied are mini-narrations in the format of headlines, which while intensely stirring people's emotional nervous nets do no more than hint at the actual sensation. Internet psychologists and digital consultants, who market hype recipes of this kind and design *sticky websites* for their clients, insist that using the more than well-known technique of mystification in a particularly excessive manner creates a curiosity gap, a sort of uncertainty, which is obviously very difficult to bear mentally and which rivets attention in a reflex manner.[157] The danger inherent in the excesses of dramatisation, the mechanisms of data-driven tabloidisation, and the direct fusion of audience observation and publication processes, is that the public internet sphere will slowly be divided into two parts. There will be the quiet, unobserved, practically unknown, lonely internet—an infinite sphere of undiscovered ideas and brainwaves, forgotten postings, rarely clicked videos. And there will be the internet centred in the midst of scales of favourites and hit lists, the internet of calculated shockers and emotionally infecting stories, which everybody will suddenly be talking about because universal key stimuli of interestingness are reinforced systematically and with as much power as possible.[158] In an apposite analysis media scientist Dannah Boyd writes:

> Our bodies are programmed to consume fat and sugars because they're rare in nature. Thus, when they come around, we should grab them. In

the same way, we're biologically programmed to be attentive to things that stimulate: content that is gross, violent, or sexual and that gossip which is humiliating, embarrassing, or offensive. If we're not careful, we're going to develop the psychological equivalent of obesity. We'll find ourselves consuming content that is least beneficial for ourselves or society as a whole.[159]

The kind of relevance distortion potentially effected by orientation towards singular shockers is well illustrated by an incident in a National Park in Zimbabwe, made public by the environmental organisation Zimbabwe Conservation Task Force 28 July 2015.[160] The statement issued on that day says that American dentist Walter Palmer has killed a lion named Cecil that was regarded as a central tourist attraction in Hwange National Park because of his striking mane. Shortly afterwards there are worldwide outbreaks of hate against the big game hunter. It is claimed that he shot the lion illegally, that he had had him lured from the National Park using a dead animal so as to be able to kill him on legal terrain, which did not immediately succeed anyway because Palmer used a bow and arrow and only injured the animal. A petition accusing the dentist collects up to 280,000 signatures within a short span of time. "Cecil the Lion" and "Walter Palmer" become trend topics on Twitter; it is stated there that he is the "most hated man in the world". Numerous celebrities, from British comedian Ricky Gervais and South African model Candice Swanepoel to singer Cher, make public statements. There is a storm of hate messages, curses and threats—culminating in a call for murder in a tabloid newspaper. The British reporter Piers Morgan, for instance, writes in the online edition of the *Daily Mail* as early as the evening of 28 July 2015 that "fat, slimy, egoistic, murderous business men" like that dentist ought to be hunted down "in their natural environment", that he should be skinned alive, that his head should be cut off, and a few photographs be taken.[161] Outside the dentist's surgery only one day later journalists appear and document the protest of shocked people mourning the death of the lion, placing roses and stuffed animals at the entrance to the building. "Justice for Cecil" and "I am Cecil" is written on the cardboard signs they hold up in the air. False news is spread on Facebook saying that Walter Palmer had actually been shot in a bar in Mexico. Inventive business people meanwhile produce diverse merchandising articles, trying to exploit the excess of attention. Stuffed animals with the name of the lion or T-shirts showing a group of lions with the caption "Where's that Dentist?" go on sale. The case demonstrates clearly that there is a bizarre focus on the emotionalising hype, a massive disproportion between the comparatively insignificant event of the killed lion and the intensity of global reception grinding on for weeks. Even *The New York Times* and the magazine *The New Yorker* deal with this topic; others, seek to find a new angle, giving the story some hitherto untried twist in panic-fuelled exertions to secure even more profit from the traffic wonder. On Vox it is stated: "Eating chicken is morally worse that killing Cecil the lion." On BuzzFeed one can read: "A psychic says she spoke with Cecil the lion after his death." In short, what comes to light here is a primarily emotion-governed hierarchy of relevance, i.e., the diktat of interestingness assuming dominance. Important is what moves. Significant is whatever creates an uproar in an immediately comprehensible and directly intelligible manner. The Zimbabwean journalist Joseph Maramba has reviewed this transformation of the incident into an endless spectacle in a very thoughtful essay. The real shock for him is that such an incident could have generated such shock waves. He writes:

> Cecil's death has shown on a grand scale how selectively the international media represent topics that they consider worth reporting, whereas the problems that ordinary Africans have to battle with every day are obviously forgotten. Lavishing such massive attention on a widely unknown animal was thought to be foolish by most Zimbabweans. The media could have spent all the energy that they invested into this topic on the adequate depiction of the circumstances responsible for the suffering of the local population.[162]

The death of the lion, he states, was really the least of the worries of the population in a world of poverty, of deficient medical resources and of political persecution. He himself and large portions of the population had never been aware of the existence of this lion that had now been stylised as an icon of Zimbabwe.

What remains is the knowledge that the international public has more love for savage animals than for that other, the human, animal. Now we know that these people who own more than they need feel more compassion for an animal that was bred only to be killed at some stage, than for a hungry child that is starving in some faraway region of this world.[163]

The Misguided Praise of Ignorance

How to react to the troubling effects of permanent emotionalisation, uncontrollable conflicts and the images of horror? How to live with the "integration of personal and public awareness" invoked by Marshall McLuhan, the prophet of digitalisation, as early as 1964 in his book *Understanding Media: The Extensions of Man*? "We live today in the Age of Information and of Communication because electric media instantly and constantly create a total field of interacting events in which all men participate. Now, the world of public interaction has the same inclusive scope of integral interplay that has hitherto characterized only our private nervous systems."[164] Naturally, we can try to pull out of this interactive game—and simply leave it. In the last few years, even at the centre of the culture of the internet, movements of refusal have sprung up attempting to escape at least temporarily from the constrictions exercised by the information and the interactivity of the digital present.[165] Media and culture critics like Evgeny Morozov declare publicly that they sometimes, for self-discipline, lock their smartphone into a timer-controlled safe, and they praise the productive power of boredom, the inspiration through the communicative nothingness. Books about self-awareness propagate the blessings of inaccessibility. Former internet enthusiasts like Douglas Rushkoff criticise the tug of permanent distraction and, together with Howard Rheingold, recommend daily meditative immersion in order to sustain the spiritual focus and the personal capability of concentration.[166] In the USA the Digital Detox movement celebrates the cult of media-free immediacy. Enterprises like Google and Facebook encourage *contemplative computing* and send their employees to attend Wisdom 2.0 conferences in California, which serve as the contact zone between the protagonists of mindful meditation (Jon Kabat-Zinn) and the engineers of consciousness in Silicon Valley. *Search inside yourself* is the slogan of a popular guidebook composed by a Google member of staff to contain the worrying negative effects of permanent accessibility (corresponding diagnoses are: *I-disorder, digital restlessness, digiphrenia*). It would be wrong to pour scorn and condescension on this mixture of spirituality and self-optimisation because all this is also a characteristic of the times, a symptom, revealing a feeling of overburdening in a world of collapsing contexts as well as the need for tranquillity and concentration. The point is the reconstitution of the zone of complacency by intermittent asceticism and self-exploration, the transformation of the world problem of information organisation into a personal concept of wellness. The question remains open, though, how much distress, how much spectacle and horror must be stomached by the individual and by society so as to preserve committed contemporaneity. What must be endured, what can safely be suppressed, knowing full well that there is "no right to a life unmolested by history",[167] as was formulated by the publicist Nils Minkmar? Under the conditions of networking, the interconnection between the *cycle of the senses* and the *cycle of the actions* has been fundamentally disturbed, the connection between what is publicly visible and what can be shaped and moulded by the individual is no longer balanced in an acceptable way, thinks the philosopher Rüdiger Safranski. He writes: "The circuit of the senses, artificially extended by media prostheses, has been totally separated from the circuit of actions. One cannot react any more in an appropriate way, i.e. transform excitement into relieving action. Whereas the individual possibilities of action are dwindling, on the one hand, the inexorable logic of the media market with its streams of information and images, on the other hand, only increases the influx of excitations."[168] We must, therefore, "in analogy to the medical practices of blocking ways of transfer, prevent the dissemination of horror news, which however would violate the duty of information".[169] Rüdiger Safranski recommends—vacillating between the diagnosis of senseless destruction and the duty of information—a sort of immunising protection of the mind, an individually determined balance of attention and avoidance, self-assured autism and sensible perception. Such a balance may help to avoid the overstraining of individuals and the feeling of helplessness and powerlessness. Others have simply abandoned the search for a personal balance of world dedication and world aversion. They propagate the undiluted praise of ignorance. The writer Botho Strauß, for instance, wishes his self-encapsulation to be understood as the reaction of an aesthetically educated personality that is still fully aware of what a genuine individual is. His critical views of the networked worlds are an attack on mass taste and the democratisation of all areas of life, where "broadness is declared to be the top" and "swarms of bacteria in the form of new media" only reinforce given opinions and general conformism. Strauß, by contrast, glorifies the "unconnected" individual who cultivates the "aristocracy of being with oneself", and escapes into "new inaccessible gardens". And he invokes the happiness and serenity of "the unaffected" who manages "to live without a stirring of future unrest, free from anxiety".[170] What is presented here is a sort of wellness concept for admirers of Spengler, the reinterpretation of the disgust with the present into a heroic nonconformism. Here again, as with the followers of mindful meditation, the perspective has been diverted: away from the tumult and the impositions of the real world to the individual self that is bent upon avoiding at all costs being moved inside or affected by external noise.

However, perhaps there is still another possibility—beyond all these ego-related recipes which in any case are usually only options for a few. Perhaps individuals and society must invent a kind of didactics for managing emotion and agitation, which will permit a more prudent and more careful handling of personal affects.[171] The key questions of such didactics for the management of emotions and agitation could be: what must we really know? What is really important for committed contemporaneity knowing full well that a democracy always thrives on involvement and interference? How do we combine excitement and relevance and how do we combine the reflexes of human perception and attention control (the orientation by the concrete, the imaginative, the emotional) with an agenda that possesses more general significance? It would suffice as a noble aim to use the feelings of outrage and emotional outbursts in as targeted a way as possible, to check them always for meaningful application, and to dose them accordingly. The escape into ignorance cannot be maintained for long anyway. Furthermore, it declares as absolute the perspective of those who are either privileged or reactionaries pretending to be avant-garde, and who regard news messages about suffering, poverty and humiliation as undesired interference with their own personal cosmos of complacency.

6

The Crisis of Reputation: Or the Omnipresence of Scandals

The Digital Pillory

One day in the year 2006, Aleksey Vayner, student at the elite American university Yale, hits upon an idea that will ruin his life. He wants to apply for a job with the financial services provider and property manager UBS and prepares a six-and-a-half-minute video entitled "Impossible Is Nothing", which he then sends to UBS. His video appears at first glance to be a parody, but it is meant to be serious. "When people tell you that you won't be able to achieve something, cross them out of your life because they're directly interfering with your success. Ignore the losers", he states on camera. "Impossibility is just another term, another opinion." He is shown pumping iron, hitting tennis balls with enormous power, dancing rumba with a scantily clad woman and smashing six bricks to pieces with a single karate blow. He is then shown racing down a skiing piste and doing a spectacular stunt. Then it is discovered, however, that Aleksey Vayner has simply inserted this clip of someone else into his video, and

B. Poerksen, *Digital Fever*, https://doi.org/10.1007/978-3-030-89522-8_5

furthermore that the CV attached to his application is full of fabrications. Slowly mean and gloating laughter arises, at first in small circles, and finally swells to loud peals of laughter around the globe.[172] The people at UBS have to laugh at this involuntary caricature of cold obsession with success and hand the video round. It circulates on Wall Street. Someone uploads it on YouTube, still a very young platform at the time. And many millions of YouTube visitors have to laugh. *The New York Times, The New Yorker* and other media report. Bloggers on the website Ivy Gate—used by students and graduates of elite American universities—comment on Aleksey Vayner, follow his footsteps and hound him for years. They publish details about his lies and misfortunes and his renewed attempts to start a new life under a different name somewhere in New York. It is a fake life that they present to a great public. The book that he claims to have written about the Holocaust proves to be plagiarised. The venture capital society that he claims to have founded is non-existent. Neither is the charity organisation for children in need that he claims to have built up. The letter of reference for Yale University allegedly written on his behalf by the Dalai Lama is obviously an invention. Aleksey Vayner appears to be the prototype of a narcisstically infested culture where show is uppermost. We are facing a singular ego trip, the great gala of an ego-maniac. Ever more disclosures, ridiculing articles and parodies follow, unearthed by the resourceful researchers and bloggers on Ivy Gate. Aleksey Vayner threatens legal action but remains unsuccessful in all his attempts to stop the chorus of laughter dogging him now wherever he moves. In January 2013 the press reports that he is dead. Rumours circulate that he had taken drugs or the wrong pills. Shortly before his death a friend posts the following message on Vayner's Facebook site: "Nobody should sell this idiot any pills!" After that he disappears in the digital universe without trace. "Was it suicide? If so then I believe that many of us are responsible", one can now read in the commentary forum on Ivy Gate, as the news of the death begins to circulate. And someone else writes: "Nobody deserves to be ridiculed. This is all very sad and should make us contemplate for a moment how hastily we judge other people." Whether Aleksey Vayner did actually die due to the consequences of his total disgrace cannot be ascertained with definitive certainty; the information available is too diffuse. But the spectacle of a manhunt and the mobbing on the world stage of the internet are robust evidence for the fact that scandal in the digital age has attained a new level of escalation. Some of the previous diagnoses conceived as fundamental must now be revised. It is important "to know the phenomenology of scandals", wrote the publicist Johannes Gross in the year 1965, for example. A scandal always has a polemical tendency, directed against elites, the establishment, the powerful. "No scandal will erupt against powerless or insignificant people", he concludes.[173] Only those ensconced at the top have to fear attacks because only they meet the essential media-dramaturgical criterion of the fall from a certain height. "No scandal will erupt against an unknown citizen who neither has nor represents power, simply because it is pointless. An insignificant citizen will without further ado be handed over to the courts of justice", seconds the journalist Christian Schütze in 1985 in a similar vein.[174] Only the moral "trespasses of high-ranking persons and institutions"[175] are at all scandal-worthy, agrees the sociologist Karl Otto Hondrich in the year 2002. Scandalisation is based on hierarchisation, he affirms. And he believes: only someone high up can fall. Nobodies seem to be scandal-immune, thanks to the grace of non-celebrity status and their relative invisibility in the public sphere.

It is questionable whether this assertion, more or less the central dogma of scandal research, has ever been correct in this absolute sense, because it has been and still remains the business model of the popular press to attack persistently even so-called simple people who have become allegedly or factually guilty, particularly in crime reporting and in its headlines about "murderous beasts". However, it has meanwhile become clear that the assumed phenomenology of scandal is in fact a selective phenomenology of the mass media age. For what was presented as apparently the timeless features of scandals, in truth grasps only the logic of outrage of the classic mass media and established journalism, which no longer generally applies in the conditions of agitation of the digital age as they are being rearranged at present.[176] Naturally, there are still large numbers of mass media that scandalise powerful and famous people in their operations of scandalisation, and derive energy fuelling fascination and excitement from the height of the tumble and the depth of the plunge. However, in the gradually emerging democracy of outrage even unknown, powerless and totally insignificant people lacking any influence are pilloried, quite independently of their societal status. Prominence is then no longer the prerequisite and condition of the possibility of scandalisation but its consequence.

The extent to which the public that was once condemned to passivity has meanwhile gained in influence is clearly demonstrated by another case that caused an international stir. It concerns Justine Sacco, a successful PR manager in New York.[177] On 20 December 2013 she is on her way to South Africa for her Christmas holiday. During the trip she tweets unremittingly. She is annoyed by the smell of the person sitting in the aeroplane next to her, she is disgusted by a sandwich and tells her 170 followers about it. In London she has to change planes and shortly before continuing her journey sends out the following tweet: "Going to Africa. Hope I don't get AIDS. Just kidding. I'm white." She thinks that this is an ironic joke poking fun from the perspective of a white person in the filter bubble of prejudices. Still at the airport in London she seems rather disappointed that nobody has yet reacted to a message whose harmlessness she is convinced of. While she is still in the air, however, the journalist Sam Biddle discovers her tweet. Biddle has 15,000 followers. He is a *prominent mediator*, an important node and connector in a network of communication from which everything is distributed because now one single communication impulse connects diverse groups and publics.[178] Justine Sacco is still sitting in her aeroplane without suspecting anything, when the criticism of her tweet turns into a worldwide Twitter trend. Thousands of outraged people enter the fray with their own comments. Within the shortest span of time, as BuzzFeed reports, 100,000 tweets are collected, among them even a message by her employer saying that the employee in question is on an international flight and cannot be reached but that the commentary is indeed infuriating and shameless.[179] Others demand that she be sacked, her racism is disgusting and shocking. Under the hashtag #HasJustineLandedYet the masses collect for the manhunt. There are death threats. Someone discovers the aeroplane she is travelling on and publishes the corresponding flight data. The Twitter message is: "Looks as if @JustineSacco will be landing in ca. 9 minutes, should be thrilling."

Another message is: "No one in Cape Town going to the airport to tweet her arrival? Come on Twitter! Would so like to see images!" She will actually be photographed at the airport, her face hidden behind sunglasses. She had in panic deleted the original tweet that triggered the scandalisation in real time shortly after landing, but of course there are already copies of it swirling around together with corresponding commentaries saying, for instance, "Sorry @JustineSacco – but your tweet will live forever." BuzzFeed meanwhile digs up other Twitter messages of hers and puts together a list of dubious-sounding messages. The article is entitled "16 Tweets Justine Sacco regrets". She breaks off her South Africa holiday. It is reported that the hotel employees threaten to strike should she appear. Her PR agency fires her, and she becomes the symbolic figure of the spoilt white woman whose arrogance and racism has accidentally been disclosed. In accordance with this image, rumours circulate on the internet that she is the daughter of rich parents and has inherited several million dollars—which is incorrect but apparently proved by an Instagram photograph showing her mother in front of an expensive car. One day, six months after she has lost her job and her old life, Justine Sacco hits on the idea of contacting Sam Biddle, the journalist with his many followers, who triggered the avalanche of anger in the first place. She wants to meet him, just like the culprits wishing to look into the eyes of their executioner. But at their first meeting he apologises to her for destroying her career and says that he believes her when she claims that everything was just a joke gone wrong, irony misunderstood. "Twitter is a fast machine that almost begs for misunderstanding and misconstrual— deliberate misreading is its lubricant", he writes in an essay following the meeting. "The same flatness of affect that can make it such a weird and funny place also makes it a tricky and dangerous one. Jokes are complicated, context is hard. Rage is easy."[180]

Sam Biddle is of course quite right in his late reflection. For it is a particular dynamic of outrage in its own right that is revealed here, an interplay of the distribution technology, i.e., the 140 characters allowed per tweet enforcing shortening and reduction, with highly inflammable anger. A concluding survey yields the identification of seven mechanisms and patterns.[181] The example of the public execution of Justine Sacco shows, first, that the development of judgements takes place at high speed. The attack is carried out in *live mode* and takes shape along hashtags following the principles of spontaneous self-organisation. The media framework of Twitter only supplies a corset of communication forms (reduced utterance, direct contact with other users and organisations, etc.) but at the same time permitting all users with an account to hook up and join the ad-hoc connective of the angry.[182] Second, the online image, or perhaps even the online grimace, of the accused in question is formed by only a handful of at best fragmentary items of information, which are used largely context free as evidence of guilt. The lawyer Daniel J. Solove explains in his book *The Future of Reputation*: "But now someone reading an online report about some faraway stranger rarely knows the whole story – the reader has only fragments of information, and when little is invested in a personal relationship, even information that is incomplete and of dubious veracity might be enough to precipitate ridicule, shunning, and reproach."[183] Third, there is a typical asymmetry of offence and punishment, because the offence of a strangely vacillating Twitter message is in no way proportionate to the consequences caused, the loss of reputation and job, the impact and the violence of the sudden surge of outrage. Fourth, the attack illustrates the high-speed condemnation in the medium of a public sphere that knows no instance of appeal, permits no explanatory inspection nor any effective defence for the accused. At work here is ad-hoc indictment on a doubtful basis coupled with simultaneous instant punishment—without rule-governed procedure, without the option of appeal, without any chance of effective defence that would uphold the presumption of innocence until the final clarification of the facts and their contexts. Fifth, in such processes of digital manhunts we can experience a particular pressure of conformity. The chorus of the outraged is usually dominated by the loudest voices. And those who may have doubts either join the presumed majority, articulate their doubts with hanging heads, or prefer to remain silent so as to avoid becoming themselves the object of anger and hate and free-floating aggression. The journalist Helen Lewis has voiced her reflections on her own failure relating to this case and the muscle of majority opinions. She writes:

Tentatively, at the time, I tried to suggest that perhaps the tweet wasn't that bad: certainly not bad enough to warrant the rape and death threats that were flooding in. Fellow tweeters began to argue that I was being a typical white, middle-class feminist, sticking up for a powerful PR executive and ignoring the voices of wronged people of colour. So I did something I have been ashamed of ever since. I shut up and looked on as Justine Sacco's life got torn apart.[184]

Sixth, this example allows us to study the logic and the sequence of steps of a *public-driven scandalisation*. The public can, quite independently of the filtering instances of the classic media, establish publicity by means of tweets, wikis and weblogs, use smartphones or digital cameras to document and publish objectionable things, set agendas as well as determine the pace of events. In the era of the powerful key media there was a three-step process of scandalisation, relegating the public to a comparatively passive role. At the outset there was an alleged or factual norm violation, then came the publication by journalists, who as gatekeepers had to decide whether and with what reasons publication was justified. Finally, the public could react. Readers, listeners and television viewers could vent their anger at the end of the communication process—or not. They could telephone the editors, or write a letter trusting in the grace of unedited publication. They were, however, condemned to react in any case in the largely interaction-free world of the classic media.

This three-step sequence may be reversed today as the networked Many have become a media power themselves capable of introducing their own topics and agendas. The new logic can also entail that there is first the eruption of the fury of a new self-activated public consisting of only a few or of many thousand members articulating themselves on Twitter or in another social network. Then the classic media pick up the outrage offer, follow the direction of thrust of the comments or create greater publicity for the case by criticising what is happening in the social networks, i.e., they actually use internet publicity as a news factor in order to legitimate their own news reporting. Open societies with free media and therefore varying views have always known what the sociologist Roland Hitzler condensed into the pithy formula: "scandal is a matter of opinion". What seems to be a grave norm violation to some, others may see as something marginal not deserving attention, let alone public complaint. Hitzler, who owes his insights to the observation of the classic mass media, thinks that such controversiality is definitely communicative normality "in segmented societies like ours, which are split into many views, ideologies and persuasions".[185] However, if anyone is able to publish, as is the case today, then agitation will continue to grow and aggravate general indignation because the outrage of either side will be considered the actual irritant, and conflicts about interpretation will clash with ever greater acerbity. The consequence is the proliferation in endless bouts of the *scandalisation of scandalisation*. This is another lesson to be learned from the special drama around Justine Sacco's tweet, for the vehemence of the attack is—with the irritation ebbing away—criticised vehemently itself as limitless and exaggerated. Under the given communication and media conditions, the phenomenon has to be defined thus: a scandal is a particular matter of opinion, invariably manifesting itself in highly different media milieus as a subject of passionate public debate.

Seventh and finally, the spectrum of supposed or factual scandalous content and topics is being extended radically. Still referring to the world of the classic mass media, the philosopher Peter Sloterdijk formulates the following diagnosis:

> Day after day journalists try to infiltrate new irritants into the arena and observe whether the scandal they are expected to trigger is beginning to flower. We must never forget that in every modern nation 20-30 irritation proposals are launched every day, most of which naturally do not lead to the desired results. Our modern societies may be a life form that enjoys scandalisation but it does not fall for every single proposal of scandalisation. Most proposals of irritation are rejected or studied with only limited interest.[186]

Nowadays, however, it is no longer only journalists who test whether their topic takes off. The very fact that each and every person can now switch themselves into circuits of agitation and can freely contribute chosen content, makes factual and assumed injustices and real deficiencies known and compete for attention at high speed. Without prefiltering and a minimum of declared relevance, today even the banal and perhaps totally unimportant norm violation is laid open to public criticism and censure. It is enough that a single individual is annoyed and enabled to generate participation and subsequent communication. Scandalised is what dissatisfies. The neighbours dumping their rubbish in the street are punished by being photographed, the hazardous overtaking manoeuvres of car drivers are documented, or the images of users of mobile phones are uploaded to the photo and video platform Flickr because they have been talking too loudly. By turns, pillory sites may show students taking drugs, doctors performing abortions, tax evaders, people defaulting payment, extremists of the right or the left, adulterers, visitors of prostitutes, battering fathers, alleged animal molesters, bad teachers, awful professors and terrorist chiefs.[187] Even targeted embarrassment for educational purposes is documented. Thus, a mother filmed her son in a state of total drunkenness and subsequently posted the video on YouTube, a father felt impelled to punish his daughter with a confession film on Facebook urging her to admit to having cheated several boys about her age. In short, the journalists who were still suspiciously eyed by the philosopher Peter Sloterdijk have long become part of a whole society operating in the business of exposure and scandalisation.

What does this mean? It means that the public sphere has been transformed into a laboratory for testing proposals of agitation of all kinds, which may be submitted by anyone who has access to the internet. Relevant information and banal narration exist in close proximity on one and the same channel. And this means that the new power of the public in combination with the technologies of documentation and barrier-free dissemination creates a situation in which the risk of losing reputation has become omnipresent and that excesses of attention, once alive, can hardly be stopped. One never knows exactly what others know about oneself, how they have gained their knowledge, what portion of it and how much of it might one day, perhaps even epidemically, be spread all over the world.

The Experience of the Loss of Control

What such loss of control may entail in concrete cases, and what accidents and events may exert additional influence, is revealed by the story of Lindsey Stone. Having once committed a mistake she tried everything in her power, even with professional support, to restore her damaged reputation, but nevertheless ended in failure.[188] Lindsey Stone, until her dismissal, worked for LIFE (Living Independently Forever), an organisation looking after people with learning difficulties. Together with a few youngsters and her friend Jamie Schuh, who also works for LIFE, she travels to Washington in October 2012. It is an excursion taking them to different places, among them Arlington National Cemetery. Stone notices a sign demanding "Silence and Respect" and spontaneously places herself in front of it pretending to scream while raising her middle finger. This is her joke, a sort of running gag between two friends who find it funny to smoke in front of a "No Smoking" sign or to make a noise and behave vulgarly where people are requested to behave and be quiet, and to take their pictures at the same time. Jamie Schuh posts the Arlington photo on Facebook. There are a few friendly and a few critical reactions from friends and acquaintances. And Stone briefly considers deleting the picture but then leaves it online because she does not really consider the matter important. "Whoa whoa whoa … wait", she writes to her commentators, "This is just us, being the douchebags that we are, challenging authority in general." Four weeks later the joke photo explodes into a scandal, although who copied and passed it around can still not be reconstructed in detail. It is spread on the internet. Her address and telephone number are circulated online. She receives a deluge of threats for having soiled the reputation of fallen soldiers. People demand that she should be shot or banished from the USA. A Facebook group and the initiators of a petition demand her dismissal. Journalists appear at her apartment and want a statement on camera. Here are a few samples of the hate she receives on the internet illustrating the extent of the anger: "Hope this cunt gets raped and stabbed to death"—"Die cunt"—"You should rot in hell"—"Fuck You whore"—"Spoke with an employee from LIFE who has told me there are Veterans on the board and that she will be fired."

As in the case of Justine Sacco, the employer dissolves the contract with her, bowing to public pressure. This is another demonstration of the power of the media-transported anger, the characteristic asymmetry of offence and punishment, and the interplay of ad-hoc defamation and context ignorance. There is, however, a special feature of the incident: Lindsey Stone makes intensive efforts to dampen the indignation and to remove the entire story from general visibility. "It was just a spur of the moment, total lapse of judgement", her father tells the press. "She wasn't reacting to the place; she was reacting to the sign and she apologizes to everybody.",[189] Together with her friend Jamie Schuh, who has also been fired, she writes an open letter:

> We sincerely apologize for all the pain we have caused by posting the picture we took in Washington DC on Facebook. While posted on a public forum, the picture was intended only for our own amusement. We never meant any disrespect to any of the people nationwide who have served this country and defended our freedom so valiantly. It was meant merely as a visual pun, intending to depict the exact opposite of what the sign said, and had absolutely nothing to do with the location it was taken or the people represented there. We never meant to cause any harm or disrespect to anyone, particularly our men and women in uniform. We realize it was in incredibly poor taste, and are deeply sorry for the offense we have caused.[190]

Some time later she is contacted by British journalist Jon Ronson, himself a victim of online attacks, who is investigating her story for a book about the power of public shaming. She tells him that, after a year filled with anxiety and depression, she still fears that her new employer might find out about her online past. So Ronson offers to support her with the help of professional reputation managers. He would himself make the necessary contacts and it would cost her nothing. And so it happens, at least for a few months. The professionals of Reputation.com try with all their power to edge out the photograph, to have contributions about other people accidentally also called Lindsey Stone moved to the upper ranks of the web search engine results, because they know that the first hits decide the general impression. And they create a digital twin, they write blog contributions and internet commentaries in her name, which deal with films, ice cream, tapas and the use of a hotel safe when travelling ("Stay vigilant, travelling friends!"). A substitute personality composed of banalities and agreeable inoffensive niceties is intended to help paint over the online image of a woman who ransacks a memorial cemetery for soldiers. The photo had nearly disappeared, reports Jon Ronson, who is following the experiment. "There was still a scattering of them, maybe three or four, but they were interspersed with lots of photographs of Lindsey doing nothing bad. Just smiling. Even better, there were lots of photographs of *other* Lindsey Stones – people who weren't her at all", he notes.[191] At the beginning of 2015, he publishes and markets his book, while the reputation managers in the background apparently terminate their work, as is suggested by an analysis of the Google search results. The chapter about the case appears in advance in the *Guardian* newspaper, and it includes the fateful photograph selected for illustration. Many reviews and public reactions in England and the USA follow, and they all present Lindsey Stone once again as the woman that she definitively didn't want to be any longer: the victim of a misunderstandable and offensively scandalised gesture. Anyone who googles her today will instantly be confronted by the photograph. The first ten hits that colour the initial general perception are entirely concerned with the story that she so desperately wanted to leave behind her. A reconstruction of the Google search questions over the years documents that the interest in her case has been rekindled by the publication of the book. Jon Ronson's experiment does not show, therefore, what he originally wanted to demonstrate, i.e., the final removal of a digital stigma with the help of professionals seeking to exploit the system architecture of search engines, platforms, networks and the principles of the economy of attention in the service of their clients. What he presents instead is that the old online identity, despite being retouched over a certain span of time, is retained as a sort of *information zombie*. It may be revived again, whenever needed, also for different occasions, (e.g., as in this case, in the service of a marketing campaign for a book), and it is then given new life and will return to the originating self in other shaming contexts.

One could say that Jon Ronson wanted to show the effectiveness of attempts at controlling things, but he merely proved the ever-present experience of the loss of control and the phenomenon of a shift of control—and has thus shown the interplay of three basic patterns, which structure communication under the conditions of digital networking. What does this mean now? The *attempt at control* consists in the attempt at targeted management of reputation, which fails because the author Jon Ronson revealed the backstage story of image cosmetics in his book, published it online and made it thus accessible to a world public.[192] The *shift of control* circumscribes the fact that, with search engines and social networks, world-view machines and authorities of reality construction have emerged, forming a system obeying special rules for the creation of attention. They focus general perception in association with classical journalism and the activities of a public that has acquired media power. They regulate how images arise, how they become stable or disappear again. They determine what information we are offered immediately about a person, and they suggest—solely by the more or less prominent placing of search results and auto-complete indications—what one is supposed to think of the person in question.[193] Finally, and in conclusion: the *loss of control* is the experience of powerlessness and enslavement that an individual or an organisation is bound to feel in the given framework. As nobody can know and determine forever who exploits our personal data trails, or who recombines and updates them, and in what way the information generated in this way will then, directed by algorithms, be diffused through social networks and be rearranged and placed within the perceptual field of a world public by the intransparent filter mechanisms of search engines, this experience has now already become everyday normality. "We no longer know what data are gathered at what time, because at the moment the whole world is being digitalised by the ubiquitous spreading of sensors", the internet theorist Michael Seemann puts it succinctly. "We no longer determine ourselves what happens with these data, where they are stored, where they are copied, who has access to them. And we are not able to assess what things these data may potentially tell. In brief: data of which we did not even know that they existed, find pathways they were not intended to enter, and reveal things that we would never ever have thought of."[194]

Control attempt	Personal attempts at controlling self-image and targeted self-presentation ("impression management", self-marketing), attempts at correction and censorship, professional reputation management
Control shift	Search engines and platforms, which function as powerful authorities of image construction in association with classic journalism and the publicist activities of a public with acquired media power. Their interplay determines what appears to be relevant
Control loss	The basic experience of individuals and organisations: they can no longer control the interaction of items of information due to their wide dispersion and linking, their permanence and presence, their quick searchability, light-handed recombinability and transferability into new contexts

The chart shows three patterns structuring communication, which may determine the reputation fate of individuals and organisations in the digital age

At this point the perspective should be expanded. The triad of control attempt, control shift and control loss is conceived of as representing three patterns structuring all communication. The question is now: how can the relationship between these phenomena be captured, how can the positive and negative interplay of control attempt, control loss and control shift in the digital age be described? Three features of the current media development scene directly catch the eye when we apply the conceptual-analytical schema outlined above. First of all, we notice a *new quality* of control loss. It goes without saying that communication, whether analogue or digital, always transcends itself in a surprising and ultimately incalculable way, if only for the simple fact that any act of communicating is irreversible, i.e., that an utterance once made cannot be unmade and may in different circumstances be received and interpreted in extremely different ways. "Whoever keeps silent, may still talk", says the sociologist Niklas Luhmann, but "who, by contrast, has spoken, cannot keep silent about it."[195] Under the conditions of digitalisation and networking the loss of control immanent to all communication becomes more probable, its experience also considerably more drastic and dramatic, because hitherto unimaginable possibilities of copying, storing, transferring, linking, evaluating, and barrier-free publication of data and documents of all kinds are now available. Nobody can even basically imagine what may happen with their Facebook postings, photos, personal Twitter or SMS messages, how they may be interpreted and instrumentalised by others at this very moment or some distant day ahead. Quite obviously the "complexity of the interaction of items of information surpasses the imaginative power of a subject",[196] and human beings are inevitably *blind to possibilities*, blind to the possible future of all the data and documents circulating about them, which may eventually one day return to them in shaming combinations and inseparably associate themselves with their personalities.[197] One might then be able to observe that *control attempts* by potentially affected persons become more intensive, due also to reports about reputation risks, attacks by hackers, leaks, disinformation and smear campaigns.[198] Image and PR consultation expands,[199] the numerical proportion of journalists and PR consultants changes, most drastically in the USA. There we have nearly five PR consultants to one journalist, who on the average earn 40 per cent more than the colleagues at the other end of the news market.[200] Not only enterprises but also individuals and even states and nations invest massively in marketing efforts and image campaigns.[201] And reputation and scandal management has become a business field in its own right in the digital age, thriving on the promise that one can unravel the system architecture of search engines and platforms, that one can comprehend the novel authorities of control shift, that one can accordingly remove negative images from the internet and replace them with positive reports. In short, the promise of control appears particularly attractive in times of looming control loss, the powers causing the shift of control being the novel object as well as the point of attack of actions. And it may be shown, finally, that under the given media conditions censorship, activities of intimidation, counterattacks, injunctions, etc. are frequently counterproductive, i.e., that a control *attempt* often leads to a control *loss.* Anyone practising censorship will be attacked. Anyone triying to remove undesirable content from the internet will merely make it appear more interesting and will in this way generate the very attention they wanted to avoid at all costs in the first place. And anyone wanting to suppress information will make themselves generally suspicious. The free flow of information—"information wants to be free" is a statement by the cybernetician Stewart Brand, founder of the first online community and initiator of the first hacker conference—under digital conditions appears to be a norm in its own right whose violation will be pilloried. A prime example of the sudden change of a control attempt into a control loss is the *Streisand effect*, which of course owes its name to the singer Barbra Streisand. Streisand discovered one day that the photographer Kenneth Adelmann, who was documenting the erosion of the coast of Northern California in a long-term project, had also published an aerial photograph of her own beach house on the internet. It was one photo among 12,000 others. She took action against Adelmann, tried to have the photo removed from the internet by means of a court order and demanded US$50 million in damages, but as a result not only lost the lawsuit but drew the attention of many people to the picture of the beach house, who copied it—marking the house with rings and red arrows—in protest against the singer's action. The attempt at suppression was enough evidence of relevance, an indication of the need to examine things more closely. The computer scientist Constanze Kurz comments on the underlying logic:

> It is like the natural reflex of the information immune system. If something is important enough to be censured or prohibited, it must obviously be of interest and worth general attention. ... The removal of potentially interesting items of information from the Internet becomes impossible precisely when they rouse attention. It is a hopeless endeavour to want to calm the waves. Although the Net seems to consist largely of cat stickers and other trifles, as soon as the general interest passes a certain threshold – which can happen as a matter of minutes nowadays – the information control reflexes of the past millennium stop functioning.[202]

Under the keywords "Streisand effect" one will today find not only the photo that was actually meant to disappear, but also Wikipedia articles reconstructing the controversy in detail together with the presentation of the incriminating picture. What can be concluded from all this? A phenomenon of a universal nature is revealed here. The complete changing of things into their opposites is already described in the fragments of Heraclitus, who thought it was a law of existence that he called *enantiodromia*—a fundamental principle that was adapted to the analysis of communications and ideologies by the psychotherapist Paul Watzlawick. In his many articles and books Watzlawick demonstrates how solutions turn into problems, how well-meant actions engender fatal consequences, and how ideologues and utopianists, in their striving to create a perfect world and to bring about happiness and peace with violence if necessary, bring about the opposite of what they actually wished to achieve.[203] Streisand exemplified this principle with her approach in the sphere of digital communication—but not only that. For her example makes us experience the loss of control as a universal factor that now affects the powerful as well as the powerless and the prominent as well as the non-prominent with a severity and intensity hitherto unknown, because information flows are much more difficult to govern today than ever before, and because classic forms of defence are no longer necessarily apt to work adequately. Her example also shows that influence, contacts, money and the hiring of aggressive lawyers to fight in the court arena no longer guarantee effective control: undesirable items of information can now be spread by anyone who wishes to do so, and the now more or less undefinable public has become a central player in the arena of agitation of our time.

How is all this to be evaluated? It would be wrong, by all accounts, to pretend that the old world of mass media and professional gatekeepers had been a sphere of information control and always seriously founded decisions of relevance, and that now, due to the publicist activities of a wider public, the situation had changed in an intolerable way. Good–bad dichotomies of this kind do not work here, for several reasons. On the one hand, it is simply not the case that a process of ad-hoc publishing washes up only trash topics and banal narrations. There certainly are quite relevant disclosures of injustice, violence and assault, which only become known because someone shoots a video with their smartphone at the right moment and publishes it online. On the other hand, even the classic media work with pseudo-irritants, pillory methods and freely invented stories, which promise record numbers of clicks, publication figures and quotas. To what extent even journalists, possessed by the furore of scandalisation, can lose their orientation by the ethos of enlightenment, can be illustrated by three recent examples. When former German Federal President Christian Wulff was accused by the media in January 2012 of being a bargain hunter, three journalists working for the *Financial Times Deutschland* researched the question of whether Wulff might really have tried, when still a pupil at his *gymnasium*, to bribe fellow pupils with small change and After Eight chocolates to support his application for pupil representative, and whether he had asked them at a later stage to keep silent about this attempted bribery. The background to all this was a report printed by a Danish newspaper, in which a former school friend of Wulff's had been trying, as it was formulated there, "to open the next chapter in the scandalous history of the Federal President", reviling him at the same time as the "After-Eight politician". On the basis of this kind of nonsense tip-off, journalists actually began seriously researching the circumstances of former fellow pupils, sent urgent enquirieis to one of the lawyers representing Christian Wulff and demanded statements on whether there was anything in all this. The subtext of this monstrously embarrassing disclosure research operation was: After-Eight bribery in conjunction with cover-up attempt in the confectionery milieu.[204]

That one can try to score points in the fight for attention even with totally unverified and possibly even freely invented claims is well known. But it rarely happened in such an unscrupulous way as in September 2015, when the British tabloid *Daily Mail* spread the story that Prime Minister David Cameron, during an initiation ceremony at the all-male Piers Gaveston Society, had committed "an obscene act with a dead pig's head" and had "inserted a private part of his anatomy into the animal".[205] The paper said that a member of the British House of Commons had affirmed it and claimed furthermore to have seen photographs of the action. A few days after publication—#Piggate had meanwhile been established as a hashtag on Twitter—the *Daily Mail* reporter responsible, Isabel Oakeshott, affirmed that she did not know either whether the story was true; but it was a fact that it was in circulation. Asked for evidence, she simply said: "It's up to other people to decide whether they give it any credibility or not". The *Guardian*'s chief editor Katharine Viner, however, criticised this kind of argumentation technique: "It seemed that journalists were no longer required to believe their own stories to be true, nor, apparently, did they need to provide evidence. Instead, it was up to the reader – who does not even know the identity of the source – to make up their own mind. But based on what? Gut instinct, intuition, mood?".

A similar kind of argumentation was practised by the chief editor of BuzzFeed, Ben Smith, when he justified the complete publication of the disclosure dossier on Donald Trump in an article for *The New York Times*. In the 35-page dossier about the American president, written by a former British Secret Service agent, it is alleged that the President's election campaign team had exchanged information with Russia, that he himself had tried to start dubious business operations with Russia, and that he had paid prostitutes in a hotel room in Moscow for bizarre services. In this case, too, the journalist simply stated that the dossier was in circulation, it was in the world—considering this as apparently a good enough reason for just publishing according to the motto: "Publish first, check later!" What had been written down might after all be true, it might in fact be proved true one day. And then one would be in the front line of the contest for the scoop with this ad-hoc publication.[206] In other words, a public that has acquired media power is no suitable scapegoat. And transgression is not a speciality of the Many. Established journalists, tabloid reporters with an economic interest in smut and dirt, as well as the chief editors of dubious media goods like BuzzFeed, work with extremely questionable means and methods whenever convenient—which could easily be illustrated by further salient examples.

The Balancing Act of Enlightenment

What are the consequences of all this if we broaden our perspective once more? Is there a real threat of perpetual scandal(isation)? Will the public world drown in an unbroken flood of spectacles, as cultural pessimists imagine? And how must scandals be generally assessed as communication events? Two positions have formed in this debate, a fairly optimistic one, and a rather pessimistic one. Protagonists of the *functionalist scandal theory* assume that violations of boundaries and norms initiate moral communication in a mode of delimitation ("It must not be!") and ultimately strengthen the cohesion of a society. An assumption inspired by the sociologist Emile Durkheim is that the publication of grievances allows "the modern unsettled society that is composed of many partial publics to redefine fundamental values by the critical analysis of particular norm violations, i.e. to reform and restore itself".[207] Scandals are—in this view—extremely useful communication events encompassing positive learning effects. They enable us to solidify norms, to remember them in point of fact, to revise them if necessary, and they can serve as catalysts in the great moral discourse of a society about itself, as "courses about what the society does not want to be but unavoidably is, too: an unattractive and intrinsically contradictory reality".[208] They engender deterrence effects and exact responsibility because the media and the public want to know who is to blame for the misconduct. And they help to terminate corruption, contribute to the elimination of grievances and the correction of misguided developments. The functionalist optimist fraction therefore follows the motto formulated by the sociologist Karl Otto Hondrich, a prominent supporter of this view: "Nothing is more beneficial for good morals than scandal."[209] Representatives of the *negativist scandal theory*, who do not use this designation for themselves but herald their approach as an empirically founded commentary claiming the aura of a special kind of objectivity, suspect journalists of purposeful campaigning and exaggerated stage management. They deplore the unjust humiliation, criticise the uninhibited attack, the occasional engineered discreditation, the plotting behind the scenes. They cannot really recognise impulses for the positive re-ordering of circumstances in scandals, they see there primarily irrationality-driven pack behaviour generating conformism and oriented by exaggerations and pseudo-certainties that are nevertheless asserted with the claim of absolute truth. Anyone who supports other views and refuses to join in the general howling anger will either be ignored or directly stigmatised. One of their protagonists, the communication scientist Hans Mathias Kepplinger, therefore states: "Thus all scandals exhibit totalitarian features: their aim is to bring everyone into line because the public deviation of some would call into question the authority of the scandalisers and their adherents. The great scandals can therefore be considered as the democratic variants of propaganda trials."[210] In short: from the perspective of the negativists the scandal is doubly destructive. It ruins the life of the victims and uses up the resources of the systemic trust that nourishes the agents and institutions of a democratic community, and it may therefore, on the whole, tend to encourage "resignative apathy rather than critical commitment".[211]

Obviously both perspectives are legitimate. For, naturally, there are documents and examples supporting one side or the other. The scandal opens up a complex debate about values, or it leads to the instant destruction and the social death of a human being. Both positions reveal their deficiencies, however, if illuminated solely by the sun of universality. The functionalists do not possess a sufficiently developed sense of the sensationalism of the old and the new media, nor for the suffering of the victims sacrificed on the altar of a debate of values, which might be considered useful from the macro-perspective of the society. For independently of whether scandalisation is justified or not, the sheer impact of the reports can traumatise, generate painful contradictions between self-image and other-image, release phases of depression and helpless anger, feelings of persecution and unsettledness.[212] All this is well documented. But it does not entail that scandalisation must be condemned outright. This is, however, precisely the problem of the negativists in the field of scandal research. They present their allegedly purely empirical media criticism in such a fundamentalist way and in such a tone of painfully controlled anger, that the question must be raised as to whether they truly recognise and appreciate the task of journalism to control and criticise power, whether they are prepared to accept as at all adequate any scandalisation process and any disclosure, however painful for the individual – beyond the strict concentration on exaggeration, overstatement and dramatisation. The journalistic stage management and dramatisation of societally relevant topics and grievances, which may be an urgent requirement for the benefit of explanatory disclosure, appears to be basically suspicious to them.[213] Whether more conservative or rather more inclined towards the political left, they use the special case of an alleged or factual transgression to intone—on the basis of their own prejudices, their political beliefs and their own empirically unverifiable value judge-ments—the same assertion time and again: journalists are *campagneros,* they abuse their power.[214]

Despite all the differences between these two schools of thought in the analysis of scandals, there are revealing commonalities. Both schools argue pre-digitally, they orient themselves by the classic gatekeepers, the disclosure logic of powerful mass media, and they insist on their discourse-determining authority, which however no longer exists in the traditional way. Because of their sweeping mode of argumentation, they are equally blind to the ambivalence of scandalisation processes. For disclosures are in fact neither good nor bad per se; they may serve enlight-enment and topple the powerful for good reasons; or they may serve counter-enlightenment and further the senseless spectacle, which injures the innocent or barely guilty in an indefensible manner. As suggested, there are documents confirming both the functionalist and the negativist positions, and sometimes one may even hit upon forms of public outrage that are unfair and overextended with regard to individuals but never-theless, from a macro-perspective, put relevant topics on the agenda. Then of course a final assessment will be really difficult because the differentiated evaluation requires the strict distinction of person-related injustice and general thematic relevance. An appropriate example in this connection is the scandalisation in the form of a shitstorm, for as a rule the intrinsic cruelty of such an attack results directly from the sheer number and pace of the comments. At the same time, in the course of such a suddenly exploding storm of outrage even topics of general relevance are repeatedly articulated—the discrimination of minorities, sexist or racist attacks, bad working conditions, exaggerated advertising promises, "greenwashing", etc. Thus, the ambivalence of scandalisation may be apparent in one and the same communication event. The deci-sive guiding standard for judging whether a public attack is legitimate and whether the collective outrage is adequate or not, is therefore not that scandalisation is in any case a positive lesson, or that it must, as a rule, be condemned as a manoeuvre of journalistic arrogance. The motto of this position, which I would, in contradistinction to the function-alist and negativist schools of thought, designate as *situationist,* is the following: *it all depends.* One has to be familiar with the conditions of the situation and the particular context, one must check the sources, assess the relevance, balance out public interest and personality rights, and one must train one's own hermeneutics of anger in order to be able to decide whether or not the norm violation in question is really significant, whether or not publication is justified and outrage then appropriate. At times, attacks are overhasty. At times, perhaps arising from mistaken consideration, matters that should urgently be made public and thus subjected to criticism are withheld. Disclosure in the medium of the sphere of the public is, from the perspective of a situationist theory of scandal, a balancing act that is nowadays required not only of classic journalists but also of all those who publish and commentate. Once upon a time powerful journalists decided primarily whether some event was to be classified as a scandal—and the public could only acclaim in an act of outrage or ignore the story. Today each and every one with access to the internet has become a gatekeeper in their own right who co-determines the climate of the public sphere and co-decides whether genuine items of news or empty spectacle reports are disseminated. The classic questions of relevance, of credibility and the verifiability of pieces of information, are today the business of every single internet-inhabiting individual. What all this might and should entail for educational processes will be shown in the concluding chapter of this book.

7

The Tangible Utopia of an Editorial Society

Principles of an Editorial Society

It is a dramatic moment in the life of Jordi Mir, a moment of affect, as he gazes into the street from his apartment a few minutes before midday on 7 January 2014.[215] He notices two hooded figures holding and aiming machine guns. Jordi Mir grabs his mobile phone, films for 42 seconds. Policeman Ahmed Merabet is lying in the street raising his hands begging for mercy. Then the lethal shots are fired. The two assassins, who had just murdered several editors and employees of the satirical magazine *Charlie Hebdo*, leap into their car and bolt. Jordi Mir is not really aware of what he has just filmed. He is thinking of a bank robbery, uploads the video as if in a trance to Facebook but deletes it again after a quarter of an hour, beginning to suspect that his ad-hoc publication might not have been a good idea. It is, however, already too late. The pictures of the execution spread like wildfire. Jordi Mir has delivered the iconic moment of the attack as a reproducible document. Not even an hour later, French television broadcasts the shooting, the rest of the media world follows, the film recordings are shared on the social networks, distributed by journalists. Suddenly they are everywhere. The brother of the murdered

B. Poerksen, *Digital Fever*,
https://doi.org/10.1007/978-3-030-89522-8_6

man will later say on camera: "How dare you broadcast this video? I heard his voice. I recognised him. I saw how they slaughtered him." A debate arises among the journalists as to whether it is defensible to show all this, unpixellated, in anonymised form or best not at all. Are the pictures relevant, of public interest, documents of a kind of cruelty that would otherwise remain incomprehensible? Jordir Mir also appeals to the public. He asks the family of the murder victim for forgiveness, calls his action a "stupid reflex", an idiocy that just happened to him in an overwhelming moment. As the journalist Friedemann Karig writes in a level-headed essay, one can consider this scene as a warning that society needs an *ethics of sharing*, a sensitive morality urging users not to pass on content thoughtlessly, not to publish execution pictures online nor perchance spread mere rumours.[216] Responsibility for the public sphere has meanwhile actually also permeated the camp of those who had once been called the public. And in fact, *also* determined by the decisions of the networked Many is what will become of the public sphere. A gigantic pool of gory pictures and exciting hit lists of ever funnier cat videos? A sphere of spectacles? A circus arena for hyped-up clowns and all those who roar the loudest and provoke most effectively? Or after all, as the doyen of publicity analysis, the philosopher Jürgen Habermas hopes, a world in which "the phenomenon of the strangely hassle-free compulsion of the better argument"[217] is still valid?

The demand for an ethics of sharing is obviously somewhat nebulous. It is like a well-meaning sermon lacking an all-encompassing framework of values, principles and concrete standards that could guide reflection in moments of decision. It lacks the foundation of a potential institution because it knows only one addressee, i.e., the individual who posts, tweets, commentates. In short, an individualistically conceived ethics of sharing is the wrong answer to the correct question as to how publicist responsibility can be re-thought in view of the active networks of the digital age, where one can, by means of the smartphone in one's hand, directly and quickly transmute from an external observer into the participant who might publish the decisive documents. Jordi Mir posts his video on Facebook, someone passes it on, classic journalism reacts, established television stations publish what was already public on Facebook. And everything explodes in a sudden surge of excessive attention. This interplay demonstrates the power centres of the digital public sphere as if under a burning glass: the media-empowered public, the existing real journalism with its direct broadcasting pressure, the impacting power of platforms.

This situation of media upheaval harbours an as yet uncomprehended challenge to education, still barely undeciphered in its true dimensions. It is not enough to start with the individual, with an ethics of sharing or, as in media pedagogy, with a diffuse, politically deflated concept of media competence[218]; it is necessary to involve all the players of the public world—the individual with internet access, the journalists, as well as all those who dominate the currents of information and opinion on social networks. To use a formulation of the philosopher Carl Friedrich von Weizsäcker, the mission is *to design the space of freedom*, i.e., to devise productive and useful maxims of communicative and publicist self-control, which seem ever more important as the legal and institutional control mechanisms of the networked world continue to diminish in effectiveness.[219] The fundamental questions of relevance are: how can we do justice to this interplay of old and new gatekeepers, take equal account of all the diverse agents flooding the public sphere? What could a unifying framework of values look like that combines the general postulate with concrete categories for assessment? How can a balance be found between abstraction and concretion in the value discourse of the digital world, permitting precise argumentation, on the one hand, and excluding, on the other hand, patronising paternalism and know-all moralising stifling the dialogue about values throughout the entire society? And how do we connect the guiding purpose of a concrete normativity with the required openness and the kind of liberal elasticity appropriate to the democratic ideal of maturity, in fact lending it its dignity by granting all the opportunities for individual development and personality formation? The answer to these questions, which will be detailed in the following, is the utopia of the *editorial society*.[220] It is a suitable target of education for digital modernity and can help to engineer the revolutionary opening up of the communicative space. This utopia should, as must be shown in due course, inspire not only the media-empowered public both theoretically and practically, but also journalism under pressure from profitability and business interests, whose representatives may possibly lack clear value conceptions and integrity and, furthermore, political independence and discursive vitality. In an editorial society, as I would like to define it, the norms and principles of an ideally conceived journalism have become part of general education together with a natural ethos that constantly stimulates everyone to reflect competently on what their own communications might entail. The practical application of these norms will be taught in schools, universities and public-oriented journalistic training colleges, and will serve as a framework of values for public discourse. They will provide impulses for the development of a platform ethic and will serve as general guiding lights in the great conversation of society about the state of the publicist world and the directions in which it is developing. These principles do not have to be invented afresh, they have been described over decades in ethical codes in Europe and the USA. They are documented in the relevant theoretical and practical literature and also in the form of interviews with journalists, as is documented by available comparative analyses.[221] The implication is that the maxims of an editorial society are already available, and that they only need to be released from their all too narrow association with a single profession and made presentable as elements of a general ethics of communication—a task that will be undertaken in what follows here. They will then not only serve the orientation of journalists but also a greater superordinate goal: they must allow society to describe itself in the most direct, unsparing and truth-oriented way, to sort and express its many-layered and disparate interests and, furthermore, to lend voice and visibility to powerless and marginalised members whose insights and views are otherwise not available in public. In this understanding they are indispensable for a living democracy.

The First Principle: Orientation by Truth

Obviously, *truth* is an epistemologically sensitive concept, but it also lends itself all too easily to moral self-aggrandisement. In times, however, in which forged news messages whirl through social networks in unbroken series, and PR specialisations and the business of disinformation become ever more professionalised, the concept of truth is a crucial guiding value of an editorial society. Nowadays the claim to be in possession of absolute truth and to command it like some substance or some material entity, is merely testimony of blatant naivety. No one who has immersed themselves in the history or foundation of epistemological scepticism would ever claim absolute objectivity and neutrality for their knowledge because it is more than apparent that the description of an allegedly independent reality is unavoidably always conditioned by selective choices and value judgements.[222] However, the principle of truth orientation as it appears in journalistic ethical codes is, as a rule, not understood in the sense of naïve realism, but as a set of working techniques and procedures—which is a real advantage. Truth orientation means, notwithstanding all the fundamental questions of the theory of knowledge, to describe what one finds to the best of the available knowledge as derived from all kinds of independent sources, in full awareness of the fact that absolute certainty is unobtainable. It means to create an appropriate picture as far as is humanly possible. It means to reckon with deception and systematic disinformation, always to listen to the other side in controversies, to compare and evaluate the perceptions of events by different observers in order to gain as comprehensive an impression as possible, and to achieve a precisely argued general assessment, which also contains clear statements as to what cannot be clarified, what is still unknown or will possibly never be discovered. The techniques of research (the two-source principle, suspicion of informants' motives, awareness of the cleverness of a PR spin, etc.) are concrete working tools here; they are primarily, however, means and possibilities to escape the bubble of personal prejudices and to attack the mental barriers blocking unprejudiced perception, as is stated by the journalism analyst Horst Pöttker.[223] His summary: "Truth is not to be seen as objectivity realised by a message, which could be taken home as a substance, black on white. It can only be seen as a *communicative process of permanent completion*, which is oriented towards the unattainable goal of complete correct information."[224] Truth orientation in the full awareness of the inescapable provisionality of knowledge is—in this understanding—a guiding value of communication in the editorial society.

The Second Principle: Scepticism

"If your mother says she loves you, check it out", American journalists may be heard to say jokingly, although there is a serious point to this common saying. For good journalism is based on an attitude of fundamental scepticism and the penetrating questioning of everything, however self-evident it may seem, because we know how powerful paradigms, beliefs, prejudices, greater and smaller ideologies, how strong pressures of conformity and groups, how influential mechanisms of manipulation and the general human desire for confirmation can be. "For the most part we do not first see, and then define, we define first and then see", Walter Lippmann formulated in 1922 in his foundational work *Public Opinion*. "In the great blooming, buzzing confusion of the outer world we pick out what our culture has already defined for us, and we tend to perceive that which we have picked out in the form stereotyped for us by our culture."[225] This general insight into the conditioning of our own perception of the world suggests that we should cast doubt on our own certainties as well as those of others and on all overhasty judgements passed in hectic moments. We are encouraged to wait and hesitate with our assessments and, ideally, to turn into "managers of our own bias",[226] as Bill Kovach and Tom Rosenstiel formulate in their book *The Elements of Journalism*, because we know about the danger of our blindness and the potential blindness to our own blindness. However, today this self-reflexive scepticism is no longer the only guiding principle for a journalism striving to be precise and to avoid mistakes. It has long mutated into a general requirement under the high-speed conditions of the digital age, especially in a media environment that permanently demands quick action and reaction and favours the reflex behaviour of commentating instantism.

The Third Principle: Understanding- and Discourse-Orientation

In the present societal situation, the rigidification of fronts and the withdrawal into self-fabricated milieus of affirmation imply a kind of nightmarish incapability of understanding and discourse, recalling Heinrich Mann's *duck pond problem*.[227] In the year 1938, Heinrich Mann considered joining the communist Walter Ulbricht in order to fight the abhorred Nazis. He came to the conclusion, however, that it was impossible. His bonmot: "You know, I can't sit down at the table with someone who suddenly declares that the table at which we are sitting is not a table but a duck pond, and who wants to compel me to agree."[228] In the digital present we can re-enact Heinrich Mann's experience without further difficulty. All we need to do is, for example, to surf back and forth between the sites of the so-called climate sceptics and the Facebook manifestations of conspiracy theorists who are convinced that our country has become the plaything of secret powers planning a *population exchange*. How can we still speak with each other in such a constellation, one must ask oneself, how to find a common basis, if only to clarify the measure of disagreement, of ideological and world-view disparity? And what does it mean if conflicts in a society no longer consist in simple differences of opinion but are grounded in the fact that one no longer shares the fundamental standards of finding the truth, or of rational argumentation, i.e., that a kind of *polarisation of the second order* has come to rule? What does it entail that the basis for mutual understanding has thus been pulled from under our feet?

Of course, in times of alienation, discrimination and rampant hate communication there can be no patent remedies, but one thing may be regarded as certain: the orientation of an ideal-type journalism by understanding and discourse will for various reasons be of even greater significance in such times. For one, it is obvious that discrimination and vilification are inescapably bound to work as blockades against understanding and discourse. They entail rhetorical escalation; they strike the insecure and the marginalised with silence. The other thing is that the journalistic guideline *audiatur et altera pars* ("the other side be also heard") may serve as the maxim of an effort towards understanding and discourse, for those who listen to the opposite side, even take it seriously and follow its argumentation, substantiate the discourse through the variety of considered positions and objections. As the communication scientist and former journalist Tanjev Schultz notes, "The norm 'audiatur et altera pars' points to a minimal measure of openness towards other positions. It requires that another view be at least taken into account and suggests to search for counter-arguments and pick up some of the burden of the argumentative process."[229] But what is meant by the virtue of understanding being the foundation of discourse? The concept itself has an intellectual-cognitive component and a moral connotation.[230] On the one hand, new things and things of a different nature must be comprehended in the first place, must be penetrated in their otherness and perhaps even strangeness. On the other hand, a minimum of *understanding* (not *agreement*) for other, antagonistic positions is the basis for any debate intent on elucidation, on resolving conflicts, on targeting compromise and settlement through appropriate argumentation.[231] To bring about comprehension and to develop understanding, one must take note of the insights of others, accept them as being fundamentally legitimate and at the same time take partial leave of one's own world perceptions. Heinrich Mann decided to stop talking with Walter Ulbricht, the prototype of an ideologue. He chose to break off the communication, perhaps for good reasons and on the assumption that a conversation was impossible anyway. A society cannot sustain such an attitude because it will bring about its disastrous fragmentation. It needs spaces of communicative integration, contact zones and hotspots for the engineering of compromises. It needs a sufficiently large reservoir of shared value conceptions, a minimal consensus on what topics are of general relevance and potential explosiveness, and it needs forums and forms of debate in order to explore the differentiated dialogue and the balancing of majority and minority interests in a fundamentally respectful manner.[232] The virtue of the orientation by understanding, and discourse orientation—thus viewed—can be seen as an implicit plea for the capability of compromise and the plurality of perspectives in social co-existence, which instils life into a vibrant democracy.

The Fourth Principle: Relevance and Proportionality

Good journalism can be conceived of as the *publicist cartography* of the given realities of life. It sketches out, every day and every hour, a map of what is going on for those who desire direction with regard to events in the world—a selection, an analysis and evaluation of what is significant and interesting in as comprehensible a manner as possible. The central feature of this form of cartography is that it reports comprehensively, nuanced and with a feeling for relevance, proportionality and distinctions. The journalists Bill Kovach and Tom Rosenstiel write in a reflection on this metaphor:

> The concept of cartography helps to clarify the question as to what journalists are expected to report. Journalists who spend more time and space for a sensational court case or a celebrity scandal than necessary – because they think they will sell better – are like cartographers who expand England or Spain to the size of Greenland, because it was once customary to do so. ... The image of journalism as an act of cartography helps us to see that proportionality and completeness are the key to precision.[233]

This orientation by relevance, proportionality and the question as to what seems *actually* important from a comprehensive perspective, is of general importance in a novel way under the digital communication conditions for three reasons. First, due to worldwide networking, real-time quotas and the reinforcement mechanisms of platform managers, banal spectacles and the alignment with hypes and the hit lists of popular content have become everyday experiences. These developments contain the hidden danger that available energies and resources for dealing with topics that are actually relevant will be cannibalised. In this situation the act of weighting information has long been a general core competence. Second, intransparent filtering systems (Facebook's EdgeRank, the algorithms of Twitter, Google, YouTube, etc.) define their own concepts of relevance, guide perception and influence opinion formation, without anyone knowing or enabled to know in detail how these programmes and secret recipes of reality construction actually function. Against this background, reflected relevance determination by individuals is an act of autonomous focussing of attention and concentration. And finally, classic media enterprises struggling for recapitalisation are under enormous pressure and constant temptation to subject themselves to the diktat of interestingness, to pay too much attention to senseless provocations and extreme positions, and to misuse their audiences as mere click machines. The nuanced sense of relevance and proportionality will therefore always be an important corrective and a basis of criticism regarding existing real journalism in the editorial society of the future.

The Fifth Principle: Criticism and Control

Digitalisation has made the critical commentating of topics of all kinds infinitely easy—no less, however, the betrayal of secrets and the dissemination and publication of alleged or factual scandalous material. In addition, we can see that the roles of whistle-blowers, disclosure activists and journalists who uncover a scandal and criticise the powerful, have become more transparent, and that every individual—whether communicator or recipient—needs a compass to distinguish between a genuine scandal, a merely alleged grievance or a totally insignificant norm violation. We must prepare our own proper standards in the exchange with others, train our moral imagination against the background of the basically vast possibilities of activity on the world stage of the internet, and develop our sensitivity to the adequacy and validity of our critical appeals. Here the journalistic ideal of criticism and control provides useful categories, because any unmasking and even any robust attack is coupled with the public interest, i.e., with the question as to whether a publication apt to injure, compromise or irreversibly damage other people is appropriate and warranted in light of the function of criticism and control exercised by the media. Obviously, there are neither patent solutions nor ready remedies for the necessary assessments and efforts to achieve justice. What may be legitimate criticism and absolutely necessary disclosure for one, may to another appear to be nothing but intolerable arrogance and false scandalisation. It would be naïve and, in accordance with the cultivation of a pluralism of opinions and general capability of autonomous decision, even wrong and counterproductive, to hope for a final consensus and the harmony of the well-meaning. But questions of usefulness for the general public, and respect for privacy and personality rights, compel us to look beyond the horizon of our own interest in sensations, our private cravings for revenge and our personal injuries. It subjects criticism and disclosure to a productive pressure of explanation and validation, because we have to reflect our own actions with regard to a superordinate goal, and the rights and needs of other people. And the question of usefulness for the general public ideally inspires politically committed contemporaneity, i.e., pledging oneself personally to tackle the correction of misguided developments in our democracies.

The Sixth Principle: Ethical-Moral Assessment

Working as journalists means, in the ideal case, that we balance out contradictory claims and conflicts of value in as reflected a manner as possible—and that we do so in clear view of the goal to publish in an ethically-morally responsible way and in full awareness of the possible consequences of the procedures and practices we employ.[234] A few examples of the paradoxes of the profession, which cannot really be evaded and which must be treated in a most circumspect manner: we must be quick, especially in times of live reporting, and we must, at the same time, use accurate language, orient ourselves equally by the guiding values of speed, on the one hand, and precision, on the other.[235] It is one of the core duties of the profession to reduce complexity—and to avoid, at the same time, all distorting simplification. It is a challenge of a particular kind to do justice to entertainment needs, but nevertheless to inform with substance, and to combine a pleasing presentation with serving goals of enlightenment. We must weigh up the right proportion of closeness and distance when dealing with informants. For if we are too intent on maintaining our distance, we will not be supplied with sufficient background information. If, however, we immerse ourselves too deeply in the milieu that we intend to describe, we endanger our impartiality and possibly turn from observers into agents involved in the events about which we are supposed to report. We must in any case follow our personal ideals and our own conscience, knowing full well about the attempts of PR agencies or political and marketing professionals, also the potential interests of our own editors-in-chief and the marketing departments of our own enterprises, to exert influence upon us. It is part of the fundamental tasks of the profession to reveal misconduct and abuses of power with complete determination and ruthlessness—but nevertheless to respect personal rights and the presumption of innocence, to avoid pillory attacks and perpetual petty-minded sanctimonious nit-picking with regard to unimportant transgressions. We must weigh up carefully whether to mention the nationality or the religion of someone suspected to have committed a crime—or whether to omit it to avoid discrimination. In our digital age, these are no longer just the *aporias* and paradoxes of the profession of journalism. They apply to everyone who comments and publishes and creates attention on the platforms of the digital age, perhaps even makes personal revelations. To make contra-dictions of this kind understandable as well as imaginable is already a decisive step on the way to a reflected and autonomous kind of decision-making, for such contradictions provoke the right kinds of question. They are suitable catalysts in a debate, they permit us to exercise our moral sensitivity, and they generate—without spelling out specifications for potential decisions, which would militate against the idea of personal responsibility—the necessary awareness of problems and dilemmas in individuals who have meanwhile become gatekeepers in their own right.

The Seventh Principle: Transparency

Transparency—the disclosure of our own procedures and working prac-tices—is a guiding value of the editorial society, and for three reasons. First, transparency secures and signals independence of news reporting. Anyone who discloses attempts to exert partisan influence as well as potential conflicts of interests and roles (consultancy contracts, activities in politics and in the PR sphere, etc.), makes these amenable to critical analysis and subjects them to a debate about the limits of what is accept-able. Second, transparency minimises mistrust and helps to preserve the acceptance of media, because we confront a potentially nonsen-sical suspicion of manipulation with openness and concrete information, and enter into a dialogue with the media public. Third, the guiding value of transparency opens up the possibility of advancing educational processes in the editorial society. When people experience how media enterprises function, how topics are discovered, researched and weighted, what sources, surveys and experts are deemed to be serious, they can gain a more precise picture of how selections are made and according to what rules news reporting is carried out. A debate shaped by openness about such standards is indeed a value in itself, because in this process they become clearly recognisable and reproducible. The imperative of transparency in the editorial society may therefore be formulated in the following way: *Offer your public every imaginable opportunity to assess the quality of the information you provide!*

Some Objections to the Idea of an Editorial Society

Particularly in these times of burgeoning media discontent, media sensationalism, and palpable insecurity of the trade, recommending the ideals of journalism as a framework of values for the public entails the discussion of various possible objections advanced against the idea of an editorial society. The first objection could be named the *argument of the pointless extension of the concept of journalism.* This objection rests on the assumption that journalism is to be perceived exclusively or primarily as a profession, as the domain of a closed society of more or less well-trained professionals. The concept of journalism, however, is protean and cannot be reduced to what the professionals in the trade actually accomplish today under the given media conditions. Such a view would universalise the image of an editorial and organisation-dependent journalism as it arose around the middle of the nineteenth century. Journalism is certainly a *vocation* and an *activity* but it is also a *business* and not least a *life form and a state of mind* in the sense of the sceptical search for truth and the critical distance with respect to power and authority. And journalism is also, in the understanding of the perspective chosen here, an equally idealistic and concrete *cultural technology*, which can be practised either in dependence or independence of an organisation, either inside or outside a classic media enterprise. This openness of the trade permits the proper recognition of publicist achievements that have not been reached on the basis of stable employment, nor in direct association with a particular editorial office. It is furthermore in no way corroborated, as the historian Timothy Garton Ash has noted, "that the journalism that best serves the public good described in this principle is always best provided by professional journalists working for media business. The profit imperative, and the heavy hands of owners, advertisers, PR, lobbyists and political forces, may outweigh the employees' advantages of time and resource. The activity of journalism needs the businesses and full-time professionals, but cannot be confined to them."[236]

The second objection to the idea of the editorial society could be called the *argument of clandestine arrogance and hidden paternalism.* This objection suspects that the ultimate point here is to save the traditional media system and to preach to an increasingly media-discontented society how wonderful and systemically relevant journalism really is for democracies of the Western type.[237] It is indeed conceivable that the established journalism in an editorial society will be regarded with new eyes because the public has gained a clearer view of the economy of quality. But it might also happen that the critique of the spectacle business, the anger about the complicity of journalism and populism, the reproach of a narrowed vision favouring established elites and the urban middle classes, will be articulated in even sharper tones and more energetically and knowledgeably. However, the accusation of clandestine arrogance and hidden paternalism as well as partisanship fails to take into account that *all* participants in the game must measure up to an ideal of journalism and that consideration of the relationship between so-called lay persons and the professional experts in a fresh and less asymmetric-hierarchical way is long overdue—in the sense of a *collaborative intelligence,* as will be shown in due course.[238] This form of intelligence can arise only when journalists and the networked Many actually inspire each other, i.e., when the fourth power starts to learn from the fifth power, listens to it with genuine interest, takes it seriously with a dialogical attitude.

The third objection to the idea of an editorial society as it has been delineated here in bright colours, I will call the *argument of normative over-emphasis.* It claims that the kind of critical, truth- and discourse-oriented journalism sketched out here exists only as a castle in the air devoid of all reality, just as there are journalists who pay neo-Nazis for Hitler salutes, organise photographs of fresh casualties ("widow shaking"), spy on celebrities, and, in the rat race for sensations, destroy biographies, print forgeries, launch contributions in exchange for booking advertisements and systematically run their public relations business under the cover of seemingly independent news reporting. Yes, this is correct. There is a lot of bad journalism around, nauseating "racket" news, pointless sensationalism, dishonest scandalisation, exaggeration and distortion, herd and pack behaviour. Yes, quite correct. There is definitely corrupt and wretched journalism, particularly in times of falling turnovers and intensified battling for attention, and it deserves to be criticised and societally ostracised.

We must add, however, that an ideal does not lose its value simply because it is constantly impaired in reality. Ideals are effective precisely because of their contrast to reality. Ideals throw into relief the unfulfilled promise, they show up what is thinkable though not yet in existence. In this understanding the idea of an editorial society is an ideal. And we can further add that it is especially the present phase of media evolution, where we can observe both the opening up and the re-feudalisation of the communication space by platform giants, that is in dire need of an energy boost in the form of idealistic considerations, certainly not on the basis of the claim that these ideals have already been completely and fully realised somewhere, but because the proclamation of ought-to demands may function as catalysts in discourse and debate. A society that understands itself as liberal and enlightened needs differentiated thinking spaces in order to be able to renew the question of publicist responsibility in the public sphere, and to deal with it properly independently of general appeals, resigned shoulder shrugging or horrified screams. Here the ideal *and* reality of journalism may be equally helpful—as a collection of glorious pathos-filled ought-to statements that deal with enlightenment, orientation by truth and relevance, but also as a reservoir of stories, negative examples and case studies, telling us about failures, media victims and pack behaviour, about prejudices and discrimination and the traumatising effects of aggressive, unjustified scandalisation.

Expansion of the Zone of Publicist Responsibility

But how can we transcend the level of mere proclamation? How do we create—enduring—spaces of thought and action, which retain their proximity to reality and yet remain autonomous, and in which the principles sketched here can be tested, checked, discussed and changed? I shall offer three proposals. In a first step I shall describe a special school subject as a sort of laboratory of the editorial society. I shall then outline how the relationship between journalism and public could be conceived in a different and a novel way, and finally I shall show how the managers of search engines and social networks could be induced to face their societal responsibilities.[239]

The First Proposal: A Special School Subject as a Laboratory of the Editorial Society

The education to achieve media maturity has long been in need of a special school subject. I imagine it as a sort of laboratory of the editorial society, as a protected space, but fully adapted to deal with the actually existing media realities, where all the mechanisms of public life can be studied, free from private business interests, without any hectic rush, but with the intention of exercising the moral imagination and the publicist potential of all participants. Why in a school context? The answer: the laboratory situation of the school is equipped to realise the feat of strength required to adopt a reflected distance from a reality that has apparently developed as if by natural law and therefore seems to us to have no alternative. It offers comparatively independent spheres of a relative freedom for those who have already actually lived in the digital world for a long time and will one day determine its future. There they may think through networking and digitalisation in all their personal and societal consequences, seek to understand them with a view to social environments and personal cognitive inner worlds, and debate their social compatibility. That would be the kind of basic pedagogical task of this new and inevitably interdisciplinary subject at the interface of philosophical ethics, social psychology, media and computer sciences. The initial phase would comprise a media-technologically based *history of the rise of the digital world*, to show in what measure media changes—from the introduction of writing systems to the invention of the printing press, of radio, film, television and the computer—are effectively ecological, because they radically transform a society, the organisation of knowledge, the character of authority and truth, and the forms of discourse.[240] The following phase could deal, again in the protected laboratory situation of the school, untouched by direct commercial exploitation interests, with an *analysis of power in the digital world*, which would show what big data, quantified self, the platform monopolists Facebook or Google, or the automation of the world of labour and the measuring of humans mean in terms of practical life, what realities are created by algorithms, and who is really connected with the blessings of the digital world. The third comprehensive topic and learning objective would be the teaching of epistemological sensitivity by means of a discipline that I would like to call *applied science of error*. It owes its illustrative examples and fundamental insights to the social-psychological literature on group and confirmation thinking, to the casuistic analysis of forgeries and misjudgements, and to the historical and epistemological study of prejudices, manipulation, and persuasion. This kind of study of the science of error provides knowledge about how knowledge is gained and how faulty and manipulation-prone the perception of individuals or even whole groups and entire societies can be.[241] It immunises in the ideal case against the temptation of unconditional certainty, the seduction by dogmatism and ideologies. "We must introduce and develop the study of the cultural, intellectual and cerebral properties of the human knowledge, its processes and modalities, and the psychological and cultural dispositions which make us vulnerable to error and illusion", writes the philosopher Edgar Morin in a book about the challenges of a pedagogy that includes the relativity of knowledge. "Knowing about knowledge should figure as a primary requirement to prepare the mind to confront the constant threat of error and illusion that parasitize the human mind. It is a question of arming minds in the vital combat for lucidity."[242] Finally, the *practice of media use in the digital world* will be a pivotal topic. Here the topic would be the assessment of the reliability and objectivity of sources and the concrete criteria that can guide us in the classification of more or less trustworthy items of information. Here we would have to deal with the potential effect of our own postings and publications in the digital networks and the power of cleverly masked advertisements and propaganda potentially circling the globe in the extreme case. And here we would have to deal with the ethics of our own talk, the rules of a rationality-oriented debate battling for the right argument, the disinhibiting effect of anonymity or pseudonymity, the concrete measures to safeguard our privacy, but also the protection of our own capability to concentrate and exercise deep attention in times of perpetual distraction and information bombardment. A vital, democratically founded public sphere, which would be the kind of driving basic insight of this new school subject, requires mindfulness and attention. It is not something natural and constantly given, it is dynamic, vulnerable, inevitably under perpetual threat in the game of interests and aggressive polarisations. In this way, step by step, a new understanding of the public sphere could emerge—a sphere that, as the spiritual life-space of a society, has to be protected against abuse and manipulation, against disinformation and intransparently active monopolies of power.

The Second Proposal: Dialogical Journalism

In the editorial society of the future, journalists must fundamentally rethink their relationship with an active and media-empowered public, design it differently, give up the arrogant simulation of omniscience, the role of the preacher, the pedagogue and truth proclaimer, and become listener and moderator and discourse partner with equal rights. The decisive re-orientation is that journalists take leave of the idea of asymmetrical tutoring,[243] the notion that there are informed (journalists) and uninformed readers, viewers, listeners. According to this notion the basic goal is the transfer of knowledge and the instruction of the general public by people who know precisely and long before any direct interaction takes place, what subject matter should be transferred and what the optimal manner of its presentation is, i.e., dissecting a body of knowledge into digestible portions, and by gradually raising the level of difficulty progressing from simple ideas to complicated processes of thought. The counterpart has the role of passive recipient, who must try to re-enact in a mode of quasi-natural toleration reflex what journalists mean when they tell us about unknown strange worlds. The underlying theory of knowledge of such a procedure is the strictly hierarchical distinction between experts and lay people as well as the belief that knowledge can be instilled into the ignorant—like a substance—so as to lead them out of their crude uneducated state to salvation (quite in keeping with a traditional metaphor of learning theory, which speaks of an alchemistic transformation of originally worthless materials into precious ones).

Knowledge is seen as something static, not as something processual. The assumption is simply that there is a transferrable entity, a resource that can be handled like a thing. In the editorial society of the future we need a new and less asymmetrically organised pact between journalists and their public, a great conversation at eye level, which casts the immemorial virtues of dialogue—approachability and tangibility, genuine, not just strategically or commercially motivated interest, and real listening, the readiness to change perspectives—into modern forms.[244] The editor-in-chief of the *Guardian* newspaper, Katharine Viner, described in an essay entitled "The rise of the reader" a number of central changes to bring about a new conception of our trade and a new attitude, which I would like to call *dialogical journalism*.[245] She reflects on the path to a different matrix of communication:

> What does it mean when we move away from a one-way dissemination of information, achieved by editorial processes which had been honed over centuries? ... Digital is not about putting up your story on the web. It's about a fundamental redrawing of journalists' relationship with our audience, how we think about our readers, our perception of our role in society, our status. We are no longer the all-seeing all-knowing journalists, delivering words from on high for readers to take in, passively, save perhaps an occasional letter to the editor. Digital has wrecked those hierarchies almost overnight, creating a more levelled world, where responses can be instant, where some readers will almost certainly know more about a particular subject than the journalist, where the reader might be better placed to uncover a story. That's why Jay Rosen calls readers 'the People

Formerly Known as the Audience'; why Dan Gillmor calls them 'the former audience'. In the era of the newspaper, there were few writers and many readers. Now, it can be hard to tell the difference. The People Formerly Known as the Audience don't just sit there.[246]

In brief, from the point of view of dialogical journalism, audiences are no longer passive masses but participants in a great and never-ending conversation in the search for truth, relevance and sense. They co-determine the agenda of topics in a direct and immediate way, they occasionally become involved in research processes according to the pattern of *crowdsourcing*, as has for instance been demonstrated by the editors of the *Guardian* newspaper in various ways: readers helped to disclose the expense fraud of politicians, they supplied material for investigative reports (e.g., on police violence on the fringe of the G20 summit in London), they discussed proposals to cap the oil spill of the *Deepwater Horizon* oil rig.[247] The basic principle revealed and made concrete by these examples is that the public becomes a partner in dialogue and discourse in a climate of mutual inspiration. Information is from this perspective no longer static. The rise of knowledge is conceived of as a process, not as a result of conclusive and exclusive proclamation. The professional expert knowledge of organised journalism is thus no longer based on the advanced superior information and knowledge of journalists but on the art of initiating communication processes and moderating and curating creative dialogues. *Sovereignty of the first order* (superiority on the basis of greater knowledge and certainty of truth) gradually changes into *sovereignty of the second order*, consisting in the virtuosity with which processes of knowledge generation and collaborative productions of intelligence are enabled.[248]

One condition of the possibility of dialogical journalism are heterogeneous editorial offices representing the diverse realities of a country, ombudsmen and ombudswomen and publicity editors, who promote the interests of the public, and a diversity-oriented personnel management of media enterprises. An editorial office must contain migrants, non-academics, a greater number of women and generally persons with deep biographical experiences, not least to avoid too expansive homogeneity of world views focussing too strongly on urban middle classes and academic and military milieus.[249] In addition, the classic *gatekeeping* of the mass-media age must be supplemented by *gatereporting*, i.e., the journalism of the future must in addition to the transportation of content provide more systematic information about the processes of the generation of these contents and offensively promote the criteria of rationality applied.[250] What is meant here? Gatekeeping means selecting information, flagging it as relevant. This is the classic and still indispensable core competence in a time in which rumours and dangerous nonsense circulate at high speed. *Gatereporting* means, on the contrary, disclosing criteria of selection and sources whenever possible, and making every effort to justify relevance, validity and claims to truth. Nowadays it is no longer adequate merely to proclaim what is considered right and important. It is now time to supply the meta-recipes of the checks applied to sources and knowledge, and the established rules of the game of fact research. It must be declared time and again—in editorial blogs, forums, social networks, by internet tutorials, the publication of raw materials— why what is said is said, and why what is selected is selected. Mistakes and transgressions must be made transparent, hazards and impediments of the independent observation of societal processes must be described without apprehension, and the actual realities of journalistic work must be explained publicly through programmes of further education and training, and citizen-oriented down-to-earth schools of journalism.[251] This means that there is an unavoidable second job for journalists in an editorial society, i.e., the self-organised illumination of the laws of their profession in a collective effort to reach the general goal of media maturity and publicist responsibility of all participants in media activities. The categorical imperative for this kind of changed journalism aimed at the great conversation is: *Always understand your own communication as the beginning and the impulse of dialogue and discourse, never as the terminal point.*

The Third Proposal: The Discourse and Transparency Duties of the Platform Monopolists

Social networks like Facebook, search engines like Google and microblogging services like Twitter are hybrid and meta-media and operate as such in a grey area that is difficult to define and even more difficult to regulate in a practical way. It is a mistake to see these as media enterprises with editorial responsibility for all their contributions, because that would give them implicit accountability for the character of individual messages, which they do not possess—and thus corresponding attempts to limit their influence will paradoxically enough increase their power. To see them as totally neutral platforms that only enable communication for everyone ignores the fact that they do indeed make editorial decisions by means of the algorithmic filtering of information—but in a largely intransparent manner. It further ignores that they do not just delete—like Facebook, for example—images of nipples and penises, but that they behave inconsistently in the cases of national and international conflicts, jam profiles, obstruct sites and content arbitrarily, leaving others that match their, or North American, ideas of freedom of opinion. And it is not sufficiently critically appreciated that these platform giants of our digital times are profoundly transforming public spheres simply by virtue of their sheer market dominance, and their cannibalising of the markets of publicity and advertising. We thus have to face the problem of how to regulate platforms in an editorial society without crashing either in the direction of total dictation (one extreme) or in the direction of all-too-cavalier laissez-faire (the other extreme). That such regulation is needed is obvious because at present the platforms tend to combine different contradictory positions—depending on whim, political-legal opportunism or topical occasion. They may appear as subjects insisting on the right to the free voicing of opinions, but then editorial decisions become known that appear to be totally arbitrary and situation dependent.[252] And finally they adopt—probably the most frequent mode of reaction—the "technocratic pose" (an expression coined by the internet critic Evgeny Morozov), claim neutrality, and behave as if their algorithms were nothing but dull justice-delivering automata computing along and sorting items of information in purely mechanical and indiscriminate ways. Consequently, the messages from the platforms declare, for instance, that they do not generate content of their own making but only represent user interests, that they employ computer scientists and engineers, and not journalists, and that there is no editorial interference by humans in the flow of information. All these arguments of last resort are simply inadequate in this form and absolute-ness, as the political and communication scientists Philipp M. Napoli und Robyn Caplan have shown.[253]

The solution that suggests itself in our endeavour for general media maturity is that filter transparency, disclosure of decision practice, and the ability of the general public to influence the decision practice must be promoted and, if necessary, enforced by law. For media (as well as media-resembling enterprises and platforms) must, in the words of the philosopher Onora O'Neill, be readily "available and assessable".[254] We have to know who in what ways and with what agenda selects, person-alises and evaluates information, possibly programmes relevance and reality distortions, and finally decides how we wish to assess these items of information and whether we want to expose ourselves to them.[255] In the area of the classic mass media and established journalism, assess-ability is given in much greater measure, although there is of course filtering and selection, too. And of course, here too the rules of selec-tion are not totally transparent, but they may be evaluated more exactly because the political-ideological alignment, editorial statutes and codes of the medium are known, and the media producers are approachable and more easily accessible. When we open a magazine with left- or right-wing orientation or switch on a television station like Fox News, then we quite consciously don tinted spectacles, as it were. We know what we are about to get, what we have to reckon with, the spectrum of topics is known, the agenda and world view are comparatively clear.[256] And it is this degree of awareness, when voting for a form of reality interpretation and an editorial programme, which is decisive. For this awareness changes the personal consumption of media and the delegation of decisions of choice to a media power into a sovereign act, because the medium has been chosen for its special approach and in full knowledge of possible alterna-tives. Only this act of choice makes a certain degree of filter sovereignty possible,[257] because it can thus be ascertained more precisely in what way lines of selection and interpretation have already been fixed beforehand.

What could a viable path to filter sovereignty look like in connection with platforms? How could individuals learn to understand a platform as a medium? My proposal here is that platforms must set out appropriate detailed guidelines and ethical codes amenable to public discussion. They will require ombuds-committees of the public in every country. They require—also in every country—publicity editors taking care of the dialogue with their audiences, who are accessible through analogue and digital channels and obliged to react immediately in cases of complaints or controversies.[258] The enterprises themselves must be obliged to reply to the following questions in transparency reports: how is the public sphere changed—by their own position in the market? What are the publicist effects of the algorithms they use, what tendencies and what discursive effects do they support? What values are inscribed? How does the enterprise generally deal with hate communication, with political and religious extremism and complaints?[259] How does the enterprise meet its publicist responsibilities, specifically in relation to its monopolistic status (e.g., by media education programmes)? What are the guidelines of the enterprise in the battle against disinformation and in the handling of propaganda, of ideologically or religiously founded fanaticism?[260] How are varieties of seriousness and quality to be differentiated? In what ways are the limits to the freedom of opinion specified? Who is charged with the curating of contents? Which processes of information filtering involve humans, which do not? How are employees treated whose job it is to filter the internet round the clock for videos that show beheadings, abuse, rape and sadism in all their gruelling varieties?[261] And how may, on the journey to greater individual filter sovereignty, news messages and streams of information be configured independently and without too much trouble?[262]

The logic of a meta-medium and the proposals introduced here require that these transparency reports are in turn to be evaluated by ombuds-committees and independent scientists, and that these assessments are to be communicated and debated prominently on the platforms themselves. For this purpose, the creation of the institution of a special *platform council* could be useful as a point of contact for refereeing and correcting misguided decisions and looking after obligations relating to discourse and transparency.[263] Concretely: such a platform council would unite platform managers, journalists, publishers, scientists and delegates from different societal groups. They would discuss complaints and critical issues, react to debates about the transformation of the digital world, articulate reprimands or disapproval, or deny and reject allegations wholly or in part. The debates and the alleged or factual violation of standards would have to be published by the platforms themselves and made glaringly accessible to the users. In this way—in a mixture of top-down and bottom-up procedures, of deduction and induction— the general principles of the editorial society would be concretised step by step in the direction of a particular platform ethics that would thus become identifiable and transparent for the wider public, in the first place. And it would become clearer, too, to what degree of seriousness the guiding values of orientation by truth, discourse and understanding are respected, what concept of relevance is promoted and to what degree the awareness of the employees of the guiding ethical-moral questions is raised.[264] What would be achieved? The answer: the intransparency of the publicist pre-decisions taken by the platforms, which meanwhile appear perilously normal and strangely natural, would in this way be made accessible to general analysis and public criticism. The public would thus be placed in a position from which it could assess the editorial programme that had previously been largely invisible and essentially removed from public discourse, it could deal with the question as to whether it was still acceptable or whether it might want to change platform and provider, a change to alternative platforms being possible, of course. This would entail more generally that obligations of transparency and meta-principles of discourse organisation could well be implemented but not special conceptions of truth, morality or freedom of opinion, because the latter would—apart from clear violations of the law—mean treading on the slippery slope of prescribing mental attitudes. So, it is not the level of content that is interfered with, it is individuals' freedom of decision that is expanded with regard to their options of considered choice, permitting them to find and pass their very own judgements.

All this certainly implies plodding down a long and laborious path. But only this Sisyphean labour of continual debate is really appropriate to the ideals of democratic co-existence in the editorial society of the future. Why? Because educational efforts of this kind presuppose the maturity of others, involve accepting them as independent counter-parts—for what other reasons should one involve oneself in discourse? And because only the readiness for continual debate makes the great conversation about publicist responsibility possible that could mark out the editorial society of the future as something special. This plea and appeal does not involve a static system of norms and rules, it is geared towards open spaces and therefore needs the continual debate, not the relaxing bench of rigid truths and supposedly eternal certainties. It takes for granted, in its choice of means—and that may be its weakness but perhaps also its strength and attraction—what must still be achieved as its goal: the autonomy and self-responsibility of human individuals and their capability of living together with others in a decent way and in freedom.

Acknowledgements

A book of this kind is a medium that works monologically but emerges through dialogue where it gains its meaning—if the dialogical impulse carries on. Without the exchange with colleagues, friends and supporters I could not have written it. I would like to thank Dorothee Börner, Melinda Crane, Hanne Detel, Bernd Engler, Alexander Filipović, Manfred Geier, Martin Giesler, Manuel Hartung, Friedemann Karig, Adrian Lobe, Daniela Nagy, Andreas Narr, Gunhild Poerksen, Julian Poerksen, Uwe Poerksen, Horst Pöttker, Julia Raabe, Jan-Lüder Röhrs, Andrea Schaub, Armin Scholl, Wolfgang Schulz, Tanjev Schultz, Friedemann Schulz von Thun, Michael Seemann, Eberhard Stahl und Surjo Soekadar. Tobias Heyl of the Hanser Verlag, Lauriane Piette, editor with Palgrave Macmillan, the translators Alison Rosemary Koeck and Wolfram Karl Koeck, Daniel Graf and Karin Graf of the Literatur- und Medienagentur Graf & Graf, I would like to thank for their faith in my work and for a plethora of stimulating ideas on my journey to completing this book, Kati Trinkner for wide-ranging research work executed with crime-solving intuition during the decisive phases of writing. Thanks are also due to the editorial offices of newspapers and radio stations in Germany, Austria and Switzerland that invited me

© The Editor(s) (if applicable) and The Author(s), under exclusive license to Springer Nature Switzerland AG 2022
B. Poerksen, *Digital Fever*,
https://doi.org/10.1007/978-3-030-89522-8

to write commentaries and essays on current affairs during the last few years. These were used for the book, wherever relevant, enlarged, corrected and nuanced, as registered in the notes. These invitations have helped me in the preparation of this book. For the need to formulate in an animated style generates a particular bracing climate for creating knowledge. And the exodus from the ivory tower has in this light proved to be an inspiration and a productive irritation of its own peculiar quality, not at all a bothersome debt to be discharged to the public but an opportunity to comprehend my own thoughts better in these acts of exchange. In short, this book has arisen out of conversations from which I have myself profited enormously, and it will have fulfilled its function if it adds a few concepts and ideas to the great conversation taking place in the public sphere.

Notes

1. McLuhan, Marshall (1964), Notes on Burroughs. In: Nation, 28 December 1964, p. 517.

2. Cf. an exemplary embarrassing-playful interview with the media theorist Jean Baudrillard, in which he maintains that the Gulf War of 1991 is not really taking place and that it is nothing but a gigantic show. Seidl, Claudius/von Festenberg, Nikolaus (1991), "Der Feind ist verschwunden". Spiegel interview with the Parisian philosopher of culture Jean Baudrillard on the perceptibility of the War. In: Der Spiegel 6, pp. 220–221.

3. My summary is based on diverse commentary pages and television reports as well as on the following articles: Ivits, Ellen (2016), Angebliche Vergewaltigung—Russland wirft deutscher Polizei Vertuschung vor. In: Stern (26.01.2016). http://www.stern.de/politik/ausland/lisa-f----russland-wirft-der-deutschen-polizei-vertuschung-von-vergewaltigung-vor-6666758.html (retrieved 25 April 2017); Kopietz, Andreas (2016), Von der Vergewaltigungslüge zum diplomatischen Gewitter. In: berliner-zeitung.de (29.01.2016). http://www.berliner-zeitung.de/berlin/13-jae hrige-lisa-aus-marzahn-von-der-vergewaltigungsluege-zum-diplomati schen-gewitter-23544190 (retrieved 25 April 2017); Wehner, Markus

© The Editor(s) (if applicable) and The Author(s), under exclusive license to Springer Nature Switzerland AG 2022
B. Poerksen, *Digital Fever*,
https://doi.org/10.1007/978-3-030-89522-8

(2016), Unser Mädchen Lisa. In: FAZ.net (31.01.2016). http://www. faz.net/aktuell/politik/russlands-informationskrieg-hat-angela-merkel-als-ziel-14043618.html (retrieved 25.04.2017).

4. I have developed the concept of the indiscreet medium on the basis of the work by the sociologist of technology, Geoff Cooper, an essay by Uwe Justus Wenzel, and the analyses by Joshua Meyrowitz. See: Cooper, Geoff (2002): The Mutable Mobile: Social Theory in the Wireless World. In: Barry Brown/Nicola Green/Richard Harper (Eds), Wireless World. Social and Interactional Aspects of the Mobile Age. London: Springer, pp, 19–31. Also: Wenzel, Uwe Justus (2006), Zeitzeichen. In: NZZ 02.10.2006, p. 23. And finally: Meyrowitz, Joshua (2003), Global Nomads in the Digital Veldt. In: Kristóf Nyíri (Ed.), Mobile Democracy. Essays on Society, Self and Politics. Wien: Passagen Verlag, esp. p. 98.

5. Mann, Thomas (1957), The Magic Mountain. London: Secker & Warburg, p. 682. (Transl. H. T. Lowe-Porter).

6. Arendt, Hannah/Heidegger, Martin (1998), Briefe 1925-1975 und andere Zeugnisse. Aus den Nachlässen herausgegeben von Ursula Ludz. Frankfurt am Main: Klostermann, p. 40. See also: Schirrmacher, Frank (2013), Sein letztes Jahr. In: FAZ.net (23.02.2013). http://www.faz. net/aktuell/feuilleton/buecher/themen/thomas-manns-zauberberg-sein-letztes-jahr-12092273.html (retrieved 15 July 2016).

7. I am here drawing on considerations first presented in the following essay: Poerksen, Bernhard (2015), "Es entsteht eine grell ausgeleuchtete Welt, ein monströses Aquarium, in dem kaum noch etwas verborgen bleibt". In: Zeit Online (21.02.2015). http://www.zeit.de/2015/08/med ien-macht-angst-anpassung-oezdemir-cannabis (retrieved 12 April 2017).

8. On the concept of de-territorialised simultaneity, see: Thompson, John B. (2005), The New Visibility. In: Theory, Culture & Society, vol. 22/6, p. 37.

9. Just a brief note on the theoretical and methodological approaches chosen in the book. I use both narration, analysis and argumentation because I am anxious to reach a wider public. As for the theoretical foundation, I feel indebted to media theory (cf. the exemplary work by Paul Levinson, Marshall McLuhan, Joshua Meyrowitz, John B. Thompson and Lance Strate). As for the empirical-analytical aspects, I use the instrument of qualitative case study. The case studies carried out for the book are based on the analysis and evaluation of published documents as well as the relevant literature on the topic. In particular cases, embedded interviews with journalists, editors and editorial staff are included as well as conversations

with individuals who had been dragged into a process of scandalisation and public pillorying – for whatever reasons. My prime concern is a theory of digital media independent of the traditional singular fixation on particular media (print, radio, television, etc.), a theory tackling the analysis of the "mobility" of digitalised materials as the cause of collapsing contexts and an irritation-driven view of the world.

10. The trend of internet pessimism is the subject of an article by Tim Hwang, which includes a stimulating and moderately ironical typology of internet critics. Cf. Hwang, Tim (2018), The Four Ways That Ex-Internet Idealists Explain Where It All Went Wrong. In: MIT Technology Review (22 August 2018). https://www.technologyreview.com/s/611805/the-four-ways-that-ex-internet-idealists-explain-where-it-all-went-wrong/ (retrieved 04 June 2019).

11. On these ideas see further: Poerksen, Bernhard (2015), Pöbeleien im Netz ersticken Debatten. Wir brauchen endlich Regeln! In: Zeit Online (09.07.2015). http://www.zeit.de/2015/26/journalisten-medien-verantwortung-debatten-regeln (retrieved 03 March 2017).

12. For details see: Erken, Rebecca (2014), Urlaubslüge nach Thailand. Interview mit Zilla van den Born In: Spiegel Online (11.12.2014). http://www.spiegel.de/lebenundlernen/uni/facebook-luege-hollaendische-studentin-taeuscht-asien-reise-vor-a-998943.html (retrieved 07 February 2017).

13. See on the following: Lobe, Adrian (2015), Nehmen Roboter Journalisten den Job weg? In: FAZ.net (17.04.2015). http://www.faz.net/aktuell/feuilleton/media/automatisierter-journalism-nehmen-roboter-allen-journalisten-den-job-weg-13542074.html (retrieved 14 February 2017). Also: Lobe, Adrian (2017), Prosa als Programm. In: FAZ.net (21.02.2017). http://www.faz.net/aktuell/feuilleton/media/roboterjourn alism-prosa-als-programm-14873449.html (retrieved 25 February 2017).

14. See further on this (and also, in addition, the at best crude estimates of there being ca. "100 million fake accounts" on all the big platforms) the analysis of Fuchs, Martin (2016), Warum Social Bots unsere Demokratie gefährden. In: NZZ.ch (12.09.2016). http://www.nzz.ch/digital/aut omatisierte-trolle-warum-social-bots-unsere-demokratie-gefaehrden-ld. 116166 (retrieved 22 November 2016).

15. Numerous examples of fake news can be found in the following book: Wannenmacher, Tom/Wolf, Andre (2016), *Die Fake-Jäger. Wie Gerüchte im Internet entstehen und wie man sich schützen kann.* München/Grünwald: Verlag Komplett-Media.

16. On the following see: Lobe, Adrian (2016), Das ist doch nicht wahr. Im Netz laufen gefälschte Nachrichten immer besser. In: FAZ.net (16.08.2016). http://www.faz.net/aktuell/feuilleton/media/im-netz-lau fen-gefaelschte-nachrichten-immer-besser-14389442.html (retrieved 29 August 2016).

17. See: Schröder, Jens (2016), Fake News: Warum Facebook verdammt nochmal seiner Verantwortung gerecht werden muss. In: meedia.de (18.11.2016). http://meedia.de/2016/11/18/fakenews-warum-fac ebook-verdammt-nochmal-seiner-verantwortung-gerecht-werden-muss/ (retrieved 15 December 2016).

18. Silverman, Craig/Singer-Vine, Jeremy (2016), Most Americans Who See Fake News Believe It, New Survey Says. In: BuzzFeed (07.12.2016). https://www.buzzfeed.com/craigsilverman/fakenews-survey?utm_term=. evb9BgKeeA#.ko6EBKRDD6 (retrieved 07 February 2017).

19. Liebelson, Dana/Bendery, Jennifer/Stein, Sam (2016): Donald Trump Made Up Stuff 71 Times In An Hour. In: *The Huffington Post* (30.03.2016). http://www.huffingtonpost.com/entry/donald-trump-fact-check_us_56fc375fe4b0daf53aee9175 (retrieved 12 September 2016). On the "reality content" of Donald Trump's speeches and comments see: Haberman, Maggie (2018), A President Who Believes He Is Entitled to His Own Facts. In: *The New York Times* (18.10.2018). https://www. nytimes.com/2018/10/18/us/politics/donald-trump-foreign-leaders.html (08.04.2019).

The campaign techniques of Donald Trump in 2016 and 2020 are analysed in the following publications: Benkler, Yochai/Faris, Robert/Roberts, Hal (2018), *Network Propaganda. Manipulation, Disinformation, and Radicalization in American Politics*. New York: Oxford University Press; Coppins, McKay (2020), The Billion-Dollar Disinformation Campaign to Reelect the President. How New Technologies and Techniques Pioneered by Dictators Will Shape the 2020 Election. In: theatlantic.com (10.02.2020). https://www.theatlantic.com/magazine/arc hive/2020/03/the-2020-disinformation-war/605530/ (retrieved 24 April 2020).

20. It would be a mistake, however, to ascribe all the propaganda successes of the individual Donald Trump exclusively to his use of social media. The man who was elected American president in 2016 incorporated the worst of two media systems and can be seen as a hybrid figure of reality-TV star and internet troll. Trump began testing his political ambitions in 2011 in the morning show *Fox & Friends*. And he did it by spreading racist

conspiracy theories. He claimed that Barack Obama was not a true-born US-American and therefore not actually a legitimate president. Other media took up his baseless speculations and reinforced them—even when attempting to dissolve them, more often though out of a clandestine fascination with provocation as it would promise higher ratings. Here we have, if you will, the original sin of journalism, i.e., to grab a marginal nonsense topic from the gutter of the internet and propel it to the centre of attention and, by claiming to debug it, jazz it up to an outrage. On the precursors inspiring Donald Trump, see the historical analyses by Nicole Hemmer, in particular Hemmer, Nicole (2016), *Messengers of the Right. Conservative Media and the Transformation of American Politics.* Philadelphia: University of Pennsylvania Press.

21. On the fundamental question of the rationality of our convictions, see the following essay: Kolbert, Elizabeth (2017), Why Facts Don't Change Our Minds. In: *The New Yorker* (20.02.2017). https://www.newyorker.com/magazine/2017/02/27/why-facts-dont-change-our-minds (retrieved 28 May 2020).

22. On the backfire effect, see the following fundamental study: Nyhan, Brendan/Reifler, Jason (2010): When Corrections Fail: The Persistence of Political Misperceptions. In: *Political Behavior*, vol. 32/2, pp. 303–330. In addition: Brodnig, Ingrid (2016), *Hass im Netz. Was wir gegen Hetze, Mobbing und Lügen tun können.* Wien: Christian Brandstätter Verlag, pp. 139ff. On the effectiveness of corrections see also Ecker, Ulrich K.H./Lewandowsky, Stephan/Chadwick, Matthew (2020), Can Corrections Spread Misinformation to New Audiences? Testing for the Elusive Familiarity Backfire Effect. Cognitive Research: Principles and Implications. In: *Cognitive Research: Principles and Implications.* No. 5. pp. 1–25. Up-to-date analyses of the backfire effect may be found here: Swire-Thompson, Briony/ DeGutis, Joseph/ Lazer, David (2020), Searching for the Backfire Effect: Measurement and Design Considerations. In: *Journal of Applied Research in Memory and Cognition.* No. 9. pp. 286–299. A meta-analysis on the effectiveness of fact checking in general is offered by the following article: Walter, Nathan/Cohen, Jonathan/Hobert, R. Lance/Morag, Yasmin (2019), Fact-Checking: A Meta-Analysis of What Works and for Whom. In: *Political Communication.* No. 37. pp. 350–375.

23. In the case of propaganda, furthermore, people usually retain concrete content longer in their memories that the sources from which this content derives. The consequence is that information from dubious channels gradually gains in credibility. On this so-called *sleeper effect* of defaming messages whose convincing power increases with time because

their origin is forgotten, see Dobelli, Rolf (2012), *Die Kunst des klugen Handelns. 52 Irrwege, die Sie besser anderen überlassen.* München: Carl Hanser Verlag, p. 82f.

24. The concept of the doctrine of equal validity originates in epistemological debates; see: Boghossian, Paul A. (2006), *Fear of Knowledge. Against Relativism and Constructivism.* Oxford: Clarendon Press, p. 3.

25. The trend towards source ignorance is reflected by the following figures: in the USA only 52 per cent of readers on social networks notice from which medium a message derives; only 49 per cent do take notice if they receive information from aggregators. In Japan and South Korea, a quarter of the people take notice of the media brand if they consume offers from aggregator services. Source loyalty is additionally weakened, as already indicated, by the fact that Facebook and other platforms determine the presentation of news offers and thus generally have the means to completely delete the origins of messages. Relevant research is: Khorana, Smitha/Renner, Nausicaa (2016), Social Media Is on the Rise, but Not Like You'd Expect. In: *Columbia Journalism Review* (21.06.2016). http://www.cjr.org/analysis/reuters_report.php (retrieved 13 July 2016). On the lack of defining signals for sources and credibility see also: Müller von Blumencron, Mathias (2016), Trennt Propaganda von Wahrheit! In: FAZ.net (05.02.2016). http://www.faz.net/aktuell/politik/inland/luegen-im-internet-spannen-ein-netz-der-verwirrung-14052436.html (retrieved 08 February 2016).

26. On the spreading of this rumour see the meticulous research by BuzzFeed and the editorial staff of *The New York Times*, also the exemplary article by: Rehfeld, Nina (2016), In America herrscht die Lüge. In: FAZ.net (09.12.2016). http://www.faz.net/aktuell/feuilleton/debatten/wie-sich-in-America-die-herrschaft-der-luege-festigt-14565557.html (retrieved 16 December 2016).

27. On this case see further: Poerksen, Bernhard (2017), Schöne falsche Welt. In: *Chrismon* (21.03.2017). http://chrismon.evangelisch.de/article/2017/33307/kampf-gegen-fakenews-im-internet (retrieved 08 April 2017).

28. Del Vicario, Michela/Bessi, Alessandro/Zollo, Fabiana/Petroni, Fabio/Scala, Antonio/Caldarelli, Guido/Stanley, H. Eugene/Quattrociocchi, Walter (2016), The Spreading of Misinformation Online. In: *PNAS*, vol. 113/3, p. 558.

29. On the following analysis see: Poerksen, Bernhard (2016), Die postfaktische Universität. In: Zeit Online (29.12.2016). http://www.zeit.de/2016/52/wissenschaft-post-faktisch-rationalitaet-ohnmacht-universitaeten (retrieved 07 March 2017). Also: Poerksen, Bernhard (2017), Das peinliche Zeitalter. In: *Forschung & Lehre*, vol. 24/2, p. 97.

30. See: Davies, William (2016), The Age of Post-Truth Politics. In: NYTimes.com (24.08.2016). http://www.nytimes.com/2016/08/24/opi nion/campaign-stops/the-age-of-post-truth-politics.html?_r=0 (retrieved 06 December 2016). And: Lepore, Jill (2016), After the Fact. In the History of Truth, a New Chapter Begins. In: newyorker.com (21.03.2016). http://www.newyorker.com/magazine/2016/03/21/the-int ernet-of-us-and-the-end-of-facts (retrieved 19 July 2016). The alleged discovery of post-factual phenomena has engendered numerous book publications; see the exemplary illuminating essay of 2017 by the media critic Brooke Gladstone: Gladstone, Brooke (2017), *The Trouble with Reality. A Rumination on Moral Panic in Our Time*. New York: Workman Publishing.

31. Even the debates about post-factual phenomena and the maturity and informedness of citizens are everything but new; basic patterns of these debates are described by Carl Bybee with regard to the dispute between the journalist Walter Lippmann and the philosopher John Dewey. Cf. Bybee, Carl (1999), Can Democracy Survive in the Post-Factual Age? A Return to the Lippmann-Dewey Debate About the Politics of News. In: *Journalism & Communication Monographs*. No. 1/1, pp. 28–66.

32. Cf. Fuest, Benedikt (2016), Der absurde Krieg der Wikipedia-Roboter. In: world.de (27.09.2016). https://www.world.de/wirtschaft/web world/article158396690/Der-absurde-Krieg-der-Wikipedia-Roboter. html (retrieved 11 October 2016).

33. I owe the formulation *deregulation of the truth market* to Michael Seemann; see: Seemann, Michael (2017), Digitaler Tribalismus und Fake News. In: ctrl-verlust.net (29.09.2017). http://www.ctrl-verlust.net/digita ler-tribalismus-und-fakenews/ (retrieved 10 October 2017).

34. For the detailed chronology of events see: Pick, Yussi (2013), *Das Echo-Prinzip. Wie Onlinekommunikation Politik verändert*. Wien: Czernin Verlag, p. 103f.

35. "Technology is neither good nor bad", so Melvin Kranzberg, "nor is it neutral." For further elucidation see: Kranzberg, Melvin (1986), Presidential Address. Technology and History: "Kranzberg's Laws". In: *Technology and Culture*, vol. 27/3, pp. 545f.

36. Cf. for basics: Rushkoff, Douglas (2014), *Present Shock: When Everything Happens Now*. New York: Penguin Group.

37. Personal communication.

38. I also deal with this example in the following: Poerksen, Bernhard (2015), Trolle, Empörungsjunkies und kluge Köpfe: Die fünfte Gewalt

des digitalen Zeitalters. In: cicero.de (17.04.2015). http://cicero.de/ber liner-republik/trolle-empoerungsjunkies-und-kluge-koepfe-die-fuenfte-gewalt-des-digitalen (retrieved 03 March 2017).

39. Quoted from: Pick, Yussi (2013), *Das Echo-Prinzip. Wie Onlinekommunikation Politik verändert.* Wien: Czernin Verlag, p. 29.

40. I have presented these considerations for the first time in the following essay: Poerksen, Bernhard (2015), Extremismus der Erregung. In: Zeit Online (06.04.2015). http://www.zeit.de/politik/2015-04/germanwings-absturz-journalism-berichterstattung-media-pilot (retrieved 08 March 2017).

41. In other cases the reaction to this vacuum of visualisation consists in the presentation of photo forgeries and sham visual evidence of what can trivially be expected. In this connection one may remember the photo fakes circulated after the killing of Osama bin Laden.

42. On this phenomenon of commentating instantism, see also the following conversation: Huber, Joachim (2016), "Die Simulation von Einordnung lässt einen frösteln". Interview mit Bernhard Poerksen. In: tagesspiegel.de (20.01.2016). http://www.tagesspiegel.de/medien/medienwissenschaft ler-bernhard-poerksen-zu-koeln-die-simulation-von-einordnung-laesst-einen-froesteln/12851788.html (retrieved 06 March 2017).

43. See Brodnig, Ingrid (2016), *Hass im Netz. Was wir gegen Hetze, Mobbing und Lügen tun können.* Wien: Christian Brandstätter Verlag, p. 132.

44. Feuz, Martin/Fuller, Matthew/Stalder, Felix (2011), Personal Web Searching in the Age of Semantic Capitalism: Diagnosing the Mechanisms of Personalisation. In: *First Monday* (07.02.2011). http://firstm onday.org/article/view/3344/2766 (retrieved 08 February 2017). On this investigation see also: Tißler, Jan (2011), SEO-Studie: Personalisierte Suche macht Ranking unberechenbar. In: t3n.de (19.04.2011). http:// t3n.de/news/seo-studie-personalisierte-suche-macht-ranking-306470/ (retrieved 08 February 2017).

45. On criticism of Eli Pariser's assumptions, see the comprehensive discussion by Christoph Kappes. Kappes, Christoph (2012), Menschen, Medien und Maschinen. Warum die Gefahren der "Filter Bubble" überschätzt werden. In: *Merkur. Deutsche Zeitschrift für europäisches Denken,* vol. 66/754, pp. 256–263. Equally critical: Passig, Kathrin/Lobo, Sascha (2012), *Internet. Segen oder Fluch.* Berlin: Rowohlt, pp. 267ff. A study by Facebook employees advocating a relaxed view is reported and criticised by Ingrid Brodnig: Brodnig, Ingrid (2016), *Hass im Netz. Was wir gegen*

Hetze, Mobbing und Lügen tun können. Wien: Christian Brandstätter Verlag, pp. 33f.

46. See here the study of the forms of asymmetric polarisation in the American presidential election campaign, which stresses the importance of ideologies and organised campaigns: Benkler, Yochai/Faris, Robert/Roberts, Hal/Zuckerman, Ethan (2017), Study: Breitbart-Led Right-Wing Media Ecosystem Altered Broader Media Agenda. In: *Columbia Journalism Review* (03.03.2017). http://www.cjr.org/analysis/breitbart-media-trump-harvard-study.php (retrieved 29 March 2017). See also: Seemann, Michael (2017), Digitaler Tribalismus und Fake News. In: ctrl-verlust.net (29.09.2017). http://www.ctrl-verlust.net/digitaler-tri balismus-und-fake news/ (retrieved 10 October 2017).

47. Seemann, Michael (2011), Breivik, Queryology und der Weltcontrolverlust. In: ctrl + verlust.net (07.08.2011). http://www.ctrl-verlust.net/breivik-queryology-und-der-weltcontrolverlust/ (retrieved 09 December 2014).

48. Glaser, Peter (2009), Kulturelle Atomkraft. In: berliner-zeitung.de vom 25.08.2009. http://www.berliner-zeitung.de/die-digitalisation-zersetzt-alte-medienformen---ihre-atome-suchen-hitzig-nach-neuer-synthese-kul turelle-atomkraft-14979222 (retrieved 23 July 2017).

49. Michael Seemann has termed the emergence of such public spheres of querying and wishing *queryology* (a *query* is the result of a search question). See Seemann, Michael (2014), *Das neue Spiel. Strategien für die Welt nach dem digitalen Kontrollverlust.* Freiburg: orange-press. pp. 58ff. and pp.179ff.

50. See the fundamental book by David Weinberger, who celebrates the liberation from the cumbersome carrier medium of paper. Weinberger, David (2007), *Everything Is Miscellaneous. The Power of the New Digital Disorder.* New York: Times Books (Henry Holt & Company). In addition, very well worth reading, the analyses by Katharine Viner and Jayson Harsin on digital information and truth organisation; see e.g.: Viner, Katharine (2016), Die Wahrheit in Zeiten des Internets. In: freitag.de (28.09.2016). https://www.freitag.de/autoren/the-guardian/die-wahrheit-in-zeiten-des-internets (retrieved 28 September 2016). Also: Harsin, Jayson (2015), Regimes of Posttruth, Postpolitics, and Attention Economies. In: *Communication, Culture & Critique*, vol. 8/2, pp. 327–333.

51. The perils of online reinforced group thinking has been described by Cass R. Sunstein in many books; see as outstanding example: Sunstein, Cass R. (2006), *Infotopia. How Many Minds Produce Knowledge.* New York: Oxford University Press.

52. Payne, Martha/Payne, David (2012), *NeverSeconds. The Incredible Story of Martha Payne*. Glasgow: Cargo Publishing, p. 25. (I have used the story of Martha Payne in various other lectures and articles.).

53. For the concept of the gatekeeper, which was originally developed in connection with the shopping behaviour of North American women, the early article by Kurt Lewin is still well worth reading. Lewin shows how the shopping housewife regulates family-internal feeding processes by selecting what goes into her shopping bag and what not. The transfer of the concept to the flow of information and of news messages is already indicated there, although not pursued any further. Lewin, Kurt (1947), Frontiers in Group Dynamics II. Channels of Group Life; Social Planning and Action Research. In: *Human Relations*, vol. 1/2, pp. 143–153.

54. Morozov, Evgeny (2013), *To Save Everything, Click Here. Technology, Solutionism and the Urge to Fix Problems That Don't Exist*. New York: Public Affairs, Perseus Book Group, p. 165. On the phenomenon of *disintermediation with simultaneous hyperintermediation* and the algorithmic filtering see also: Poerksen, Bernhard (2015), Pöbeleien im Netz ersticken Debatten. Wir brauchen endlich Regeln! In: Zeit Online (09.07.2015). http://www.zeit.de/2015/26/journalisten-medien-verantwortung-debatten-regeln (retrieved 03 March 2017).

55. The ideal-type distinction between media democracy and outrage democracy, as developed in the text, was first presented in the following article: Poerksen, Bernhard (2012), Wir Tugendterroristen. In: Zeit Online (08.11.2012). http://www.zeit.de/2012/46/Digitales-Zeitalter-Mediendemokratie-Tugendterroristen (retrieved 06 March 2017).

56. Bruns, Axel (2009), Vom Gatekeeping zum Gatewatching. Modelle der journalistischen Vermittlung im Internet. In: Christoph Neuberger/Christian Nuernbergk/Melanie Rischke (Eds), *Journalismus im Internet. Profession – Partizipation – Technisierung*. Wiesbaden: VS Verlag für Sozialwissenschaften, p. 107.

57. Luhmann, Niklas (1996), *Die Realität der Massenmedien. 2., erweiterte Aufl*. Opladen: Westdeutscher Verlag, p. 9.

58. On the economic situation in the print area see: Schnibben, Cordt (2015), "Knast, wenn du lügst!" In: *Der Spiegel* 10, pp. 80–86. The often dramatic situation of journalism in many countries, even in the USA, is described by Jill Lepore in a contribution to *The New Yorker*: cf. Lepore, Jill (2019), Does Journalism Have A Future? In: *The New Yorker* (28.01.2019). https://www.newyorker.com/magazine/2019/01/28/does-journalism-have-a-future

(retrieved 23 April 2019). The actual dangers journalists are exposed to are comprehensively analysed by Arthur Gregg Sulzberger. Cf. Sulzberger, A. G. (2019), The Growing Threat to Journalism Around the World. In: NYTimes.com (23.09.2019). https://www.nytimes.com/2019/09/23/opi nion/press-freedom-arthur-sulzberger.html (retrieved 04 May 2020).

59. Lobo, Sascha (2016), *Das Ende der Gesellschaft – Von den Folgen der Vernetzung. Schriftenreihe zur Tübinger Mediendozentur.* Köln: Herbert von Halem Verlag, p. 19.

60. The meeting and the combination of counterculture and computer culture was brilliantly described by Fred Turner; see: Turner, Fred (2006), *From Counterculture to Cyberculture. Stewart Brand, the Whole Earth Network, and the Rise of Digital Utopianism.* Chicago/London: The University of Chicago Press.

61. See on this: Baumgärtel, Tilman (2013), Das Ende der Utopie. In: NZZ.ch (04.07.2013). http://www.nzz.ch/feuilleton/das-ende-der-utopie-1.18110281 (retrieved 10 November 2015).

62. The expert in American studies, Michael Butter, states that conspiracy theories had a much better image and a different status in the Europe of the eighteenth century—they were comparatively recognised interpretative patterns supported by members of the social elite. See on this: Butter, Michael (2017), Dunkle Komplotte. Zur Geschichte und Funktion von Verschwörungstheorien. In: *Politikum*, vol. 3/3, pp. 8ff.

63. It is symptomatic that even scientists try to rid conspiracy theories of their negative image and to present them as interpretative patterns that are all too rashly marginalised and unjustly stigmatised. On this attempt at rehabilitation see the programmatic introductory contributions in: Anton, Andreas/Schetsche, Michael/Walter, Michael K. (2014) (Eds): *Konspiration. Soziologie des Verschwörungsdenkens.* Wiesbaden: Springer Fachmedia.

64. For elucidation of the concept see: Lehman, Joseph G. (2010), An Introduction to the Overton Window of Political Possibility. In: Mackinac Center for Public Policy (08.04.2010). http://www.mackinac.org/12481 (retrieved 20 March 2017).

65. Tufekci, Zeynep (2016), Adventures in the Trump Twittersphere. In: NYTimes.com (31.03.2016). http://www.nytimes.com/2016/03/31/opi nion/campaign-stops/adventures-in-the-trump-twittersphere.html?_r=0 (retrieved 20 September 2016).

66. Stein, Joel (2016), How Trolls Are Ruining the Internet. In: time.com (18.08.2016). http://time.com/4457110/internet-trolls/ (retrieved 21 March 2017).
67. Duggan, Maeve (2014), Online Harassment. In: Pew Research Center (22.10.2014). http://www.pewinternet.org/files/2014/10/PI_OnlineHar assment_72815.pdf (retrieved 20 March 2017).
68. See: Suler, John (2004), The Online Disinhibition Effect. In: *CyberPsychology & Behaviour*, vol. 7/3, pp. 321–326.
69. On this formula see: Poerksen, Bernhard (2015), Der Hass der Bescheidwisser. In: *Der Spiegel*, vol. 2, pp. 72–73.
70. Sunstein, Cass R. (2006), *Infotopia. How many Minds Produce Knowledge.* New York: Oxford University Press.
71. Cf. as an excellent example: Brodnig, Ingrid (2016), *Hass im Netz. Was wir gegen Hetze, Mobbing und Lügen tun können.* Wien: Christian Brandstätter Verlag.
72. See: Edelmann (2017), 2017 Edelman Trust Barometer Reveals Global Implosion of Trust (Press Release). In: edelman.com (15.01.2017). http://www.edelman.com/news/2017-edelman-trust-barometer-reveals-global-implosion/ (retrieved 15 March 2017).
73. See for example Hatr.org.
74. These forums were the chosen fields of activity of an American individual, who operated under the pseudonym *Violentacrez*. It was considered one of the most malicious trolls until it was unmasked. On the details see: Brodnig, Ingrid (2013), *Der unsichtbare Mensch. Wie die Anonymität im Internet unsere Gesellschaft verändert.* Wien: Czernin, pp. 95ff.
75. Nuhr, Dieter (2015), Wir leben im digitalen Mittelalter. Bericht aus dem Shitstorm. In: FAZ.net (17.07.2015). http://www.faz.net/aktuell/feuill eton/media/dieter-nuhr-ueber-shitstorms-digitales-mittelalter-13706268. html (retrieved 28 August 2015).
76. Frank, Arno (2013), *Meute mit Meinung. Über die Schwarmdummheit.* Zürich/Berlin: Kein & Aber, p. 14.
77. For the specification of the fifth power I am making use of passages from the following essay: Poerksen, Bernhard (2015), Trolle, Empörungsjunkies und kluge Köpfe. Die fünfte Gewalt des digitalen Zeitalters. In: cicero.de (17.04.2015). http://cicero.de/berliner-republik/ trolle-empoerungsjunkies-und-kluge-koepfe-die-fuenfte-gewalt-des-dig italen (retrieved 03 March 2017).
78. Wolf, Fritz (2015): *"Wir sind das Publikum!" Autoritätsverlust der Medien und Zwang zum Dialog. Eine Studie der Otto Brenner Stiftung.* Frankfurt am Main: Otto Brenner Stiftung.

79. On the critical objectives of the commentators and the question of the representativeness of the critics see: Prochazka, Fabian/Schweiger, Wolfgang (2016), Medienkritik online. Was kommentierende Nutzer am Journalismus kritisieren. In: *SCM*, vol. 5/4, pp. 454–469.
80. On such threats of violence see e.g. the pamphlets by the author Akif Pirinçci.
81. Schultz, Tanjev (2016), "I'm a Serious Reporter". Profi- und Amateurjournalismus im Lichte deliberativer Demokratietheorie. Ein Zentrum-Peripherie-Modell. In: *Media Journal*, vol. 40/2, p. 57.
82. The concept of the connective that I am introducing here owes decisive input to the analyses of the political scientists W. Lance Bennett and Alexandra Segerberg, who contrast the logic of collective and connective action in an illustrative way. See: Bennett, W. Lance/Segerberg, Alexandra (2012), The Logic of Connective Action. Digital Media and the Personalization of Contentious Politics. In: *Information, Communication & Society*, vol. 15/5, pp. 739–768.
83. Quoted from: Viner, Katharine (2015), The Rise of the Reader: Journalism in the Age of the Open Web, *The Guardian*, Wednesday 9 October 2013 (retrieved 24 September 2019).
84. On the details of the public perceptibility of Roosevelt's paralysis: Pressman, Matthew (2013), The Myth of FDR's Secret Disability. In: time.com (12.07.2013). http://ideas.time.com/2013/07/12/the-myth-of-fdrs-secret-disability/ (retrieved 19 April 2017). Also: Associated Press (2013), Prof: FDR Film Shows Wheelchair. In: politico.com (10.07.2013). http://www.politico.com/story/2013/07/franklin-delano-roosevelt-wheelchair-footage-093942 (retrieved 19 April 2017). And: Berndt, Christina (2014), Vom gut gehüteten Geheimnis zum Gesundheits-Liveticker. In: SZ.de (12.01.2014). http://www.sueddeutsche.de/politik/kranke-politiker-vom-gut-gehueteten-geheimnis-zum-gesundheits-liveticker-1.1860204 (retrieved 19 April 2017).
85. On the unfolding of events See: Medick, Veit (2016), Der Mann, der Clintons Kampagne ins Wanken brachte. In: Spiegel Online (19.09.2016). http://www.spiegel.de/politik/ausland/hillary-clinton-hob-byfotograf-filmte-kollaps-am-ground-zero-a-1112834.html (retrieved 22 November 2016). Also: Lapowsky, Issie (2016), The Making of Hillary Clinton's Most Unwanted Viral Video. In: Wired (09.12.2016). https://www.wired.com/2016/09/making-hillary-clintons-unwanted-viral-video/ (retrieved 19 April 2017).

86. See Poerksen, Bernhard (2015), "Es entsteht eine grell ausgeleuchtete Welt, ein monströses Aquarium, in dem kaum noch etwas verborgen bleibt". In: Zeit Online (21.02.2015). http://www.zeit.de/2015/08/med ien-macht-angst-anpassung-oezdemir-cannabis (retrieved 12 April 2017).

87. On the revision of the interaction and situation sociology of Erving Goffman see: Meyrowitz, Joshua (1990), Redefining the Situation. Extending Dramaturgy into a Theory of Social Change and Media Effects. In: Stephen Harold Riggins (Ed.), *Beyond Goffman. Studies on Communication, Institution, and Social Interaction*. Berlin/New York: Mouton de Gruyter. Especially pp. 87ff.

88. Meyrowitz, Joshua (1985), *No Sense of Place: The Impact of Electronic Media on Social Behavior*. New York: Oxford University Press, p. viii (Author's emphasis).

89. Altman, Lawrence K. (2016), How Healthy Is Hillary Clinton? Doctors Weigh in. In: NYTimes.com (18.09.2016). http://www.nytimes.com/ 2016/09/19/us/politics/hillary-clinton-health.html?_r=0 (retrieved 30 September 2016).

90. Enzensberger, Hans Magnus (1997), *Zickzack. Aufsätze*. Frankfurt am Main: Suhrkamp Verlag, p. 116.

91. See Bentham, Jeremy (1791), *Panopticon: Or, the Inspection-House*. Dublin: Thomas Byrne.

92. Foucault, Michel (1977), *Überwachen und Strafen. Die Geburt des Gefängnisses*. Frankfurt am Main: Suhrkamp Verlag, pp. 251ff.

93. Mann, Steve/Ferenbok, Joseph (2013), New Media and the Power Politics of Sousveillance in a Surveillance-Dominated World. In: *Surveillance & Society*, vol. 11/1/2, pp. 18–34.

94. On these and the following figures see: Herrmann, Sebastian (2016), Wer knipst, gewinnt. In: SZ.de (12.08.2016). http://www.sueddeutsche.de/ panorama/fotografie-wer-knipst-gewinnt-1.3118844 (retrieved 10 April 2017). Also: Kannenberg, Axel (2016), "Statistisch gesehen": Das Smartphone frisst die Digitalkamera. In: Heise Online (21.09.2016). https:// www.heise.de/newsticker/meldung/Statistisch-gesehen-Das-Smartphone-frisst-die-Digitalkamera-3328281.html (retrieved 10 April 2017).

95. Stahl, Eberhard (2010), Lob der Intransparenz. In: Friedemann Schulz von Thun/Dagmar Kumbier (Eds.), *Impulse für Kommunikation im Alltag. Kommunikationspsychologische Miniaturen 3*. Reinbek bei Hamburg: Rowohlt, p. 225.

96. Morozov, Evgeny (2013), *To Save Everything, Click Here: Technology, Solutionism and the Urge to Fix Problems That Don't Exist*. New York: Public Affairs, Perseus Book Group, pp. 80f.
97. Meyrowitz, Joshua (1985), *No Sense of Place: The Impact of Electronic Media on Social Behavior*. New York: Oxford University Press, p. 66.
98. Meyrowitz, Joshua (1985), *No Sense of Place: The Impact of Electronic Media on Social Behavior*. New York: Oxford University Press, pp. 167–168.
99. Körner, Torsten (2013), Das Verzwergen der Helden. Charisma in Zeiten des Internet. In: tagesspiegel.de (17.08.2013). http://www.tagesspiegel. de/media/digitale-world/charisma-in-zeiten-des-internet-das-verzwergen-der-helden/8651514.html (retrieved 13 January 2015).
100. See on this in a different connection: Poerksen, Bernhard/Detel, Hanne (2012), *Der entfesselte Skandal. Das Ende der Kontrolle im digitalen Zeitalter*. Köln: Herbert von Halem Verlag, pp. 81f.
101. See for example: Mayer-Schönberger, Viktor (2010), *Delete. Die Tugend des Vergessens in digitalen Zeiten*. Berlin: University Press.
102. Lasica, Joseph Daniel (1998), The Net Never Forgets. In: Salon (25.11.1998). http://www.salon.com/1998/11/25/feature_253/ (retrieved 05 May 2017).
103. See SalahEldeen, Hany M./Nelson, Michael L. (2012), Losing My Revolution. How Many Resources Shared on Social Media Have Been Lost? In: Panayiotis Zaphiris/George Buchanan/Edie Rasmussen/Fernando Loizides (Eds.), *Theory and Practice of Digital Libraries*. Berlin/Heidelberg: Springer, pp. 125–137.
104. Quoted from: Brand, Stewart (1999), *The Clock of the Long Now: Time and Responsibility*. London: Weidenfeld & Nicolson, p. 84.
105. Simanowski, Roberto (2004), Erinnern und Vergessen im Netz. In: Christian Lotz/Thomas R. Wolf/Walther Ch. Zimmerli (Eds.), *Erinnerung. Philosophische Perspektiven*. München: Fink, p. 258.
106. See also in another connection and regarding another media epoch: Postman, Neil (1986), *Amusing Ourselves to Death: Public Discourse in the Age of Show Business*. London: Methuen, p. 135.
107. On the relationship between authority, acceptance and medialisation in the case of religious communication see: Hjarvard, Stig (2016), Mediatization and the Changing Authority of Religion. In: *Media, Culture and Society*, vol. 38/1, pp. 8–17.
108. Münkler, Herfried (1994), Die Moral der Politik. Politik, Politikwissenschaft und die soziomoralische Dimension politischer Ordnungen.

In: Claus Leggewie (Ed.), *Wozu Politikwissenschaft? Über das Neue in der Politik*. Darmstadt: Wissenschaftliche Buchgesellschaft, p. 237.

109. See Schertz, Christian/Höch, Dominik (2011), *Privat war gestern. Wie Media und Internet unsere Werte zerstören*. Berlin: Ullstein Buchverlage, pp. 30f.

110. On the concept of informational uncertainty and the following see also: Poerksen, Bernhard (2015), "Es entsteht eine grell ausgeleuchtete World, ein monströses Aquarium, in dem kaum noch etwas verborgen bleibt". In: Zeit Online (21.02.2015). http://www.zeit.de/2015/08/med ien-macht-angst-anpassung-oezdemir-cannabis (retrieved 12 April 2017).

111. By the way: The present hype about influencer marketing can now be explained against this background. For influencers are the *prototypes of matiness* and *heroes of commonness* in sales businesses. Their authority results from their alleged authenticity.

112. Quoted from: Köppel, Christian (2015), Einer gegen alle. In: tages-anzeiger.ch (07.08.2015). http://www.tagesanzeiger.ch/ausland/Ame rica/trump-schliesst-kandidatur-als-parteiloser-nicht-aus/story/27013588 (retrieved 08 May 2017).

113. Meyrowitz, Joshua (1985), *No Sense of Place: The Impact of Electronic Media on Social Behavior*. New York: Oxford University Press, p. 165. (Author's emphasis).

114. See on this: Drobinski, Matthias (2010), Idole in der Gesellschaft. Sehnsucht nach Vorbildern. In: SZ.de (06.04.2010). http://www.suedde utsche.de/politik/idole-in-der-gesellschaft-sehnsucht-nach-vorbildern-1. 4708 (retrieved 05 November 2016).

115. For a precise reconstruction of the events see: Backes, Thierry/Jaschensky, Wolfgang/Langhans, Katrin/Munzinger, Hannes/Witzenberger, Bene-dict/Wormer, Vanessa (2010), Timeline der Panik. In: SZ.de (01.10.2016). http://gfx.sueddeutsche.de/apps/57eba578910a46f716 ca829d/www/ (retrieved 07 March 2017). In addition: Gennies, Sidney (2016), Informierst du dich noch, oder hetzt du schon? In: tagesspiegel.de (24.07.2016). http://www.tagesspiegel.de/politik/muenchen-und-social-media-informierst-du-dich-noch-oder-hetzt-du-schon/13918410.html (retrieved 12 September 2016).

116. Cammarata, Patricia (2016), +++Ich brauche keine Liveticker+++. In: Das Nuf Advanced (23.07.2016). http://dasnuf.de/ich-brauche-keine-liv eticker/ (retrieved 01 August 2016).

117. Coupland, Douglas (2010), *Marshall McLuhan: You Know Nothing of My Work!* New York: Atlas & Co., p. 13.

118. Pariser, Eli (2011), *The Filter Bubble: What the Internet Is Hiding from You*. London: Penguin Books.

119. Meckel, Miriam (2011), Weltkurzsichtigkeit. Wie der Zufall aus unserem digitalen Leben verschwindet. In: *Der Spiegel*. H. 38, pp. 120–121.

120. The critical reflections of the notion of filter bubbles presented here were first developed in the following essay on which these passages are based: Poerksen, Bernhard (2018), Die Theorie der Filterblasen ist nicht länger haltbar – Wir leiden bereits unter dem Filter-Clash. In: *Neue Zürcher Zeitung* (12.07.2018). https://www.nzz.ch/feuilleton/die-theorie-der-filterblasen-ist-nicht-laenger-haltbar-denn-wir-leiden-bereits-unter-dem-filter-clash-ld.1402553 (retrieved 06 August 2019). On what follows see also: Poerksen, Bernhard (2020), Gesellschaft der Gleichzeit-igkeiten. In: Bernhard Poerksen/Friedemann Schulz von Thun, *Die Kunst des Miteinander-Redens. Über den Dialog in Gesellschaft und Politik*. München: Hanser, pp. 18ff. A fundamental critique of the concept was formulated by Axel Bruns, cf. Bruns, Axel (2019), *Are Filter Bubbles Real? (Digital Futures Series)*. Cambridge: Polity Press.

121. The connection between online media use and the experience of the rich variety of information is dealt with in the following article: Fletcher, Richard/Nielsen, Rasmus Kleis (2017), Are People Incidentally Exposed to News on Social Media? A Comparative Analysis. In: *New Media & Society*, vol. 20/7, pp. 2450–2468.

122. See here the classic study of network sociology by Marc S. Granovetter: Granovetter, Marc S. (1973), The Strength of Weak Ties. In: *American Journal of Sociology*, vol. 78/6, pp. 1360–1380.

123. On the analysis of asymmetric polarisation cf.: Benkler, Yochai/Faris, Robert/Roberts, Hal (2018), *Network Propaganda: Manipulation, Disinformation, and Radicalization in American Politics*. New York: Oxford University Press.

124. A study from the Massachusetts Institute of Technology (MIT) has found that on Twitter, the news channel for everyone, a factually correct piece of news takes six times longer than a piece of fake news to reach 1500 users. Faked information is therefore shared 70 per cent more frequently than factually correct news. Why is this so? Is it due to an algorithm, to social bots, i.e., software geared to spreading disinformation? Not primarily. Fake news is spread by human individuals because it can serve as a—seemingly plausible and highly infectious—irritant that endorses whatever they wish to believe anyway. The consequence:

The notion of the filter bubble neglects the human factor. It transforms social phenomena of self-siloing and the universal problem of human "confirmation bias" into technological manipulation fantasies, suggesting mistaken problem–solution procedures centring on a restructuring of software rather than the critical interaction with other human individuals and groups. The notion of the filter bubble turns algorithms into the opponents to be feared—and loses sight of the human beings as the actual agents involved who—in this theoretical cognitive image—are nothing but the victims of algorithmic sorting games sadly beyond their comprehension. On the MIT study and its interpretation cf. Yogeshwar, Ranga (2020), Journalismus im Zeitalter der Erregungsbewirtschaftung. In: Poerksen, Bernhard/Narr, Andreas (Eds.), *Schöne digitale Welt. Analysen und Einsprüche von Richard Gutjahr, Sascha Lobo, Georg Mascolo, Miriam Meckel, Ranga Yogeshwar und Juli Zeh*. Köln: Herbert von Halem Verlag, pp. 161f. On the suggestion of mistaken problem–solution procedures cf. Bail, Christopher (2018), Twitter's Flawed Solution to Political Polarization. In: NYTimes.com (08.11.2018). https://www.nytimes.com/2018/09/08/opinion/sunday/twitter-political-polarization.html (retrieved 27 January 2020). See also for reference to current research: Klein, Ezra (2018), When Twitter Users Hear Out the Other Side, They Become More Polarized. In: Vox (18.10.2018). https://www.vox.com/policy-and-politics/2018/10/18/17989856/twitter-polarization-echo-chambers-social-media (retrieved 27 January 2020).

125. Seemann, Michael (2014), *Das neue Spiel. Strategien für die Welt nach dem digitalen Kontrollverlust*. Freiburg: Orange-Press, pp. 185 und 194f. Also: Seemann, Michael (2017), Das Regime der demokratischen Wahrheit IV—It's the Culture, Stupid. In: ctrl-verlust.net (20.03.2017). http://www.ctrl-verlust.net/breitbart-alt-right-filterbubble/ (retrieved 22 May 2017).

126. On this logic of trench warfare see also the following empirical investigation: Karlsen, Rune/Steen-Johnsen, Kari/Wollebæk, Dag/Enjolras, Bernard (2017), Echo Chamber and Trench Warfare Dynamics in Online Debates. In: *European Journal of Communication*, vol. 32, pp. 257–273.

127. McLuhan, Marshall (2002), *The Mechanical Bride: Folklore of Industrial Man*. New York: Ginko Press, p. 3.

128. See on this also: Postman, Neil (1982), *The Disappearance of Childhood*. New York: Delacorte Press, pp. 83f.

129. See on this also: Meyrowitz, Joshua (1985), *No Sense of Place: The Impact of Electronic Media on Social Behavior*. New York: Oxford University Press, p. 239.

130. Radisch, Iris (2005), Phrasen, die keiner mehr kennt. In: Zeit Online (24.02.2005). http://www.zeit.de/2005/09/L-Kempowski (retrieved 30 May 2017).

131. On the connections between information integration, social tensions and the wish for societal participation, Meyrowitz writes with profound knowledge; see for instance: Meyrowitz, Joshua (1985), *No Sense of Place: The Impact of Electronic Media on Social Behavior*. New York: Oxford University Press, pp. 133f.

132. Himmelsbach, Nadine (2012), "Unser Alltag ist besser als euer bester Tag". In: SZ.de (25.08.2012). http://www.sueddeutsche.de/leben/reiche-kids-inszenieren-sich-auf-instagram-unser-alltag-ist-besser-als-euer-bes ter-tag-1.1449423 (retrieved 11 August 2016). And: Salloum, Raniah (2014), Reiche Iraner bei Instagram: Die Angeber von Teheran. In: Spiegel Online (12.10.2014). http://www.spiegel.de/politik/ausland/iran-die-richs-kids-of-tehran-verlieren-gegen-die-poor-kids-a-996415.html (retrieved 11 August 2016).

133. Lobo, Sascha (2016), *Das Ende der Gesellschaft – Von den Folgen der Vernetzung. Schriftenreihe zur Tübinger Mediendozentur*. Köln: Herbert von Halem Verlag, p. 16 (Author's emphasis).

134. Wayne, Teddy (2016), The Trauma of Violent News on the Internet. In: NYTimes.com (10.09.2016). https://www.nytimes.com/2016/09/11/fas hion/the-trauma-of-violent-news-on-the-internet.html?_r=0 (retrieved 08 March 2017).

135. A comparable case is the reviling video *Innocence of Muslims*, which depicts the prophet Mohammed as, among other things, a woman-iser, homosexual, pederast, and bloodthirsty commander. This video—allegedly a trailer for a longer film—was posted on YouTube, remained unnoticed at first, until at the beginning of September 2012 a synchro-nised version in Arabic was published. In protests involving countries like Pakistan, Afghanistan and Libya more than 50 people had lost their lives by the end of September. On the dynamics of the origin of conflicts see in detail: Garton Ash, Timothy (2016), *Free Speech: Ten Principles for a Connected World*. London: Atlantic Books, p. 93.

136. The expression "oxygen of publicity" was used by the former British prime minister Margaret Thatcher, who in 1985—after an aeroplane had been hijacked by a terrorist group—sharply attacked the media and

demanded a codex of standards for reporting about terror as well as the deliberate ignoring of assassins. On this suggestion see: Mascolo, Georg/Neumann, Peter (2016), Warum sich die Berichterstattung über Terror ändern muss. In: SZ.de (07.08.2016). http://www.sueddeutsche. de/media/journalism-warum-sich-die-berichterstattung-ueber-terror-aen dern-muss-1.3108867 (retrieved 09 September 2016).

137. On the following see: Gerhart, Ann/Londoño, Ernesto (2010), Pastor Terry Jones's Koran-Burning Threat Started with a Tweet. In: wash- ingtonpost.com (10.09.2010). http://www.washingtonpost.com/wp- dyn/content/article/2010/09/10/AR2010091007428.html (retrieved 19 June 2017). And: Kolawole, Emi (2010), Terry Jones Timeline: It All Started with a Tweet. In: voices.washingtonpost.com (11.09.2010). http://voices.washingtonpost.com/44/2010/09/terry-jones-timeline-it- all-st.html (retrieved 20 June 2017). Also: Weaver, Matthew (2010), Qur'an Burning: From Facebook to the World's Media, How the Story Grew. In: theguardian.com (10.09.2010). https://www.theguardian.com/ world/2010/sep/10/quran-burning-how-the-story-grew (retrieved 20 June 2017).

138. On this mechanism and the case analysis see: Holiday, Ryan (2012), *Trust Me, I'm Lying: The Tactics and Confessions of a Media Manipulator.* New York: Penguin.

139. It is interesting to note that this group had already carried out a Koran burning in the streets of Washington in 2008, which had not been featured by the media. There was no escalating violence. This again suggests a co-responsibility of the media for what happened. See: Knickerbocker, Brad (2010), Florida Church May Not Burn Qurans, But Kansas Church Says It Will. In: *The Christian Science Monitor* (10.09.2010). http://www.csmonitor.com/USA/Society/2010/ 0910/Florida-church-may-not-burn-Qurans-but-Kansas-church-says-it- will (retrieved 20 June 2017).

140. CNN (2010), Lessons from the Whole Quran Episode. In: edition.cnn.com (14.09.2010). http://edition.cnn.com/2010/OPI NION/09/13/quran.case.roundup/index.html (retrieved 20 June 2017).

141. On the dynamics of news spread see the details in: Myers, Steve (2011), Florida Quran Burning, Afghanistan Violence Raise Questions about the Power of Media Blackouts. In: poynter.org (06.04.2011). https:// www.poynter.org/2011/florida-quran-burning-afghanistan-violence-raise- questions-about-the-power-of-media-blackouts/126878/ (retrieved 20 June 2017). Also: Myers, Steve (2011), How the Quran Burning Story

Skipped the U.S. as It Spread from Gainesville around the World. In: poynter.org (07.04.2011). http://www.poynter.org/2011/how-the-quran-burning-story-skipped-the-u-s-as-it-spread-from-gainesville-around-the-world/126616/ (retrieved 19 June 2017).

142. Myers, Steve (2011), Florida Quran Burning, Afghanistan Violence Raise Questions about the Power of Media Blackouts. In: poynter.org (06.04.2011). https://www.poynter.org/2011/florida-quran-burning-afg hanistan-violence-raise-questions-about-the-power-of-media-blackouts/ 126878/ (retrieved 20 June 2017).

143. Fetscher, Caroline (2011), Was müssen wir wissen? In: tagesspiegel.de (27.04.2011). http://www.tagesspiegel.de/medien/interessant-heisst-nicht-relevant-was-muessen-wir-wissen/4105422.html (retrieved 19 June 2017).

144. Bercovici, Jeff (2011), When Journalism 2.0 Kills. In: forbes.com (07.04.2011). https://www.forbes.com/sites/jeffbercovici/2011/04/07/when-journalism-2-0-kills/#4d96a65f1f0a (retrieved 19 June 2017).

145. On this case see: Poerksen, Bernhard/Detel, Hanne (2012), *Der entfesselte Skandal. Das Ende der Kontrolle im digitalen Zeitalter.* Köln: Herbert von Halem Verlag, pp. 118ff.

146. Wang, Grace (2008), The Old Man Who Lost His Horse. In: *China Digital Times* (11.05.2008). http://chinadigitaltimes.net/2008/05/grace-wang-the-old-man-who-lost-his-horse-video-added/ (retrieved 26 August 2011).

147. The linguisticians Peter Koch and Wulf Oesterreicher have coined the concept of *conceptional orality.* It means that the kind and style of a contribution—the erratic, colloquial, not really well-formed formulation—signals that someone's speech is situation and moment related. In analogy to such conceptional orality and the case analysed, one could speak of the *conceptional volatility* of utterances and actions: Wang Qianyuan believes herself to be acting at a particular moment within a concrete situation, her utterances and ad-hoc activities are however recorded and presented to a larger public. On background see: Koch, Peter/Oesterreicher, Wulf (1985), Sprache der Nähe – Sprache der Distanz. Mündlichkeit und Schriftlichkeit im Spannungsfeld von Sprachtheorie und Sprachgeschichte. In: *Romanistisches Jahrbuch*, vol. 36, pp. 15–43.

148. This diagram (slightly adapted for the purposes of the present book) is taken from the publication by Bernhard Poerksen and Hanne Detel, in which the concept and the different forms of context violation are discussed more precisely. See: Poerksen, Bernhard/Detel, Hanne (2012),

Der entfesselte Skandal. Das Ende der Kontrolle im digitalen Zeitalter. Köln: Herbert von Halem Verlag, pp. 234f.

149. Glaser, Peter (2009), Kulturelle Atomkraft. In: berliner-zeitung.de (25.08.2009). http://www.berliner-zeitung.de/die-digitalisation-zersetzt-alte-medienformen---ihre-atome-suchen-hitzig-nach-neuer-synthese-kul turelle-atomkraft-14979222 (retrieved 23 July 2017).

150. This section expands the following articles: Poerksen, Bernhard (2016), Klick! Mich! An! In: Zeit Online (13.09.2016). http://www.zeit.de/2016/ 35/online-medien-aufmerksamkeit-buzzfeed (retrieved 03 March 2017); Poerksen, Bernhard (2016), Die Erregungsindustrie der Viral-Platformen. In: POP. Kultur und Kritik, No. 9, pp. 50–53.

151. Lobo, Sascha (2009), Die bedrohte Elite. Frank Schirrmacher und der Kulturpessimismus. Eine Gegenrede. In: *Der Spiegel*, No. 50, p. 143.

152. Battelle, John (2003), The Database of Intentions. In: John Battelle's Searchblog (13.11.2003). http://battellemedia.com/archives/2003/11/ the_database_of_intentions.php (retrieved 12 June 2017).

153. The power of measuring systems is confirmed by the following media-sociological investigation: Petre, Caitlin (2015), The Traffic Factories: Metrics at Chartbeat, Gawker Media, and *The New York Times*. In: Tow Center for Digital Journalism (07.05.2015). http://towcenter.org/ research/traffic-factories/ (retrieved 23 February 2016).

154. It is only fair to concede that BuzzFeed consistently also publishes excellently researched disclosure stories.

155. On this case see: Anonymous (2014), Die Umarmung, die die World seit Jahrzehnten rührt. In: world.de (25.08.2014). https://www.world.de/ vermischtes/article131576801/Die-Umarmung-die-die-World-seit-Jahrze hnten-ruehrt.html (retrieved 31 May 2017); Williamson, Dianne (2013), Twins Still Popular after All These Years. In: telegram.com (17.02.2013). http://www.telegram.com/article/20130217/COLUMN01/102179821 (retrieved 31 May 2017).

156. Williamson, Dianne (2013), Twins Still Popular after All These Years. In: telegram.com (17.02.2013). http://www.telegram.com/article/201 30217/COLUMN01/102179821 (retrieved 31 May 2017).

157. Jakob Steinschaden has assembled an instructive survey of the viral and clickbaiting formulas of the platforms working with suggestions and mystifications, see: Steinschaden, Jakob (2016), Anatomie des Click-baiting: So ködern uns Upworthy, BuzzFeed und Co. In: *Netzpiloten Magazin* (21.04.2016). http://www.netzpiloten.de/anatomie-des-clickb aiting-koedern-uns-upworthy-buzzfeed-und-co/ (retrieved 23 February 2016).

158. That it is really primarily emotional stories that spread virally is also shown by the study carried out by Jonah Berger and Katherine L. Milkman; they have, on the basis of nearly 7000 articles, investigated which articles made it onto the "most emailed list" of *The New York Times*. Here emotions like anger, joy and fear dominate as well. See Berger, Jonah/Milkman, Katherine L. (2012), What Makes Online Content Viral? In: *Journal of Marketing Research*, vol. 49/2, pp. 192–205.

159. Boyd, Danah (2009), Streams of Content, Limited Attention: The Flow of Information through Social Media. In: danah.org (17.11.2009). http:// www.danah.org/papers/talks/Web2Expo.html (retrieved 12 June 2017).

160. See i.a.: Anonymous (2015), Ein Jäger wird zur Hassfigur. In: Spiegel Online (29.07.2015). http://www.spiegel.de/panorama/getoeteter-loewe-in-simbabwe-us-jaeger-wird-zur-hassfigur-a-1045805.html (retrieved 31 May 2017).

161. See: Hertreiter, Laura (2015), Hetzjagd auf den Löwenjäger. In: SZ.de (29.07.2015). http://www.sueddeutsche.de/panorama/nach-tod-von-cecil-hetzjagd-auf-den-loewenjaeger-1.2587541 (retrieved 31 May 2017). The original article containing the call for murder is still accessible: Morgan, Piers (2015), I'd Love to Go Hunting One Day with Dr. Walter Palmer the Killer Dentist... So I Can Stuff and Mount Him for MY Office Wall. In: Mail Online (28.07.2015). http://www.dailym ail.co.uk/news/article-3177611/PIERS-MORGAN-d-love-hunting-one-day-Dr-Walter-Palmer-killer-dentist-stuff-mount-office.html (retrieved 19 June 2017).

162. Maramba, Joseph (2015), Wer bitte ist Cecil? In: Zeit Online (07.08.2015). http://www.zeit.de/kultur/2015-08/cecil-loewe-simbabwe-afrika/komplettansicht (retrieved 31 May 2017).

163. Maramba, Joseph (2015), Wer bitte ist Cecil? In: Zeit Online (07.08.2015). http://www.zeit.de/kultur/2015-08/cecil-loewe-simbabwe-afrika/komplettansicht (retrieved 31 May 2017).

164. McLuhan, Marshall (1964), *Understanding Media: The Extensions of Man*. London: The MIT Press, p. 248.

165. On the following see also: Poerksen, Bernhard (2014), Tanz um den Redwood. In: tagesspiegel.de (20.06.2014). http://www.tagesspiegel.de/medien/digitale-world/tamagotchi-gefuehle-tanz-um-den-redwood/100 77354.html (retrieved 06 March 2017).

166. See: Rushkoff, Douglas (2014), *Present Shock: When Everything Happens Now*. New York: Penguin Group; Rheingold, Howard (2012), *Net Smart: How to Thrive Online*. Cambridge/London: The MIT Press.

167. Minkmar, Nils (2016), Gereiztes Land: Kurz vorm Durchdrehen (22.02.2016). http://www.spiegel.de/kultur/gesellschaft/fluechtlingskrise-deutschland-ist-kurz-vorm-durchdrehen-a-1078368.html (retrieved 15 July 2016).

168. Safranski, Rüdiger (2003), *Wieviel Globalisierung verträgt der Mensch?* München: Carl Hanser Verlag, pp. 78f.

169. Safranski, Rüdiger (2003), *Wieviel Globalisierung verträgt der Mensch?* München: Carl Hanser Verlag, pp. 82f.

170. Strauß, Botho (2013), Der Plurimi-Faktor. Anmerkungen zum Außenseiter. In: *Der Spiegel*, No. 31, pp. 108ff. (Author's emphasis).

171. A similar direction is taken up by my proposal of a *scandal didactics*, see: Poerksen, Bernhard (2010), Scandal! In: Chrismon (28.05.2010). http://chrismon.evangelisch.de/article/2010/bernhard-poerksen-scandal-4318 (retrieved 08 April 2017).

172. This reconstruction relies primarily on the following sources: McGrath, Ben (2006), Aleksey the Great. In: newyorker.com (23.10.2006). http://www.newyorker.com/magazine/2006/10/23/aleksey-the-great (retrieved 24 July 2017); Pasternack, Alex (2013), Aleksey Vayner, Whose Tale the Internet Mocked, Has Died at 29. In: Vice—Motherboard Blog (24.01.2013). https://motherboard.vice.com/en_us/article/pgg8vb/aleksey-vayner-death-video (retrieved 24 July 2017); Trotter, J.K. (2013), Aleksey Vayner Reported Dead in New York. In: IvyGate (23.01.2017). https://www.ivygateblog.com/2013/01/aleksey-vayner-reported-dead-in-new-york/ (retrieved 23 January 2017); Anon. (2013), "'Do Not, Anyone, Sell This Idiot ANY Pills!' The Desperate Last Messages to Former Yale Student Infamous for 'Impossible Is Nothing' Résumé Who Is Reportedly, 'Dead at Age 29 from an Overdose'". In: Mail Online (24.01.2013). http://www.dailymail.co.uk/news/article-2267861/Aleksey-Vayner-Impossible-Nothing-r-sum-star-dead-overdose.html (retrieved 25 July 2017).

173. Gross, Johannes (1965), Phänomenologie des Skandals. In: *Merkur*, vol. 19/205, p. 400.

174. Schütze, Christian (1985), *Skandal. Eine Psychologie des Unerhörten*. Bern/München: Scherz Verlag, p. 326.

175. Hondrich, Karl Otto (2002), *Enthüllung und Entrüstung. Eine Phänomenologie des politischen Skandals.* Frankfurt am Main: Suhrkamp Verlag, p. 40.

176. As background literature for this chapter I would like to quote the following publications: Bergmann, Jens/Poerksen, Bernhard (2009) (Eds), *Skandal! Die Macht öffentlicher Empörung.* Köln: Herbert von Halem Verlag; Poerksen, Bernhard/Detel, Hanne (2012), *Der entfesselte Skandal. Das Ende der Kontrolle im digitalen Zeitalter.* Köln: Herbert von Halem Verlag; Trinkner, Kati (2016), Netzopfer. Das Individuum im Fokus digitaler Öffentlichkeit. Unpublished Master's dissertation, Eberhard Karls Universität Tübingen.

177. On the history of Justine Sacco see: Biddle, Sam (2014), Justine Sacco Is Good at Her Job, and How I Came to Peace with Her. In: Gawker (20.12.2014). http://gawker.com/justine-sacco-is-good-at-her-job-and-how-i-came-to-pea-1653022326 (retrieved 24 July 2017); Trinkner, Kati (2016), Netzopfer. Das Individuum im Fokus digitaler Öffentlichkeit. Unpublished Master's dissertation. Eberhard Karls Universität Tübingen; Ronson, Jon (2015), *So You've Been Publicly Shamed.* London: Picador.

178. On the concept of the prominent mediator see: Poerksen, Bernhard/Detel, Hanne (2012), *Der entfesselte Skandal. Das Ende der Kontrolle im digitalen Zeitalter.* Köln: Herbert von Halem Verlag. p. 140; Gladwell, Malcolm (2001), *The Tipping Point: How Little Things Can Make a Big Difference.* London: Abacus, pp. 34f.

179. For detailed reconstruction the following book may be mentioned again: Ronson, Jon (2015), *So You've Been Publicly Shamed.* London: Picador, pp. 63f.

180. Biddle, Sam (2014), Justine Sacco Is Good at Her Job, and How I Came To Peace with Her. In: Gawker (20.12.2014). http://gawker.com/justine-sacco-is-good-at-her-job-and-how-i-came-to-pea-1653022326 (retrieved 20 July 2017).

181. See in this connection also the story of the Nobel Prize winner Tim Hunt, who was attacked for alleged sexist sallies. Poerksen, Bernhard (2015), Der digitale Pranger. Reputationsverluste in der Empörungsdemokratie der Gegenwart. In: *Forschung & Lehre,* vol. 22/10, pp. 808–809.

182. But as with the typical connective, it is not just assent that is possible. It is conceivable to hijack the hashtag with eigeninterest. A showpiece of so-called *hashtag hijacking* is the firm Gogo, which offers Wi-Fi reception during flights. "Before you tweet something silly waiting for take-off next

time", someone writes, "make sure that you are sitting in a @Gogo plane! CC: @Justine Sacco."

183. Solove, Daniel J. (2007), *The Future of Reputation. Gossip, Rumor, and Privacy on the Internet.* New Haven/London: Yale University Press, p. 37.

184. Quoted from: Ronson, Jon (2015), *So You've Been Publicly Shamed.* London: Picador, p. 273.

185. Hitzler, Ronald (1987), Skandal: Karrierebremse oder Karrierevehikel? Inszenierungsprobleme Bonner Parlamentarier. In: *Sozialwissenschaftliche Informationen,* vol. 16/1, p. 24.

186. Sloterdijk, Peter (2007), Am Medienhimmel. Ein Gespräch mit Jana Kühle und Sugárka Sielaff. In: Jens Bergmann/Bernhard Poerksen (Eds), *Medienmenschen. Wie man Wirklichkeit inszeniert.* Münster: Solibro, p. 273.

187. Numerous examples can be found in the following book: Jacquet, Jennifer (2015), *Scham. Die politische Kraft eines unterschätzten Gefühls.* Frankfurt am Main: Fischer. See especially pp. 137ff.

188. This case analysis is based on the following sources, supplemented by research results from the internet dealing with the events around Lindsey Stone. D'Amato, Pete (2015), Non-Profit Worker Who Provoked Fury with Disrespectful Arlington Photo Tells How She Lost Her Job, Can't Date and Now Lives in Fear. In: Mail Online (23.02.2015). http://www. dailymail.co.uk/news/article-2964489/I-really-obsessed-reading-Woman-fired-photo-giving-middle-finger-Arlington-National-Cemetery-says-fin ally-Google-without-fear.html (retrieved 24 July 2017); Trinkner, Kati (2016), Netzopfer. Das Individuum im Fokus digitaler Öffentlichkeit. Unpublished Master's dissertation. Eberhard Karls Universität Tübingen, see especially pp. 50ff.; Ronson, Jon (2015), *So You've Been Publicly Shamed.* London: Picador, pp. 197f.

189. Quoted from: D'Amato, Pete (2015), Non-Profit Worker Who Provoked Fury with Disrespectful Arlington Photo Tells How She Lost Her Job, Can't Date and Now Lives in Fear. In: Mail Online (23.02.2015). http:// www.dailymail.co.uk/news/article-2964489/I-really-obsessed-reading-Woman-fired-photo-giving-middle-finger-Arlington-National-Cemetery-says-finally-Google-without-fear.html (retrieved 24 July 2017).

190. Stone, Lindsey/Schuh, Jamie (2012), Lindsey Stone and Jamie Schuh's Statement about Arlington Photo. In: WMUR-TV (21.11.2012). http://www.wmur.com/article/lindsey-stone-and-jamie-schuh-s-statem ent-about-arlington-photo/5177904 (retrieved 24 July 2017).

191. Ronson, Jon (2015), *So You've Been Publicly Shamed*. London: Picador, p. 261.

192. Jon Ronson was not willing to discuss the consequences of his experiment.

193. The potential damage to reputation caused by the autocomplete system of Google that immediately offers additional suggestions when researching a name (perhaps: "escort", "satanist", "rapist") was described in detail by Evgeny Morozov. See: Morozov, Evgeny (2013), *To Save Everything, Click Here. Technology, Solutionism and the Urge to Fix Problems That Don't Exist*. New York: Public Affairs, Perseus Book Group, pp. 142f.

194. Seemann, Michael (2014), *Das neue Spiel. Strategien für die Welt nach dem digitalen Kontrollverlust*. Freiburg: orange-press, p. 38.

195. Quoted from: Seemann, Michael (2014), *Das neue Spiel. Strategien für die Welt nach dem digitalen Kontrollverlust*. Freiburg: Orange-Press, p. 17.

196. Seemann, Michael (2011), Vom Kontrollverlust zur Filtersouveränität. In: Carta (06.04.2011). http://carta.info/39625/vom-kontrollverlust-zur-filtersouveranitat/comment-page-1/ (retrieved 30 May 2011).

197. That even digital experts—whistle-blowers, WikiLeaks protagonists, IT specialists—are not immune to a loss of control, has repeatedly been shown. Just one curious example: John McAfee, inventor of an anti-virus software that made him rich, was searched in connection with a murder case in the year 2012. McAfee allowed journalists from the magazine *Vice*, who accompanied him on his escape, to photograph him with an iPhone. When the picture was posted on a website, the metadata in the image file of the built-in GPS receiver made it possible to reconstruct the location in Guatemala where the picture had been taken. On this case see Fuest, Benedikt (2012), McAfee nach absurder Jagd in Guatemala gestellt. In: world.de (06.12.2012). https://www.world.de/vermischtes/weltgeschehen/article111867155/McAfee-nach-absurder-Jagd-in-Guatemala-gestellt.html (retrieved 10 July 2017). On the concept of blindness to possibilities see more comprehensively: Poerksen, Bernhard/Detel, Hanne (2012), *Der entfesselte Scandal. Das Ende der Kontrolle im digitalen Zeitalter*. Köln: Herbert von Halem Verlag, p. 234.

198. On the strategic use of leaks in election campaigns and the power of disinformation on the political world stage see: Rosenbach, Marcel (2017), Krieg mit den Leaks. In: *Der Spiegel* No. 3, pp. 30–31.

199. An illustrative example of the growing importance of image and reputation management are the interviews conducted with communication officers from North America, Europe, Asia–Pacific and Latin America,

which must be taken with a pinch of salt, however, because they hail from a PR agency and a business and personnel consultancy. PR agencies are of course keen to stress the importance and indispensability of PR. A summary of the central results can be found in the following press release: Weber Shandwick (2016), Studie Rising CCO: Digitale Kommunikation und Mitarbeiter-Engagement sind Top Prioritäten von CCOs. In: webershandwick.de (10.10.2016). http://webershandwick.de/press_release/rising-cco-vi-studie/ (retrieved 24 July 2017).

200. Greenslade, Roy (2014), PRs Outnumber Journalist in the US by a Ratio of 4.6 to 1. In: theguardian.com (14.04.2014). https://www.theguardian.com/media/greenslade/2014/apr/14/marketingandpr-usa (retrieved 20 February 2017).

201. The forms of influence applied, for instance, in order to polish up the negative image of Rwanda, Sri Lanka, Saudi Arabia or Kazakhstan, are described in the following article: Booth, Robert (2010), Does This Picture Make You Think of Rwanda? In: theguardian.com (03.08.2010). https://www.theguardian.com/media/2010/aug/03/london-pr-rwanda-saudi-arabia (retrieved 24 July 2017).

202. Kurz, Constanze (2010), Wenn die Zensur reichlich alt aussieht. In: FAZ.net (20.08.2010). http://www.faz.net/aktuell/feuilleton/debatten/digitales-denken/aus-dem-maschinenraum-14-wenn-die-zensur-reichlich-alt-aussieht-11027346.html (retrieved 30 August 2011).

203. See by way of example: Watzlawick, Paul (1984), Components of Ideological "Realities". In: Paul Watzlawick (Ed.), *The Invented Reality. How Do We Know What We Believe We Know? Contributions to Constructivism.* New York/London: W. W. Norton & Company, Inc., pp. 206f.

204. For details of this case see: Poerksen, Bernhard (2014), Seht her, die nackte Seele! In: *Die Zeit.* Nr. 11. p. 52.

205. The quotations and assessments are from the following article: Viner, Katharine (2016), How technology disrupted the truth, *The Guardian* 12 July 2016 (retrieved 30 September 2016).

206. Smith, Ben (2017), Why BuzzFeed News Published the Dossier. In: NYTimes.com (23.01.2017). https://www.nytimes.com/2017/01/23/opinion/why-buzzfeed-news-published-the-dossier.html?_r=0 (retrieved 08 February 2017).

207. Michal, Wolfgang (2012), Der Bobby-Car-Effekt. In: freitag.de (29.03.2012). https://www.freitag.de/autoren/der-freitag/der-bobby-car-effekt (retrieved 20 September 2016).

208. Hondrich, Karl Otto (2002), *Enthüllung und Entrüstung. Eine Phänomenologie des politischen Skandals.* Frankfurt am Main: Suhrkamp Verlag, p. 72.

209. Quoted from: Michal, Wolfgang (2012), Der Bobby-Car-Effekt. In: freitag.de (29.03.2012). https://www.freitag.de/autoren/der-freitag/der-bobby-car-effekt (retrieved 20 September 2016).

210. Kepplinger, Hans Mathias (2005), *Die Mechanismen der Skandalierung. Die Macht der Medien und die Möglichkeiten der Betroffenen. 2., aktualisierte Aufl.* München: Olzog, pp. 86f.

211. Kepplinger, Hans Mathias (2005), *Die Mechanismen der Skandalierung. Die Macht der Medien und die Möglichkeiten der Betroffenen. 2., aktualisierte Aufl.* München: Olzog, p. 156.

212. The reactions to processes of scandalisation recall the reactions of terminally ill patients to their diagnosis, which the psychiatrist Elisabeth Kübler-Ross has described in the form of a phase model: At the start there are denial and anger, then come rejection, attempts at negotiation and depression, finally acceptance of the inevitable. (This last phase is not at all the rule, however, with victims of scandalisation; the shame of public attack usually remains painful, and they rarely succeed in making peace with the situation.)

213. On this objection see also: Leyendecker, Hans (2009), Der Rechercheur. Ein Gespräch mit Sarah-Lynn Paetzel und Florian Diekmann. In: Jens Bergmann/Bernhard Poerksen (Eds), *Skandal! Die Macht öffentlicher Empörung.* Köln: Herbert von Halem Verlag, p. 211.

214. See by way of example the reasonably up-to-date publication by Thomas Meyer, who argues from the perspective of an infuriated leftie, but also adheres to the mental schemas of the negativists (strict gatekeeper orientation, theses of manipulation and campaigns, the primarily pessimistic evaluation of processes of scandalisation): Meyer, Thomas (2015), *Die Unbelangbaren. Wie politische Journalisten mitregieren.* Berlin: Suhrkamp Verlag.

215. The presentation of the case rests on the following articles: Satter, Raphael (2012), AP Exclusive: Witness to Paris Officer's Death Regrets Video. In: apnews.com (11.01.2015). https://www.apnews.com/5e1ee93021b941629186882f03f1bb79 (retrieved 28 August 2017); Altrogge, Georg (2015), Charlie Hebdo und die Medienmoral: Darf man ein Exekutionsvideo zeigen? In: meedia.de (08.01.2015). http://meedia.de/2015/01/08/charlie-hebdo-und-die-mediamoral-darf-man-ein-exekutions-video-zeigen/ (retrieved 21 August

2017). On this key scene and the following reflections see also: Poerksen, Bernhard (2015), Pöbeleien im Netz ersticken Debatten. Wir brauchen endlich Regeln! In: Zeit Online (09.07.2015). http://www.zeit. de/2015/26/journalisten-media-verantwortung-debatten-regeln (retrieved 03 March 2017).

216. Karig, Friedemann (2015), Terrorbilder im Netz: Teile und herrsche (10.02.2015). https://krautreporter.de/384--terrorbilder-im-netz-teile-und-herrsche (retrieved 12 May 2015).

217. Habermas, Jürgen (2016), *Theorie des kommunikativeen Handelns. Band 1. Handlungsrationalität und gesellschaftliche Rationalisierung. 10. Aufl.* Frankfurt am Main: Suhrkamp Verlag, pp. 52f.

218. See for criticism: Sarcinelli, Ulrich (2002), Medienkompetenz in der politischen Bildung. In: bpb.de (26.05.2002). http://www.bpb.de/apuz/ 25559/medienkompetenz-in-der-politischen-bildung?p=all (retrieved 19 July 2017).

219. See on this: Arndt, Adolf (1966), Die Rolle der Massenmedien in der Demokratie. In: Martin Löffler (Ed.), *Die Rolle der Massenmedien in der Demokratie.* München/Berlin: Beck, p. 1.

220. The concept of the editorial society was introduced by the media scientist John Hartley (he speaks of a "redactional society"). However, he uses it in the most inconceivably naïve way. He seems to believe that the fact that each and everyone is able to publish will automatically turn every individual into a journalist. He also believes that the editorial society has already arrived and follows a notion of journalism that is independent of any normative and professional embedding, is ultimately not distinguished from PR, advertising and propaganda, is ignoring all traditional boundaries. Publishing for him means simply: publishing as a journalist. I will take up this concept of Hartley's here but with a decisively different target perspective. I consider the editorial society as a concrete utopia based on a normative conception of good journalism. On the difference of the concepts see: Hartley, John (2000), Communicative Democracy in a Redactional Society: The Future of Journalism Studies. In: *Journalism*, vol. 1/1, pp. 39–48. For criticism of Hartley see also: Neuberger, Christoph (2004), Konkurrenz oder Ergänzung zum professionellen Journalismus? Teil II. In: politik-digital.de (24.10.2004). http://politik-digital.de/themen/zehn-jahre-onl ine-journalism/netzkulturneuberger_konkurrenz2-shtml-2791/ (retrieved 12 September 2016).

221. Such comparative analyses, showing a broad consensus about values across different countries, have been carried out with great precision by Claudia Paganini in her as yet unpublished habilitation thesis.

222. On the relationship between epistemology and journalism see the comprehensive treatment by: Poerksen, Bernhard (2015), *Die Beobachtung des Beobachters. Eine Erkenntnistheorie der Journalistik.* Heidelberg: Carl-Auer Verlag.

223. Pöttker, Horst (2008), Öffentlichkeit als Sisyphusarbeit. Über unlösbare Widersprüche des Journalismus. In: Bernhard Poerksen/Wiebke Loosen/Armin Scholl (Eds), *Paradoxien des Journalism. Theorie – Empirie – Praxis.* Wiesbaden: VS Verlag für Socialwissenschaften, p. 69.

224. Pöttker, Horst (2017), Wahrheit und Wahrhaftigkeit. Grundbegriffe der Kommunikations- und Medienethik (Teil 7). In: *Communicatio Socialis*, vol. 50/1, p. 88 (Author's emphasis).

225. Lippmann, Walter (1922), *Public Opinion.* New York: The Macmillan Company, p. 81.

226. Kovach, Bill/Tom Rosenstiel (2014), *The Elements of Journalism. What Newspeople Should Know and the Public Should Expect. 3rd rev. & updated ed.* New York: Three Rivers Press, p. 128.

227. On this concept and the following see also: Poerksen, Bernhard (2016), Die post-faktische Universität. In: Zeit Online (29.12.2016). http://www.zeit.de/2016/52/wissenschaft-post-faktisch-rationalitaet-ohnmacht-universitaeten (retrieved 07 March 2017).

228. Quoted from: Garton Ash, Timothy (2016), *Free Speech. Ten Principles for a Connected World.* London: Atlantic Books, p. 96.

229. Schultz, Tanjev (2016), "I'm a serious reporter". Profi- und Amateurjournalismus im Lichte deliberativer Demokratietheorie. Ein Zentrum-Peripherie-Modell. In: *Media Journal*, vol. 40/2, p. 61.

230. See on this: Schwan, Gesine (2006), Was anders werden muss in der Bildung. In: *Tempo. Jubiläumsausgabe 20 Jahre Tempo*, p. 356.

231. On the distinction between *comprehension, understanding* and *agreement* see fundamentally: Schulz von Thun, Friedemann (2010), Verstehen – Verständnis – Einverständnis. In: Friedemann Schulz von Thun/Dagmar Kumbier (Eds), *Impulse für Kommunikation im Alltag. Kommunikationspsychologische Miniaturen 3.* Reinbek bei Hamburg: Rowohlt, pp. 13–39.

232. On the communicative preconditions of democractic co-existence see also: Müller, Henrik (2016), Die Donald Trumps sind überall. In: Spiegel Online; http://www.spiegel.de/wirtschaft/soziales/populismus-die-donald-trumps-sind-ueberall-muellers-memo-a-1074896.html (retrieved 07 June 2016).

233. Kovach, Bill/Tom Rosenstiel (2014), *The Elements of Journalism. What Newspeople Should Know and the Public Should Expect. 3rd rev. & updated ed.* New York: Three Rivers Press, pp. 242f.

234. On the following see: Krainer, Larissa (2001), *Medien und Ethik. Zur Organisation medienethischer Entscheidungsprozesse.* München: kopaed Verlag; Poerksen, Bernhard (2008), Schule des Sehens. Aporien und Paradoxien des Journalismus als zentrale Elemente einer Fachdidaktik. In: Bernhard Poerksen/Wiebke Loosen/Armin Scholl (Eds), *Paradoxien des Journalismus. Theorie – Empirie – Praxis.* Wiesbaden: VS Verlag für Sozialwissenschaften, pp. 663–678.

235. On the paradox of speed exactitude see: Wegner, Jochen (2016), Die fünf Paradoxien der Livemedia und der Mythos des Oknos. In: Zeit Online (25.07.2016). http://www.zeit.de/gesellschaft/2016-07/onl ine-journalism-media-amoklauf-muenchen (retrieved 11 August 2016).

236. Garton Ash, Timothy (2016), *Free Speech. Ten Principles for a Connected World.* London: Atlantic Books, p. 201f. (Author's emphasis.).

237. This direction is taken by the argumentation presented by Wolfgang Michal in a well-balanced essay, which critically analyses the concept of a citizen-oriented school for journalism in an editorial society. See: Michal, Wolfgang (2017), Journalisten als Lehrer der Nation? In: wolfgang-michal.de (17.01.2017). http://www.wolfgangmichal.de/2017/01/journa listen-als-lehrer-der-nation/ (retrieved 14 June 2017).

238. Kovach, Bill/Tom Rosenstiel (2014), *The Elements of Journalism. What Newspeople Should Know and the Public Should Expect. 3rd rev. & updated ed.* New York: Three Rivers Press, pp. 289ff.

239. The concept of a school subject was sketched out in a previous essay; the thoughts presented there are expanded here to fit the purposes of this book. See: Poerksen, Bernhard (2016), Wir lernen Netz. In: Zeit Online (03.03.2016). http://www.zeit.de/2016/09/digitalisation-soziale-netzwerke-ueberwachung-mediennutzung-schulfach (retrieved 07 March 2017).

240. Such a media-ecological perspective is discussed by Neil Postman in the following contribution: Postman, Neil (1992), *Technopoly. The Surrender of Culture to Technology.* New York: Vintage Books, A Division of Random House, Inc., pp. 18f.

241. It is quite remarkable that Walter Lippmann, in his book *Public Opinion,* already thinking along the same lines, recommends "the study of error " as "a stimulating introduction to the study of truth ". "As our minds become more deeply aware of their own subjectivism ", he writes, "we

find a zest in objective method that is not otherwise there." Lippmann, Walter (1922), *Public Opinion*. New York: The Macmillan Company, pp. 409f.

242. Morin, Edgar (2001), *Seven Complex Lessons in Education for the Future*. Paris: UNESCO Publishing, p. 1.

243. I have described this departure from the ideal of indoctrination in the book *Die Beobachtung des Beobachters* with regard to pedagogy and didactics; I am incorporating those considerations and some of the formulations in the present book; see especially: Poerksen, Bernhard (2015), *Die Beobachtung des Beobachters. Eine Erkenntnistheorie der Journalistik*. Heidelberg: Carl-Auer Verlag, pp. 219ff.

244. Features of a dialogical attitude are described by Kenneth N. Cissna and Rob Anderson in the following book: Cissna, Kenneth N./Anderson, Rob (2002), *Moments of Meeting. Buber, Rogers, and the Potential for Public Dialogue*. Albany: State University of New York Press. See in particular pp. 9ff.

245. Dialogical journalism resembles what the former *Guardian* editor-in-chief Alan Rusbridger has called *open journalism*. Both patterns of news reporting share a different relationship with the news recipients. However, I think that dialogue orientation is the more comprehensive, more holistic approach. *Open journalism* seems to me to be too focussed upon research contributions and auxiliary services for the readers. In addition, good journalism is in principle open to inspiration from outside, otherwise it would not be journalism but mere ideological publishing; the expression is thus somewhat pleonastic. On Rusbridger's concept and his manifold suggestions see the following publications: Ellis, Justin (2012), Alan Rusbridger on *The Guardian*'s Open Journalism, Paywalls, and Why They're Pre-planning More of the Newspaper. In: niemanlab.org (29.05.2012). http://www.niemanlab.org/2012/05/alan-rusbridger-on-the-guardians-open-journalism-paywalls-and-why-the yre-pre-planning-more-of-the-newspaper/ (retrieved 21 August 2017); Anonymous (2012), Q&A with Alan Rusbridger: The Future of Open Journalism. In: theguardian.com (25.03.2012). https://www.thegua rdian.com/commentisfree/2012/mar/25/alan-rusbridger-open-journalism (retrieved 21 August 2017).

246. Viner, Katharine (2015), The rise of the reader: journalism in the age of the open web, *The Guardian*, Wednesday 9 October 2013 (retrieved 21 September 2019).

247. Cf. ibid.

248. On the distinction between sovereignty of the first and the second order see the fundamental presentation by: Bernhard Poerksen/Friedemann Schulz von Thun (2014), *Kommunikation als Lebenskunst*. Heidelberg: Carl-Auer Verlag, pp. 87f.

249. On the problem of lacking diversity in journalism see the basic analysis by: Jones, Harrison (2016), Journalism's Lack of Diversity Threatens Its Long-term Future. In: theguardian.com (04.08.2016). https://www.theguardian.com/media/2016/aug/04/journalism-diversity-newspapers (retrieved 22 November 2016).

250. The concept of *gatereporting* was invented by the media scientist Hanne Detel. Her understanding is, however, narrower than mine, as she uses it to refer to reflecting reports on internet phenomena and internet interests. In my view it is appropriate to give this concept a broader meaning in strict analogy with the elementary process of gatekeeping; see here also my essay that I draw upon here: Poerksen, Bernhard (2016), Die post-faktische Universität. In: Zeit Online (29.12.2016). http://www.zeit.de/2016/52/wissenschaft-post-fak tisch-rationalitaet-ohnmacht-universitaeten (retrieved 07 March 2017). On the original use of the concept see: Detel, Hanne (2017), *Netzprominenz. Entstehung, Erhaltung und Monetarisierung von Prominenz im digitalen Zeitalter*. Köln: Herbert von Halem Verlag, pp. 178f.

251. On corresponding programmes see: Tückmantel, Ulli (2016), Fakten und Fiktionen im Internetzeitalter: Lügen haben schnelle Beine. In: wz.de (05.02.2016). http://www.wz.de/home/politik/fakten-und-fiktionen-im-internetzeitalter-luegen-haben-schnelle-beine-1.2116595 (retrieved 08 February 2017); The News Literacy Project, About. Our Mission. http://www.thenewsliteracyproject.org/about/our-mission (retrieved 28 August 2017); Schraven, David (2017), Reporterfabrik gegründet. Web-Akademie für Journalism. In: correctiv.org (15.01.2017). https://cor rectiv.org/blog/2017/01/15/reporterfabrik-gegruendet/ (retrieved 14 June 2017).

252. On this discussion see: Garton Ash, Timothy (2016), *Free Speech. Ten Principles for a Connected World*. London: Atlantic Books, pp. 302f. An additional note: The fact that many social networks locked the accounts of the former US president Donald Trump just before the inauguration is a symptom, a sign of the times. It seems clear now that the era of internet utopias has finally come to an end. Grassroots democratic euphoria, once upon a time electrifying the computer hippies of the first hour, has long been replaced by disillusionment and the fear of

the complete disappearance of respect and rationality in a post-factual rumpus. The former mantra of Facebook "Move fast and break things" meanwhile appears even to some of the protagonists of Silicon Valley to be a devilish incantation to destabilise entire societies. But how is the so-called deplatforming of Donald Trump, the locking of the presidential accounts, to be assessed? Judgements vacillate, remain controversial and precarious. The blockade may be considered right at this historical moment because after the storming of the Capitol the fear of civil war unrest was justified. This is the argument of the necessary defence against imminent violence. But it may also be seen as erratic. For there have been immensely more massive violations of the platform rules by Donald Trump before—attacks on minorities, dissenters and nonconformists, even threats to use nuclear weapons. This is the argument of inconsistency and disproportionate severity. And finally, the deplatforming decision appears to be highly problematical simply because a very small group of internet princes determined dictatorially, without any democratic societal control, quasi as chairpersons of a global editorial office and an international court of law, what is to be deleted and what can remain. This is the argument of arrogance in principle. It entails that publicist decisions concerning an audience of billions must be taken in a democratic and transparent way. Whatever the judgement on all this, one clear fact remains: the platform enterprises are out of their depth when it comes to the global regulation of processes of information and opinion management. With regard to this discussion see: Poerksen, Bernhard (2021), Das Beispiel Trump zeigt: Soziale Netzwerke müssen reguliert werden. In: *Neue Zürcher Zeitung* (21.01.2021) https://www. nzz.ch/meinung/das-beispiel-trump-zeigt-soziale-netzwerke-muessen-reg uliert-werden-ld.1597301?reduced=true (retrieved 06 March 2021).

253. On the arguments of the platforms—and their refutation—see in detail: Napoli, Philip M./Caplan, Robyn (2017), Why Media Companies Insist They're Not Media Companies, Why They're Wrong, and Why It Matters. In: *First Monday*, vol. 22/5.

254. Quoted from: Garton Ash, Timothy (2016), *Free Speech. Ten Principles for a Connected World*. London: Atlantic Books, p. 96f.

255. It is somewhat revealing that the users seem to remain wholly unaware of the influence of algorithms, as is confirmed by various surveys. More than 60 per cent of the Facebook users interviewed claimed that all the contributions of their "friends" were shown. Others were annoyed by the enormous number of baby photos displayed to them and assumed

that young mothers were flooding the social network with infant photos, which is not the case, however. These images are prioitised by the Facebook algorithm because they tend to receive a particularly large number of likes and especially intense comments. On the different investigations see: Lischka, Konrad/Stöcker, Christian (2017), *Digitale Öffentlichkeit. Wie algorithmische Prozesse den gesellschaftlichen Diskurs beeinflussen. Arbeitspapier.* Gütersloh: Bertelsmann Stiftung, p. 14 and p. 59.

256. The analogy of the tinted spectacles is due to Eli Pariser; see: Pariser, Eli (2011), *The Filter Bubble. What the Internet Is Hiding from You.* London: Penguin Books, p. 18.

257. On the concept of filter sovereignty see: Seemann, Michael (2014), *Das neue Spiel. Strategien für die Welt nach dem digitalen Kontrollverlust.* Freiburg: orange-press, pp. 193ff.

258. The transmission of textual building blocks without a link to an identifiable communication partner is unworthy of a dialogue of minimally satisfactory seriousness.

259. It remains largely unknown, for instance, that certain complainants (e.g., the British Home Office) receive privileged treatment and systematic preferment by YouTube due to successful lobbying and pressure by governments. Their reports of objectionable content are dealt with more quickly and in 90 per cent of cases lead to the removal of posts, as one of the top managers of the platform affirms. For comparison: only 30 per cent of normal complaints lead to a deletion. See on this: Garton Ash, Timothy (2016), *Free Speech. Ten Principles for a Connected World.* London: Atlantic Books, p. 241.

260. In dealing with neo-Nazi groups the positions of various platforms (e.g., Airbnb, Google, PayPal) are very explicit by now. On particular measures see: Beuth, Patrick (2017), Kein Netz für Nazis. In: Zeit Online (17.08.2017). http://www.zeit.de/digital/internet/2017-08/daily-stormer-cloudflare-internet-infrastruktur-provider (retrieved 28 August 2017).

261. The outsourcing of such dirt and elimination jobs—under the lofty name of *commercial content moderation*—is described in the following contribution: Reuter, Markus (2016), Die digitale Müllabfuhr: Kommerzielle Inhaltsmoderation auf den Philippinen. In: netzpolitik.org (27.04.2016). https://netzpolitik.org/2016/die-digitale-muellabfuhr-kommerzielle-inh altsmoderation-auf-den-philippinen/ (retrieved 19 September 2016).

262. One could think of being enabled, for example, to choose between different variants of algorithmic structuring. Thus Konrad Lischka and Christian Stöcker propose, for example, "It could be made possible to have the personal News Feed ordered by an algorithmic system, which only shows references to news sources with transparently defined minimal requirements (like, for instance: observation of the strict distinction between editor and publisher, e.g. impressum, cooperation in self-regulation etc.)." Lischka, Konrad/Stöcker, Christian (2017), *Digitale Öffentlichkeit. Wie algorithmische Prozesse den gesellschaftlichen Diskurs beeinflussen. Arbeitspapier*. Gütersloh: Bertelsmann Stiftung, p. 26.

263. Facebook has taken a first step in this direction with its so-called Oversight Board, which started its work in 2020.

264. It is obvious that platforms must develop their own forms of concretisation in a dialogue with the media audiences and other stakeholders—due to their hybrid status in the border area between neutral broadcasting and editorial decision-making. Thus the principle of truth orientation cannot, for example, be applied in the same way as in a journalistic editorial office. This would entail the strict control of all content before publication. The special challenge is to establish signals of seriosity and informational quality, as is already practised in certain areas, without sinking into premature paternalism. See on this: Müller von Blumencron, Mathias (2016), Trennt Propaganda von Wahrheit! In: faz.net (05.02.2016). http://www.faz.net/aktuell/politik/inland/luegen-im-internet-spannen-ein-netz-der-verwirrung-14052436.html (retrieved 08 February 2016).

Author Biography

Bernhard Poerksen was born in 1969 and is Professor of Media Studies at the University of Tübingen in Germany, with particular research interest in the new media age. His writing regularly appears in both scholarly and popular science publications, and several of his books have become bestsellers in Germany. He has written or co-authored books on topics such as communications theory, journalism education, cybernetics, systemic thinking, and constructivist epistemology, and he has received accolades for the essays he wrote for newspapers and magazines. In 2008 he was voted Professor of the Year in Germany in recognition of the quality of his teaching. The following books are available in English: *Understanding Systems* (with cybernetician Heinz von Foerster, 2002); *The Certainty of Uncertainty—Dialogues Introducing Constructivism* (2004); *From Being to Doing. The Origins of the Biology of Cognition* (with neurobiologist Humberto Maturana, 2004); *The Creation of Reality. A Constructivist Epistemology of Journalism and Journalism Education* (2011); *The Unleashed Scandal. The End of Control in the Digital Age* (with media scholar Hanne Detel, 2014).

© The Editor(s) (if applicable) and The Author(s), under exclusive license to Springer Nature Switzerland AG 2022
B. Poerksen, *Digital Fever*,
https://doi.org/10.1007/978-3-030-89522-8